# Sweden and ecological governance

Published in our
centenary year
~ 2004 ~
MANCHESTER
UNIVERSITY
PRESS

Issues in Environmental Politics

*series editors* Mikael Skou Andersen and Duncan Liefferink

At the start of the twenty-first century, the environment has come to stay as a central concern of global politics. This series takes key problems for environmental policy and examines the politics behind their cause and possible resolution. Accessible and eloquent, the books make available for a non-specialist readership some of the best research and most provocative thinking on humanity's relationship with the planet.

*already published in the series*

# Sweden and ecological governance

Straddling the fence

Lennart J. Lundqvist

**Manchester University Press**

Manchester and New York

distributed exclusively in the USA by Palgrave

*Published by Manchester University Press*
Oxford Road, Manchester M13 9NR, UK
and Room 400, 175 Fifth Avenue, New York, NY 10010, USA
www.manchesteruniversitypress.co.uk

*Distributed exclusively in the USA by*
Palgrave, 175 Fifth Avenue, New York,
NY 10010, USA

*Distributed exclusively in Canada by*
UBC Press, University of British Columbia, 2029 West Mall,
Vancouver, BC, Canada V6T 1Z2

*British Library Cataloguing-in-Publication Data*
A catalogue record for this book is available from the British Library

*Library of Congress Cataloging-in-Publication Data applied for*

ISBN    0 7190 6902 5    *hardback*

First published 2004

12  11  10  09  08  07  06  05  04        10  9  8  7  6  5  4  3  2  1

Typeset in Sabon
by Action Publishing Technology Ltd, Gloucester
Printed in Great Britain
by CPI, Bath

# Contents

# List of tables

# Preface

This study is about policies and strategies for ecologically rational governance that are expected to achieve their final results in a generation from now. In some sense my work on this subject began more than a generation ago, when I wrote my dissertation on the emergence of modern environmental administration in Sweden. Some years later I did a comparative study of clean air policies in Sweden and the US. I was overwhelmed by the wide and generous reception of *The Hare and the Tortoise*, and had great plans for continuing to do work within the area of comparative environmental policy.

Life took another turn, however, and a decade of work in comparative housing policy came to pass before I returned to the environmental issue. By now, the field had grown immensely. The number of scholars and sub-fields was such as to make the earlier comprehensive overview well nigh impossible. The object of study had changed. Gone was the rather clear-cut sectoral environmental policy dealing with identifiable sources of pollution to specified media. Centre stage began to be crowded with problems of diffuse sources of environmental disturbances across sectors and scales not amenable to action by single jurisdictions. Gro Harlem Brundtland and her international group set the direction for the future discourse by bringing sustainable development to the political agenda, thus also providing a global framework for the comparative study of environmental and ecological politics and policies.

In these new waters, I was lucky to be guided by skilled and inspiring pilots. When my Norwegian colleague in environmental

policy research, Alf-Inge Jansen, invited me to a 1992 Drøbak
workshop on comparative environmental policies in Europe, it
was the beginning of a very stimulating friendship. We soon
joined with others in a comparative Nordic project, subsequently
reported in the volume *Governing the Environment: Politics,
Policy, and Organisation in the Nordic Countries* (1996). During
that project, and in the subsequent incisive encounters over the
final report from the Drøbak meeting, he never tired of discussing
and elaborating how one should really approach the political
study of what was then increasingly known as ecological
modernisation.

Participation in the EU-sponsored concerted action *Towards
the Ecological State* further emphasised the need for new scholarly perspectives on ecologically relevant political action, and
gave new insights into different national responses. In the international joint research project *Governance for Sustainable
Development: Addressing a Need for New Approaches and More
Effective Mechanisms* I have enjoyed the immensely stimulating
discussions with the project co-ordinator William Lafferty and
the other participants. Not the least have these encounters made
me quite apprehensive as to the different national preconditions
and conceptions of environmental, ecological, and sustainable
development policies and measures, and the ways in which these
differences can be fruitfully approached in comparative studies.

Why then confine this study to one single nation? My choice of
Sweden as the case for an empirical study of how political systems
try to govern so as to 'value democracy and individual autonomy
and still retain the integrity of the commons' rests on two general
and one special argument. The first general argument is
consciously *heuristic*. Sweden is viewed in much of recent scholarly debate as a forerunner in environmental and ecological
policy. The Swedish government's launching of the programme
for 'Sustainable Sweden' seemed to provide a critical case. If any
country has at all come anywhere near meeting such criteria for
ecologically rational government as the ones I have set out for this
study, Sweden might be that country. The second general argument is the need for *cumulativity*. Much has been written on how
ecological governance or an ecological state *should* be designed
and function. However, much less has been done to find out
empirically whether and how such governance *is* actually

working. I am convinced that the results from a comparison between the empirical 'front' case of Sweden and normative criteria for ecologically rational governance derived from the political theory (regardless of colour), might be able to add something to the emerging, and increasingly necessary discourse on democratic ecologically rational governance. As for the third, special argument, I have to admit that there is a streak of *parochialism* involved here. Sweden is my home country. I hope to do justice to the comparative advantage of having first-hand knowledge of this political system and its policies for ecologically sustainable development.

During the work on this book, I have enjoyed the privilege of visiting several research *milieus* outside my home department. In spring 1999, I worked at the Institute of Administrative and Organisational Studies at the University of Bergen, where Alf-Inge Jansen and his colleagues took time to discuss some of my research problems. Later that spring, I visited Forschungsstelle für Umweltpolitik at the Free University in Berlin, where Martin Jänicke and his team probed my ideas in seminars and coffee discussions. In spring 2000, I stayed with the Center for Clean Technology and Environment Policy at Twente University, where Hans Bressers and his colleagues arranged seminar discussions on some of my research ideas. In the autumn of 2000, I taught at the Institute for Public Administration and the Department of Political Science at Åbo Akademi, where I got stimulating ideas from my colleagues in the joint 1992–96 Nordic project, Ann-Sofi Hermansson and Marko Joas. Work in the European Science Foundation's TERM II Committee brought me in touch with Bernd Siebenhühner, who provided valuable comments on Chapter 4. The comments on my first full draft provided by the two editors of the MUP series *Issues in Environmental Policy*, Duncan Liefferink and Mikael Skou Andersen, gave me a valuable nudge in the ribs to proceed further with the comparative discussion of the final chapter.

The book owes much to the stimulating research environment at Göteborg University's Department of Political Science. It was recently ranked superior in an international evaluation of Swedish political science departments. Its bustling seminar culture provided valuable inputs to my work. The General Research Seminar, led by Bo Rothstein, commented on an early version of the study's general problematic. The seminar on Political Theory, led by Bengt-Ove Boström and Gunnar Falkemark, and the seminar on Public Policy and Administration, led by Jon Pierre, have been particularly valuable; designated discussants and regular seminar participants engaged in incisive and constructive discussions on different versions of several of the chapters. My doctorate students – Sverker C. Jagers, Victor Galaz, and Marie Uhrwing – earn special thanks on two accounts; first, for their continuous support and valuable comments, and second, for their sustained patience with my oftentimes absent-minded look and inflected responses. Thanks are also due to Kerstin Gidsäter for her patient and skillful adaptation of my chapters into a manuscript ready for publication.

Last but certainly not least, I enjoy my home base. My wife Solveig never tires of teaching me the intricacies of making our garden provide rich yields, and how to keep it sustainable over time. Our children and grandchildren enlighten and strengthen us. They make us feel the duty of present generations to make the Earth a sustainable base for human life. This book is dedicated to our grandchildren and their possibilities to enjoy an ecologically sustainable future, and to make their own autonomous choices for the good life.

The study received generous financial support from the Bank of Sweden Tercentenary Fund as well as from the Adlerbert Foundation at Göteborg University.

Göteborg, Ascension Day, 2003

LJL

# 1

# Where the grass is greener: criteria for ecologically rational governance

The (re)discovery of the tragedy of the commons raised a normative question that has haunted students and practitioners of politics ever since: *'How are we to govern ourselves so as to value democracy and individual autonomy and still retain the integrity of the commons?'* The question implies that the latter – interpreted as ecological sustainability – may prove a formidable challenge to presently existing democratic systems of governance.

Practical political answers addressing the full spectrum of sustainable development, and in particular its ecological aspects, are now emerging. Sweden provides an interesting case of development from environmental policy towards ecological governance. In his acceptance speech as the new Leader of Sweden's Social Democratic Party in March 1996, the then Minister of Finance Göran Persson proclaimed the achievement of an ecologically sustainable society as a new and noble mission for his party. Presenting his Cabinet Policy Platform two weeks later, Prime Minister Persson stated that Sweden should be an 'an internationally driving force and a forerunner in the endeavours to create an ecologically sustainable development' (Swedish Parliamentary Record 22 March 1996). To achieve this objective, he and his party have alluded to the building of the democratic Swedish welfare state, *the People's Home*. Ever since the Social-Democratic coming to power this metaphor has 'envisioned a democratic family in which all its members enjoyed equal status and participated collectively in decision-making' (Tilton 1990:128). Said Persson: '[Our party] once built the People's Home in broad consensus on the conditions for production, increased standards of living, and security for everyone. Now, we have a similar mission. We will realise the vision of a *green* welfare state ' (see Persson 1997, italics added).

The eighteen months following Mr. Persson's Cabinet Policy Declaration witnessed a dramatic moulding of ecological, socio-economic and political aspects into a policy for an 'Ecologically Sustainable Sweden', and the process of change continues. This book aims at answering the following question: *To what extent do policy measures taken in Sweden to achieve ecologically sustainable development shape and/or rearrange the structures and processes of governance in such a way that the collective outcome is ecologically rational and democratically acceptable* (see Barry 1999:104)?

## Governance and ecological rationality

How do we achieve democratically legitimate *and* ecologically rational governance? The suggestions offered by political philosophers and social scientists point in many directions. There are arguments for both more and less of market or state (see Eckersley 1995). Pragmatic environmentalists think it is possible to green contemporary democracies and their use of nature (see Dobson 1990:73 ff.). Eco-anarchists argue that following abolition of the state, human beings will build ecologically adapted, self-governing communities (see Bookchin 1982; Carter 1993). Calls for more local government (see Dobson 1990:145 ff.) are found alongside pleas for transferring governing powers to the global level (Caldwell 1990). Some have spoken in favour of ecocracy, i.e., rule by scientific expertise rather than rule by popularly elected trustees (Ophuls and Boyan 1992).

However, most of these suggestions can be questioned. On the one hand, they fail on grounds of autonomy, i.e., a value at the very core of liberal democracy (see Jagers 2002:90 ff.). Harsh restrictions imposed on individual choice in the name of ecological necessity seem to rule out individual control over the context of choice. On the other hand, their effectiveness in achieving sustainable development is questioned. Democratically elected policy-makers are always under strong pressures to secure votes. This tends to favour short, election-period incentives over longer-term ecological balance measures (Milbrath 1984:27 f.; Porritt

1984:122 ff.: Dryzek 1995:299 f.). Even those rare real world instances of governance that combine autonomy and freedom with sustainable resource use seem to have built-in frailties (Ostrom 1990).

Sustainable use and management of the natural environment and its resources is here seen as a problem of *governance*. This refers to the 'shaping and sustaining of the arrangements of authority and power within which actors make decisions and frame policies that are binding on individual and collective actors within different territorial bounds, such as those of the state, county and municipality' (Hanf and Jansen 1998:3). The present systems of governance have grown out of earlier political challenges and shifting power configurations in society. They thus embody different institutional logics, and provide actors with different frames for determining appropriate behaviour. Logics of democratic decision-making, based on the value of citizen autonomy, are found alongside the logic of competitive markets, based on the value of individual gain. The most profound struggle and conflict in politics is about 'the institutional logic by which the various social activities should be regulated and over categories of persons to which they should apply' (Hanf and Jansen 1998:4 f.).

Efforts to maintain a sustainable social-environmental relationship thus concern the design and logic of political *institutions*, since they determine much of the actual *policies* for sustainable development. To assess the extent to which environmental policy measures shape and sustain arrangements of authority and power that make the collective outcome ecologically rational and socially acceptable, we need specific criteria for what constitutes a system of *ecological governance* with an institutional *logic of ecological rationality*.

The concept of ecological rationality originally comprised only *functional* aspects of ecological sustainability, i.e., the consistent and effective provision of human life support (Dryzek 1987:34 ff.). But decisions on society-environment relations are made under conditions of uncertainty. This indicates a need to include also *normative* aspects that enable judgements on what is 'use' or 'abuse' of resources and on what is 'just' or 'unjust' distribution of human life support, as well as on which decision-making procedures are acceptable in terms of popular sovereignty and autonomy (Barry 1999:107 ff.). The logic of ecological rationality proceeds from the precautionary principle. This defines 'a range of outcomes that are impermissible, namely those that can not be altered in the future'. It can be viewed as an 'additional self-binding character of democracy ... [for] long-term collective interest' (Barry 1999:225). Ecological rationality is closely connected to the learning and adaptive capacities of social institutions to cope with both substantial and value-related dimensions of the society-environment relationship (see Jänicke 1997:11 f.).

The multiple spatial scales of society-environment relationships indicate that an ecologically rational system of governance is a *multi-level* endeavour. From the debate on how to order the relations between society and the natural environment we find that several crucial dimensions are involved:

- *Scale*: Where and how should the boundaries of responsibility, authority and sovereignty be drawn to best provide for both autonomy and sustainability? How can institutions of governance be designed to achieve a balance between 'cultural' boundaries and 'natural' scales, extendible among and linking jurisdictional levels upward/downward?

- *Time*: How can political institutions be arranged to take account not just of democratically relevant cycles such as election periods, but also of different life cycles and time scales important to the balance of ecosystems? How could institutions be designed to legitimately deal with issues of inter-generational safeguarding of natural resources and the distribution of present sacrifices to achieve sustainability in the future?

- *Knowledge*: How should a system of ecological governance be designed to make sure that ecologically relevant scientific knowledge is brought into resource-related decision-making and still allow for the democratic accountability of public decision-makers?

- *Integration:* If a highly centralised and holistic ecology-centred institutional structure of government is ruled out on grounds of autonomy, and a narrow sectoral environmental administration on grounds of sustainability, how could a multi-level, multi-sectoral public administration for effective ecological governance be designed to integrate both these objectives?

All these dimensions indicate a system of rational ecological governance set up to meet the double standard of sustainability and democracy. The scholarly debate indicates that *democracy* and *individual autonomy* constitute the most crucial aspect of ecological governance. On the one hand, analyses built on recent comparative studies hold that democratically elected politicians are locked into the logic of competition in global markets. The necessity to secure continued economic growth and social welfare for the citizen means they may have to tune down quests or policies for ecological sustainability coming from the electorate (Jansen, Osland and Hanf 1998:313 ff.). On the other hand, much of the literature on ecological politics argues that the relation between democracy and sustainability *ought* to be different. Communicative rather than instrumental rationality should be the procedural rule for democratic decision-making (Dryzek 1990:54). Ecological politics is said to entail new and widened forms of citizen participation. Processes such as Local Agenda 21 are interpreted as a sign of this widened citizen involvement in democratic ecological governance (see Eckerberg and Lafferty 1997).

These aspects of ecologically rational governance present several challenges to existing institutions and organisation of public government. First, it is easily said that environmental problems should be dealt with on the scale where they occur. However, the proper delineation of units of governance is not as easily done. Second, it seems right in a normative sense to build institutions for ecologically sustainable development on the principles of intergenerational justice. However, this may be found to clash with the objective of socio-economic justice within present generations. Third, the rule of expert knowledge may be disclaimed as illegitimate on grounds of autonomy. We must, however, also recognise that resource management decisions made without relevant knowledge may lead to ecologically irrational governance. Fourth, constraints on the market motivated by ecological reasons could thwart entrepreneurial creativity and the development of new technologies conducive to sustainable resource management (see Sunstein 1990:86 f.). Fifth, while ecological modernisation proponents hold that the economy-ecology relation can be made a win-win solution, interventions in resource use and management will almost inevitably clash with notions of autonomy. This means that choices of institutions and instruments for sustainable resource use must be made in ways that secure their political legitimacy (Lundqvist 2001b).

As the logic of ecological rationality is defined here, the pursuit of sustainability is normatively constrained by the value of democracy and individual freedom and autonomy. To enable conclusions about the extent to which Sweden is approaching ecologically rational governance, the following *normative* and ideal-type set of criteria for such governance will be used:

• Ecologically rational governance is adapted to ecologically relevant boundaries.
• Ecologically rational governance is adapted to natural eco-cycles and to the safeguarding of inter-generational equality without sacrificing norms of socio-economic justice embraced by the present welfare state.
• Ecologically rational governance has institutional capacities to interpret and effectively transform scientific sustainability-directed arguments into integrated and collectively binding policies and decisions legitimised by representative democratic government.
• Ecologically rational governance is able to effectively bring socio-economic activities within the scale of the ecological resource base with minimum coercion and maximum consent and without fettering initiatives conducive to efficient resource use.

*Empirical* criteria for assessing the congruence of actual environmental policy with this ideal type of ecologically rational governance will be further discussed and formulated below. They will be more fully operationalised at the beginning of each empirical chapter. The questions I seek to answer are:

• To what extent are Swedish environmental policy developments since the 1990s compatible with the criteria for ecological governance, i.e., with multilevel collective ecological management based on the logic of ecological rationality?

- What has been the role of the state in this development, and how has the state's position within the governance of society-environment relationships developed?

## Ecological governance and scale

The *territorial* limits of government are traditionally drawn along cultural and human-related lines. Language and ethnicity very much determine borders between nations. Once developed from nature-given conditions, boundaries at regional and local levels increasingly reflect efforts to optimise political and administrative jurisdictions in view of technological and infrastructural economies of scale. This has meant that culturally and socio-economically determined boundaries cut across life-supporting ecosystems, such as sea basins, river catchments, and biotopes. This 'lack of fit' (see Pritchard Jr. et al. 1998:14) does not favour resource management patterns and practices compatible with ecologically rational and sustainable governance.

This has led some to recommend the break-up of central government in favour of self-governing, self-sufficient bio-regions (see Sale 1984a and b). Apart from the somewhat astonishing neglect of the value of individual autonomy in certain proposals, one could muster empirical and instrumental counterarguments. Natural regions and areas are today so interpenetrated and trans-gressed by linked human activities at different spatial scales that autonomy for such 'ecologically' geared governance over and above present democratic institutions would be difficult to legit-imise. These multi-level linkages furthermore indicate the necessity to distribute authority and competence at different scales and levels so as to provide for degrees of autonomy accept-able also to actors with differing dependencies on, or even conflicting interests in, the region's resources. Secession – the bio-regionalist solution to the sustainability problem – simply is not acceptable on grounds of democracy and autonomy.

It has been argued that because ecological problems are inher-ently complex, non-reducible, variable, uncertain, spontaneous, and collective in nature, ecological governance must be different from conventional government (Dryzek 1987:26 ff.). A truly envi-ronmental administration ought to be non-compartmentalised, open, decentralised, anti-technocratic, and flexible (Paehlke and

Torgerson 1990:292 ff.). While these arguments point towards
flexibility in territorial terms, one should not abandon traditional
norms for administrative effectiveness and efficiency. An instrumental view of the public administration's role in ecological
governance must thus find solutions to institutional design that
are (a) acceptable in terms of democracy and autonomy; (b) efficient in achieving sustainable resource management, and (c)
adjusted to the realities of modern, larger-scale and inter-linked
social and economic entities and activities.

One such idea embraced widely during the 1990s is that of
*ecosystem management*. This is defined as 'the application of
ecological and social information, options, and constraints to
achieve desired social benefits within a defined geographic area
and over a specified period' (Lackey 1998:22, 29). Directed
towards sustaining the health, productivity, and biodiversity of
ecosystems as well as human quality of life, it involves all relevant
stakeholders in defining sustainable alternatives for the environments in which they live, also integrating social and economic
needs. Eco-system management emphasises place- or region-based
objectives with scopes and approaches defined appropriately, and
developed in a participatory process, for each given unit (Szaro et
al. 1998:3 f.).

This emphasis of ecosystem management on place- or region-
based objectives developed by participating stakeholders shows
its limitations as the sole territorial basis for building an ecologically sustainable society. Resource issues, however local the
resource, are linked to large-scale, or rather cross-scale, socio-
economic and political issues. This also indicates that centralised
management cannot be totally replaced by local ecosystem
management. The crucial problems of fit to scale for ecological
governance are thus how local ecosystem management units are
linked to institutions on higher levels without at the same time
losing their fit to the local resource or sacrificing individual
autonomy. This points to the need for inter-linked institutions.
To be effective in the cross-scale perspective just mentioned, local
institutions with recognised spheres of autonomy need connections to, and backing from, institutions at higher levels. This may
take the form of 'nested enterprises' (see Ostrom 1990: 101 f.).
Such nestedness does not necessarily imply a top-down perspective across the whole spectrum of relations. Neither does it imply

a tight, non-flexible distribution of authority (Pritchard Jr. et al. 1998:30 f.).

With respect to the spatial dimension, the following criteria for ecologically rational governance may be formulated:

- Governance is ecologically rational to the extent that ecosystem-based management units, such as air sheds, water catchments, or specific landscape types, have become constitutive elements in the collective management of environment and natural resources to achieve sustainability.
- Ecological governance is spatially rational to the extent that it defines the circles of participating stakeholders and interests in goal setting and decision-making on actual resource use and management in accordance with relevant spatial scales.

## Ecological governance and time

As an ethic principle for intergenerational equity, sustainability pits present demands on natural resources against the perceivable demands of future generations. Against the economic concept of '*sustained* development' based on expectancy of short- to medium-term growth it puts the ecological concept of '*sustainable* development' concerned with the longer-term viability of the natural resource base. It brings ecological lifecycles, varying from millennial geological changes to seasonal and even shorter time periods, to bear on political time horizons, be they election periods or long-term 'plans'.

How then could political and societal clock time be made compatible with the life cycles of the natural environment? The most often recommended political solution is collective self-binding *now* to provide autonomy for *future* generations. They are held to have the same rights to the earth's resources as earlier and present ones. This implies the need to design institutions that guarantee a transmission of the world's resources in usable shape to future generations (see Achterberg 1993:96 f.). However, quests for sustainability built on the premise of inter-generational equity must reconcile issues of socio-economic justice today. The stronger existing human and civil rights are protected, the more can present actors use natural resources without regard to their long-term viability. Questions about sustainable resource use are indeed also questions about rights to the resources. They also concern *whether*, and, if so, by *whom*, present resource users should be compensated if they are deprived of their user rights in the interest of future generations. Stretton's classic rhetorical question is still valid: Is it worth having a self-binding system of ecological governance for sustainability 'if it merely shifts hardships from rich to poor?' (see Stretton 1976:4f.).

An ecological governance in line with the 'precautionary principle' must thus get a 'normative constraining of permissible policy options' democratically acceptable and accepted (Barry 1999:133). Natural resource and land-use *planning* is a well-known form of normative constraint on future resource use. In the context of ecological governance, planning refers to 'conscious, collective determination and co-ordination of social activities' to maintain a sustainable society-environment relationship (see Barry 1999:131). In terms of sustainability, however, present planning is often found wanting (Jänicke and Jörgens 1998:47 f.; see Meadowcroft 1997a:431 ff.). Comprehensive ecological planning for sustainable development is thus presented as a permanent process of 'institutional learning and design' (see Meadowcroft 1997b:179).

However, the potential scale and pervasiveness of such planning may severely intrude on the autonomy of present resource users. Therefore, its legitimisation must come from central democratic government. The preferable way to reconcile stringent plans for sustainability with the value of user autonomy is through generous provisions for participation and influence in the planning process. Elected policy-makers can provide strategic impulses and interventions, such as consensus talks with relevant key interests and groups, and voluntary agreements for decentralised implementation in co-operative management regimes (see Jänicke and Jörgens 1998:30 f.; Meadowcroft 1997b: 182). But also the outputs from such processes of resource and land-use planning take the form of regulations binding future action, and are backed by democratically legitimised state coercion. Certain resource uses may be totally prohibited or restricted by conditions spelled out in licences or quota. Some areas or resources may be set aside for only specifically allowed activities, or spared from all forms of exploitation (see Lundqvist 2001b:461 ff.).

Another way of approaching the temporal aspect of sustain-

able resource use is to create *closed cycles* for materials and
resources flowing through society. Elaborate systems for reuse
and recycling of materials have been introduced in many nations
over the past 10 to 15 years. They involve consumers, producers,
local, regional and central governments, and market-based instruments are often applied to make recycling and reuse work. In
some systems the responsibility for a product is put on the manufacturer, and covers the entire life cycle of the product or
material. It is left to the manufacturer to develop the technicali-
ties of this system of recycling and reuse (see Ligteringen 1999:
187 ff.).

While this concept provides for individual autonomy, its relationship to sustainable development is precarious. As socially
constructed phenomena, the perceived closed cycles build on
steering the flows of materials and energy through infra-struc-
turally determined stages and locations. The closing is often made
possible only by heavy external inflows of fossil fuels. Second, the
durability of many materials and products continues beyond the
politically foreseeable future. Together with the dynamics of
markets that make companies come and go, producer liability
thus poses difficult temporal problems for the democratic governance of eco-cycles (see Lidskog 1996).

Flagging catchwords like Factor 10 and environmental certification of industries, proponents of *ecological modernisation* see
increased efficiency of resource use as a way of 'freeing' or
preserving resources for future use. Eco-technological innovation
and development opens up for a new phase of industrialisation
where fewer resources are needed to produce the same or larger
amount of services (see Gouldson and Murphy 1997:74 f.). But
for this to come about, new eco-technological markets must be
opened up by state governments through stringent environmental
legislation *and* economic incentives (Dobers 1997:63 ff., 114 ff.).
To get acceptance for this double strategy, however, proponents
of ecological modernisation must convince industry and the
public that this is a 'win-win' solution dissolving the perceived
conflict between economic growth and environmental protection
(Cohen 1998:150).

Using language that harmonises sustainability with orthodox
economic imperatives, politicians preach that 'pollution prevention pays', bringing industry to find anticipatory development of

green technology profitable (Hajer 1995:26 ff., 273; see Barry 1999:139). While ecological modernisation may provide for considerable individual autonomy, its links to sustainable development have been questioned. The 'ecological modernisation' school's major assumption – resource problems can be solved through consensual decisions with positive-sum outcomes – is held to have no explicit, logical link to the specific ecological scale at which solutions are to be reached (Langhelle 2000:303 ff.).

With regard to the temporal aspects of the society-environment relationship, the following criteria for ecologically rational governance may be formulated:

- Governance is ecologically rational to the extent that comprehensive resource planning directed towards objectives of sustainable development contains measures to secure popular participation and influence over this collective process of self-binding.
- Governance is ecologically rational to the extent that strategies of 'closed cycles' or increased 'eco-efficiency' are constitutive parts of the efforts to bring about sustainable development.

## Ecological governance and knowledge

Quite clearly, restructured or new institutions to promote ecologically prudent spatial and temporal management of the resource base imply constraints on individual autonomy. We are then faced with the question of how such restrictions might be legitimised within society. One line of argument holds that ecologically rational governance can be obtained if scientists and professionals have the last word because of their exclusive knowledge (Ophuls and Boyan 1992). However, claims for 'domination of elites embedded within bureaucratic decision-making bodies distant from democratic control' to achieve sustainability cannot be democratically legitimised (Smith 1996:43 f.). Science cannot claim a unified knowledge of what is actually sustainable (see Wynne 1994). To forecast and remedy all possible natural and social events and unintended consequences of human actions is simply too tall an order for science or any professional expertise (de Geus 1996:198).

Decisions on how to achieve sustainability simply have too far-reaching consequences for the life and welfare of all citizens to allow for limitations on the autonomy of the *demos*. A more realistic view is that scientific monitoring and assessment of positive or negative effects of certain resource uses should be subjected to socio-economic and political debate. This is because scientific conclusions and assessments imply 'losers' and 'winners' in the continuous competition for resources. In a democratic system of ecological governance, scientific recommendations for specific resource decisions 'necessary' to achieve sustainability must be weighed against other considerations, such as the provision of socio-economic welfare for present citizens.

Since resource use decisions are made under conditions of uncertainty, however, the assistance of scientific knowledge is highly needed to provide the best possible evaluation of different alternatives, both *ex ante* and *ex post*. Scientific knowledge of ecosystems and views on proper resource use should thus be an integral part of broader social, economic and other considerations, but not have the final word (see EndterWada et al. 1998). Political decision-makers striving for ecologically rational resource management should make sure that decisions are founded on the best possible scientific opinion. But they must also ensure that resource decisions are politically legitimate. Therefore, ecologically rational governance must set up institutional arrangements to 'secure that the application of science is *within* rather than *beyond* democratic regulation' (Barry 1999:203).

One way of achieving this is to build up a structure of semi-autonomous institutions to gather, assess and disseminate information on sustainable resource management to political decision-making bodies and to the general public (Jänicke 1997, Cohen 1998). A long-term strategy for securing scientific knowledge on sustainable development might involve university departments, independent research and monitoring institutes and agencies that work much like the semi-autonomous institutions presently found in the judicial and – to an increasing extent – financial spheres. Norms of democracy and autonomy mean that there should also be institutions where the scientific information on resource use alternatives could be politically evaluated and judged. Such institutions, be they judicial boards of appeal, public hearings and other devices for citizen participation, must be easily accessible for all the actors and interests wanting to influence or challenge resource-related decisions.

The following criteria for ecologically rational governance may be formulated:

- Governance is ecologically rational to the extent that the structures built up for developing, assessing and disseminating science-based knowledge allow for free exchange of complementary and competing views.
- Governance is ecologically rational when competing knowledge is made accessible to public debate and scrutiny in the policy process.
- Governance is ecologically rational to the extent that scientific knowledge is brought to bear on, and to interact with, political judgement to arrive at democratically legitimate decisions on how to use and manage natural resources in order to achieve sustainable development.

### Ecological governance and integration

Policymaking for ecologically sustainable development is embedded in the existing systems of governance with its fragmented structures, and filtered through competing logics that reflect the historic institutionalisation of different value structures (see Hanf and Jansen 1998:4 ff.). Democratic governments have a built-in respect for autonomy that makes for compromises over resource management and allocation. Interests that presently make demands on resources most often find themselves forced to act according to the logics of the increasingly globalised competitive market. National politicians are hard pressed to take the short-term and medium-term economic prospects of their own countries into account. These competitive, conflicting logics in turn tend to result in muddled or contradictory resource management objectives. Progress towards sustainability then becomes difficult to achieve, let alone to determine (see Lafferty 1996:13).

Thus a most crucial issue remains. How should a system of governance, based on the logic of ecological rationality, be organised so that ecological concerns are effectively *integrated* in policy-making and implementation? This problem of integration grows as the previous view of environment as a specific policy field among others gives way to views of ecological sustainability as a universal concern to, or constraint on, all human and societal activities.

To establish criteria for *what* should be changed and *where* to bring about such integrated ecological governance, one must observe the intricate relationship between institutions and organisations. *Institutions* are 'symbolic systems, cognitive constructions and normative rules through which actors categorise' their activities and 'infuse it with meaning and value', i.e., provide a logic of action (Hanf and Jansen 1998:4). *Organisations* are concerned with action, i.e., with mobilisation of resources to achieve certain goals and pursue specific values. Institutionalised values create, influence and develop organisational practices.

One is thus led to the conclusion that organisational changes in themselves would not be sufficient to achieve integrated governance. Value changes that enhance an ecologically benign interplay between structures and agents must somehow be injected into the organisation of ecological governance to 'influence the behaviour of agents by affecting the conditions under which they make decisions' (Barry 1999:104). Organisational changes must thus provide mechanisms for instilling common values of ecological rationality into its structures and agents. Effective ecological governance for sustainability 'can be realised only if infrastructure policies become "ecologised" and there is a build-up of "substantial environmental capacities in the non-environmental policy areas"' (Knoepfel 1995:214, 229).

'Ecologisation' can be achieved by inserting guarantees for an ecologically rational decision-making *process*. Examples are mandatory inclusion of ecological objectives and competence within all resource-related administrations, obligations to consult with ecological administrations, or mandatory requirements to develop environmental impact assessments for all resource use and management-related projects of some scale (see Knoepfel 1995:221 ff.). Another way of improving the effectiveness in ecological governance is to develop criteria for *'good' ecological performance*. Common measures 'set in parameters that have ecological and social references, and linked to agreed norms and targets' can be introduced (O'Riordan and Voisey 1997:10). One way here is to create standardised sustainability indicators (see

Thomas and Tennant 1998). Another is found in the efforts to introduce measures of good green conduct, such as green bench-marking and green certification, for both public governmental bodies and private business. Closely related to benchmarking and certification are the strategies of green labelling, green purchasing and tender and green accounting. A crucial thing to observe and judge is how and to what extent such measures are explicitly adapted to institutionalised values of autonomy.

With regard to the integrative dimension, the following crite-rion for ecologically rational governance may be formulated:

• Ecological governance is integrated in so far as 'ecological' values and norms, ecological capacities, and codes of ecologi-cally good conduct are actually internalised in the political and administrative decision-making process related to the use and management of resources.

## Ecological governance, democracy and individual autonomy

This book builds on the normative argument that ecologically rational governance must strive for sustainability *within* limits drawn by democracy and the value of individual autonomy. When laid out in ideal type fashion, such a system of governance may seem attractive in terms of sustainability. Still, its practical implementation will most certainly intensify conflicts over when, how, why and by whom resources should be used. However careful the balance is struck between sustainability and auton-omy, there will thus be 'winners' and 'losers'. The stronger the value of autonomy is pursued at present, the more individual actors today can utilise natural resources in ways not compatible with the need for long-term, sustainable resource management. On the other hand, the stronger the pursuit of long-term ecologi-cal sustainability, the more threatened may be the value of individual autonomy (see Lafferty and Meadowcroft 1996a:5). Government is the main mechanism for solving such political conflicts. But in *democratic* government, collectively binding decisions on where this balance ought to be struck are dependent on the configuration and distribution of power among actors and interests, entrenched in institutions and organisations.

Ecologically rational governance thus seems bound to meet

with political opposition and questioning of its legitimacy. How, then, could individual autonomy and political influence be safe-guarded in a system of governance geared towards ecological sustainability? In the latter half of the 1990s, it was increasingly argued that this question was wrongly put. Proponents of ecological modernisation held that promotion of green growth would do away with the presumed conflict between sustainability and individual autonomy (see Jansen, Osland and Hanf 1998:291 ff.). However, this view has been questioned on grounds of both sustainability and autonomy. As for sustainability, ecological modernisation 'follows, in essence, past patterns of economic development, particularly the equation of economic growth with human social progress' (Barry 1999:252 f.). A comparative study of West European environmental governance found general agreement that 'none of the most active promoters of ecological modernisation will achieve its goals in terms of the central categories and criteria of environmental policy' (Jansen, Osland and Hanf 1998:319). In terms of democracy and individual autonomy, ecological modernisation is criticised because its strong emphasis on market-based instruments 'addresses individuals and groups in society as consumers' rather than as 'democratic citizens under the law' (Barry 1999:227). It encourages people to think in terms of marginal behavioural change guided by the criterion of individual economic gain.

However, argue the critics, ecologically sustainable development necessitates a massive change in cultural values. This can be politically legitimised through free and informed deliberations on what the institutionalised societal values should really be about. This implies a concern with measures for participatory democracy where autonomous citizens are 'encouraged to consider the interests of all those potentially affected by the democratic process' (Barry 1999:228 f.). When individuals are addressed as citizens, their sphere of autonomy is widened. They are empowered to participate in, and deliberate over which collectively binding decisions should be made with respect to resource use and management. Democratic governance, in which citizens have a guaranteed sphere of influence also over collective matters, is after all 'a process in which we all come to internalise the interests of each other and indeed of the larger world around us' (Goodin 1996:18).

Several innovations in environmental policy provide for more varied and intense public participation. Right-to-know legislation, public hearings, impact assessment procedures, environmental mediation, and regulatory negotiation are all examples of designs which ideally bring people together under conditions of free and open discourse to reach decisions through the strength of the better argument (Dryzek 1995:302). It should be noted, however, that ecologically rational governance in terms of space and time both strengthens the need for democracy and autonomy and complicates the realisation of these objectives. The picture of ecological governance as a multi-level system of 'nested enterprises' indicates that its democratic legitimacy is dependent on each level having spheres of autonomy that allow for meaningful popular participation (Ostrom 1990:89 f.). Decentralisation and delegation of authority and responsibility are called for in this respect, as are specific programs directly addressing local and ecosystem-based entities of governance with recognised spheres of competence. The inter-generational perspective of ecological governance calls for mechanisms to enhance the interests of future generations. Arguments have therefore been raised in favour of autonomy restrictions on the individuals of today to provide autonomy of choice for future generations. There are proposals to give rights not only to future generations, and even to certain types of nature, in order to guarantee sustainability (see Wissenburg 1993).

With respect to the democracy and autonomy aspects of ecological governance, the following criteria can be formulated:

- Governance is ecologically rational in terms of democracy and individual autonomy to the extent that the management of environment and natural resources is subjected to political debate and decision-making in democratic processes open to meaningful public participation at all levels of governance.
- Governance is ecologically rational in terms of individual autonomy to the extent that the balance among different policy instruments used in such governance is explicitly tilted in favour of safeguarding individual rights across generations.

## Ecological governance and the authority of government

It was argued above that collective ecological management in accordance with the logic of ecological rationality implies and even requires a multi-level governance approach. Admittedly, governance *is* an elusive concept. It refers to an inclusive and comprehensive process of co-ordination and direction of public and private actions and resources. Governance is concerned with 'achieving collective action in the realm of public affairs', where it is not always fully possible 'to rest on recourse to the authority of the state' (Stoker 2000:93). This implies that the nation state is not the logical top rung on the ladder of governmental units involved.

But exactly what role does govern*ment* play in govern*ance*? The literature presents us with two opposing views of the 'ecology of governance', i.e., the relations among actors in the structures and processes of governing. At one end, central government is seen as dwindling to a position as one among equals within a core structure of governance consisting of inter-linked networks and communities with both public and private sector participants, mutually interdependent on each other for resources such as money, expertise, and legitimacy. Indeed, since 'integrated networks resist government steering, develop their own policies and mould their environments', new governance comes close to 'governing without government' (Rhodes 1996:652, 658).

At the other end, it is argued that hierarchical relations are still very important. Governments do indeed 'establish the basic parameters within which markets, and even social groups, function'. The role of the state is 'transforming from a role based in constitutional powers towards a role based in co-ordination and fusion of public and private interests' (Pierre and Peters 2000:25, 39). In fact, 'linkages upward towards transnational government and downward towards sub-national government should be more thought of as state *strategies* to reassert control and not as proof of states surrendering to competing models of governance' (Pierre and Peters 2000:16; italics mine). While the role and power of the state can vary between sectors, it retains control over such critical resources in the process of governance as legislation and grants, which gives it a decisive role in producing desired outcomes. The state's role may in fact be strengthened: '[I]t tends to gain control at the implementation stage by having in essence co-opted social interests that might otherwise oppose its actions' (Pierre and Peters 2000:49).

What, then, is the role and fate of the democratic state's authority in multi-level *ecological governance*? One way to analyse this is to look at the historic record of state authority in society and the economy. The pattern of state regulation and control in Sweden is one where 'the state has taken a higher profile in society, pursuing agendas of provision and distribution' (Pierre 2000:244). There is thus a historically developed institutional interest in maintaining the authority of national government. This means that there is institutional capacity (see Jänicke 1997) for the state to function as the 'needle's eye' in the multi-level institutionalisation of the logic of ecological rationality. Upward to the international and global levels, the state sovereignly enters into agreements and assumes duties in the common pursuit of global sustainability. Downward to regions and municipalities, the state may delegate responsibilities for implementing these internationally agreed upon measures. Admittedly, there are several semi-autonomous as well as politically independent branches of government. However, the state is vested with enough constitutionally legitimised resource-mobilising capacity and coercive competence to retain authority 'in its own right' (Lundqvist 2001a).

Another way is to start from the spatial character of sustainability problems. The scale of such problems as climate change necessitates a *global* approach; 'ecologism in one country' is impossible. The individual nation state becomes – at least morally – bound to implement agreed-upon international measures. Regional organisations such as the EU call for equal conditions with respect to production and consumption of goods and services. These movements towards 'nested enterprises' undermine the individual state's authority to regulate economic activities within its territory to promote ecological sustainability over and above the levels prevailing for the Union as a whole. At the same time, EU directives related to ecologically sustainable development may force national governments to delegate power and authority for the management of particular eco-systems – such as water basins – to local or even sub-local units.

How far and how intensely ecologically rational governance

challenges the authority of the *democratic* state is thus open to empirical analysis. Recent comparative research does not conclude with certainty whether or not sustainable development really is democratically obtainable. Some contend that democratic governance – particularly if it involves corporativist streaks – and traditional environmental policy are mutually enhancing (Jänicke 1997:12 f.; Crepaz 1995; Jahn 1998). Others argue that democracies seem to have severe difficulties in adopting integrated and effective policies of sustainable resource management (Eckerberg and Lafferty 1997; O'Riordan and Voisey 1997). Liberal democracy with its piecemeal style of policy-making may prove insufficient for achieving sustainability (Hayward 1996:232). The sheer comprehensiveness of public policies needed to steer natural resource use towards sustainability in both production and consumption might cause government overload. The efforts to control individual behaviour might stumble on the constitutional 'inaccessibility' of citizens' private, autonomous choices as market actors (see Ligteringen 1999). On the other hand, some aspects of the existing democratic state might be conducive to a system of ecologically rational governance that values individual autonomy. This is more likely if the capacity of the political system as a whole for public participation and administrative integration is well developed, as well as if there is a political cultural context characterised by a co-operative policy style.

Chapter 7 of this book will assess Sweden's emerging system of ecological governance in terms of their effects on the authority of national government. The approach is somewhat different from that of the other empirical chapters. Instead of establishing specific assessment criteria, the themes and patterns of the earlier chapters are brought to bear on the problem of authority. The objective is to shed further light on the *democratic* state's power and authority to actually bring public and private efforts and resources together to pursue a common objective of ecologically sustainable development. Could the democratic state also become the ecological state?

## Sweden and ecological governance – a case in point?

Developing criteria for rational ecological governance is one thing, choosing the most fruitful ways and cases for comparing actual developments and performance to these criteria another. A basic assumption underlying this study is that environmental policies have been undergoing thorough changes in the 1990s. This is particularly the case following the 1987 Brundtland Commission report and the 1992 Rio Earth Summit. The quest for sustainable development has indeed placed new responsibilities on the world community of states to integrate ecological concerns into their structures and processes of governance.

An empirical answer as to how far we succeed in governing ourselves to secure both democracy and sustainable development could be sought through some form of comparison among a randomly chosen number of nations. It could also be sought by systematically comparing some class of nations that show similarities in some characteristics crucial to the enhancement of ecological concerns in governance. This latter strategy is employed in a recent comparison of 'high consumption societies' and their strategies for implementing sustainable development. Several arguments are put forward in favour of such a comparative approach. One is *normative*. The internationally acknowledged principle of 'differentiated responsibility' obliges developed industrial nations to take special action, since their high levels of production and consumption lead to 'ecological footprints', i.e., pressure on environment and resources that transcend far beyond their geographical territories. Another is based on *cumulativity*. Several studies of environmental policy have shown the importance for environmental policy of the countries' productive, technological, financial and political/administrative capacities (see Jänicke 1997). These two arguments lead to a third; 'the affluent societies of the North' provide *critical cases* for studying how far ecological concerns have penetrated the governance of those nations. That these countries are also democracies only adds to this criticality (see Lafferty and Meadowcroft 2000a:3).

Sweden is part of that comparative study. The final assessment places the country in a group of nations whose governmental response to sustainable development is classified as 'enthusiastic'. Sweden is said to have 'an established reputation as an environmental policy innovator and this has been carried forward over the past decade into the policy realm of sustainable development' (Lafferty and Meadowcroft 2000b:412 f.). Recent comparative

studies of the implementation of Local Agenda 21 have characterised Sweden as 'setting the pace', showing 'quick progress', and
being 'at the leading edge' in the LA 21 process (see, e.g.,
Eckerberg, Coenen and Lafferty 1999:242 ff.; see also below,
pp. 168–71).

This means that *critical case* arguments for studying how high
consumption societies have gone about implementing sustainable
development within the democratic framework are even more
supportive for selecting Sweden as a case in point. If any country
has come anywhere near meeting the criteria for ecologically
rational government, a 'forerunner' like Sweden might be such a
country. This also means that concern for *cumulativity* speaks in
favour of making Sweden the case for analysis. While there is
much theoretical literature on how ecological governance or a
democratic ecological state should be designed and function,
much less has been done to find out how such governance is actually working. A comparison between an empirical 'front' case and
cumulatively established normative criteria for democratic *and*
ecologically rational governance could thus be a valuable addition to the current discourse.

Such a comparison of empirical strategies and measures with
normatively established criteria should, to be of any cumulative
value, be based on a systematic selection and treatment of data.
What of the Swedish strategies, policies and measures could be
deemed relevant here? One criterion is the timing of Swedish
action. I have predominantly selected Swedish political action
related to sustainable development in the 1990s, i.e., a period
when the perspectives of the Brundtland Commission and the Rio
Earth Summit were making themselves felt and gradually
accepted nationally as well as internationally. In terms of the
content of strategies and policies chosen for analysis, I have
concentrated particularly on the ecological aspect of sustainability. In so doing, I have tried as far as possible to cover actions that
seem pertinent to each of the dimensions of rational ecological
governance discussed above.

The reader will find that I have deliberately chosen to concentrate on the *national* efforts to bring about ecologically rational
governance. This may of course fly in the face of those arguing –
rightly – that strategies for sustainable development cannot be
successfully implemented by individual nation states. However, I

have applied this national perspective in order to be able to draw some comparative lessons about what the individual nation *can* and *cannot* achieve, thereby illuminating how and why national strategies may succeed in, or fall short of successfully promoting ecologically rational governance. It may also illuminate the particular political, institutional and other circumstances that seem to promote progress or provide obstacles to ecologically rational governance. This would – so I hope – open up an extended exchange and a closer connection between green political and democratic theory on the one hand, and the comparative study of politics for sustainable development on the other.

# 2
# 'Nested enterprises'? Spatial dimensions of ecological governance

## Do the twain ever meet? 'Natural' and 'man-made' systems and the problem of scale

*The nature–society interface: different scales, problems of fit, and nestedness*

Space is of central concern to rational ecological governance. Environmental problems and resource management issues cross the man-made scales of local, regional or national governments. The question thus becomes how 'to negotiate a better fit' in responding to very complex ecological challenges (Pritchard Jr. et al. 1998:30 f.). Elinor Ostrom's answer in her now classic *Governing the Commons* is twofold. The underlying principle in her model of stable, ecosystem-based governance is one of congruence between a natural ecosystem and the unit of governance for that system. Regimes for the use and management of natural resources must thus have *clearly defined boundaries,* and the users/managers of the resource should have their *right to organise recognised* by external governmental authorities. Pointing to the complexity posed by the crossing scales of natural and man-made systems, and thus the problems of scale and co-ordination in ecological governance, she recommends a spatial web of *'nested enterprises'.* Smaller-scale resource regimes are linked in multiple layers to form larger entities of resource governance (Ostrom 1990:90 ff., 101 f.).

Admittedly, Ostrom's classic study deals above all with single-interest, single-purpose resource regimes. Ecosystems of some size are, however, usually subjected to multiple, often conflicting claims and uses. This makes the problem of designing and co-ordinating units for ecologically rational governance even more complex. However, I argue that the idea of nested enterprises *does* imply that multi-faceted interests and uses of shared natural resources can be organised into a proper response to problems of ecological governance. I therefore examine the ideas of *ecosystem management* in order to formulate operational criteria for evaluating Sweden's performance in terms of spatially rational ecological governance.

*Ecosystem management – basic features*
The first issue of ecosystem management is to define the unit to be managed. An *ecosystem* is a community of organisms that functions as an integrated energy-nutrient processing system. As such, it has physical structures, such as soil, plants and animals, and exhibits functions of energy flows and nutrient cycling. Ecosystems do have both space and time attributes. However, 'no boundary, border or classification system can adequately categorise and organise all of the information to support an ecological approach' (Sexton et al. 1998:168). Ecosystems grade into one another and are nested within a matrix of interrelated ecosystems of different sizes (Szaro et al. 1998:2). Still, we can define certain types of ecosystems. Some are bounded naturally, like water catchments, or topographically, like mountain ranges (see Brussard et al. 1998:11 ff.).

Ecosystems provide the basis for sustenance and reproduction of human life. This human dimension means that to become meaningful units for management, ecosystems must be delineated in ways that have meaning and significance for people within and outside that area as management units. They must thus be defined in terms compatible with the problems of the actors benefiting from or dependent on the natural resources and the ecological services of the area (Lackey 1998:24). As management units, they may build on, but not be constrained by existing political and administrative jurisdictional boundaries. Governance units at local and regional levels can be modified to match such areas as water basins, air sheds, or mountain ranges. From a management point of view, however, it is important to have a core definition of the spatial area in order to enhance the effectiveness of the administrative operational unit for that area (Slocombe 1998:34).

What then should we mean by ecosystem *management* (ESM)? It is evident that there has been an evolution in the views on what constitutes the proper aims and content. In terms of our double standard of sustainability and autonomy, the traditional view of ESM showed little concern for autonomy. Many of the early definitions contended that ESM should be run by expert managers who wilfully and skilfully use and integrate an established knowledge base to achieve already decided objectives, usually framed in terms of the viability of the ecosystem. The need for participation by present users and the population of the area in decision-making was not recognised (Freemuth 1996:413).

However, this view of the ESM as best left to professionals is rapidly fading. Scientific information is important for effective ecosystem management, but is only one element in a decision-making process that is fundamentally one of public and private choice (Lackey 1998:21 ff.). Nowadays, ESM is seen as a democratic process that requires public participation to create consensus on the most proper use of resources. This is achieved on the basis of an integrative use of knowledge – ecological, economic, social and managerial – not only to maintain ecosystem sustainability and biological diversity but also to support human culture through sustainable economies and social civic communities (Berry et al. 1998:56; Szaro et al. 1998:6). ESM is thus now seen as involving relevant stakeholders in defining ecologically sustainable alternatives for the interactions of people and the environments in which they live. The implementation of these alternatives is achieved through a full integration of social and economic needs into management decisions (Pavlikakis and Tsihrintzis 2000:265 ff).

*Ecosystem management and existing units of governance: alternative ways to negotiate a 'better fit'*
The inclusion of different stakeholders and interests in ESM means that conflicting economic and social demands enter the process (see Jones et al. 1995:166). This, and the fact that stakeholders' actions have economic effects across areas of various scales, means that the distribution (read 'nesting') of authority and responsibility across natural and institutional scales becomes a core issue for rational ecological governance (see Szaro et al. 1998:3 f.).

But where should the collectively binding decisions be made to allow for a better fit to scale? The underlying premise in the more recent discourse seems to be that the actors and interests living in and/or socially and economically dependent on the ESM unit's resources should have considerable space for self-regulation, i.e., to make and apply binding resource decisions for the designated area. Given the spatial delineation of present jurisdictions, this may involve at least three designs, i.e., scaling down, scaling up, or working sideways. Scaling down means transfer of authority and responsibility to the ecosystem level, if that is smaller in size than the political/administrative unit presently vested with jurisdiction over the ESM area in question. Working sideways or scaling up denotes strategies for use when the delineated ESM area covers space across boundaries of already existing jurisdictions. These units will then have to relinquish powers horizontally or vertically to the trans-boundary ESM unit.

Used in this way, the ESM approach would mean an increase in autonomy for the stakeholders directly affected by ESM decisions. However, there could be problems in terms of nestedness. The use of natural resources and the effects thereof may have ecological, socio-economic and cultural repercussions way beyond the designated ecosystem management area. To make this alternative of self-governance at the ESM level acceptable, its mandate must thus be compatible with democratically established national and regional sustainability objectives, and bounded by authority and power at the higher jurisdictional levels, e.g., the region or the state. This means a need to create co-operative mechanisms among agencies and actors through changes in the existing institutional and organisational pattern. At a minimum, meaningful co-operation will require resolving conflicting mandates and integrating management goals among different jurisdictions and agents (Cortner et al. 1998:162; Brussard et al. 1998:14).

The state has the power to establish overarching objectives and the scale of natural resource use in society. It is the central government's responsibility to determine the 'law of the land', e.g., to provide for a decentralisation of certain decision-making authority, as well as responsibility for implementing sustainability measures that are functional in an ecological and resource management sense. Such authoritative linking of levels of governance, be it scaling down to regional or local governments, scaling up to the central level, or cross-level co-operative schemes, are strategies continuously used for restructuring governance to adapt to new circumstances. For such re-organisational efforts to be seen as ecologically rational, however, there must at least be allusions, and preferably direct adaptations to ecologically relevant scales.

*Criteria for spatially rational ecological governance*
We can now formulate some operational criteria for *spatially* rational ecological governance. First, at its core are place bound units with *clearly defined boundaries*. The delineation is based on ecologically relevant characteristics, such as natural or topographical features. Second, spatially rational ecological governance means that *the circle of relevant principal stakeholders and participants* is defined on the grounds of the area's natural or topographical characteristics. Finally, spatially rational ecological governance through ecosystem-based management units works within a larger web of *'nested enterprises'*, i.e., interlinked decision-making units and processes of scaling down, working sideways and scaling up in adherence to relevant ecological scales.

- Ecological governance is spatially rational when air sheds, water catchments, or specific landscape types are constitutive elements in the collective management of environment and natural resources to achieve sustainability.
- Ecological governance is spatially rational to the extent that it defines the circles of stakeholders and interests in goal setting and decision-making on actual resource use and management in accordance with relevant spatial scales.

**'Scaling down' – decentralisation to local government**

*Administrative decentralisation of environmental affairs in the 1980s*
Despite 'misfits' with ecosystem boundaries, local governments are of crucial importance to ecologically rational governance. In Sweden, there is a long history of local governance; municipalities have a constitutional responsibility to attend to the common interests and collective welfare of their inhabitants, and are vested

with strong tax powers for this purpose. Scaling down along traditional lines of public authority means decentralisation from central to regional and local levels of government. Over the last decades the Swedish state has transferred an increasingly heavy burden of responsibilities for implementing national policies.

What has been the pattern of such 'traditional' decentralisation in environmental affairs over the last decades? The authority to issue permits for polluting activities under the 1969 Environmental Protection Act was originally very centralised. A reform in 1981 delegated all permit issues – except those of national significance – to the Regional Administrations. The 1981 reform opened up for municipalities to take over – by agreement – some or all of the County Administration's supervision of polluting activities within the municipality. However, only few of the 286 municipalities sought such widened responsibilities during the 1980s (SOU 1987:32, p. 200).

The 1988/89 environmental reform redefined activities covered by the Environment Protection Act according to duration, scope, and effects on man and the environment. Half of the large plants and facilities covered by the National Licensing Board procedures were deferred to the Regional Administrations. Authority to issue environmental permits to about 6,000 medium-sized and small plants and facilities was decentralised from the regional level to the municipal Environment and Health Protection Committees (EHPCs). These Committees already handled more than 4,000 smaller facilities and activities requiring prior 'notification'. Decentralisation of supervisory responsibilities meant that the municipal EHPCs would from then on supervise all permit or notification activities within the local government's jurisdiction (SOU 1987:32, p. 309 f.).

While such changes may bring some gains in local autonomy, their contribution to spatially rational ecological governance is less certain. The drive for resource efficiency might encourage inter-municipal co-operation on environmental issues. Data from a 1991 survey to Swedish local Chief Environmental Inspectors show that more than half of the municipalities were engaged in formally organised co-operation on water and air quality monitoring and surveillance. Nearly 60 per cent of the registered co-operative contacts concerned neighbouring municipalities. Furthermore, almost nine out of ten reported co-operative activities with municipalities within the same region. In terms of authority, only one out of six CEIs said that the co-operative organisations had authority to make decisions on resources or actions binding on the participating municipalities (CEIS 1991).

Thus, while decentralisation along traditional administrative boundaries provides municipalities with more autonomy within their territory, it contains inter-municipal co-operation within and along traditional administrative lines. This has consequences for spatially rational ecological governance. Municipalities co-operate more with non-neighbours inside the same region than with neighbours across the county border, even if close co-opera-tion with the latter would be more rational in terms of ecosystem management (see below, pp. 36–9).

*Freedom to organise; the 1991 reform of municipal government*
The 1991 survey revealed the existence of a lively network among professionals at the local and regional levels of government. When asked about their contact network, the CEIs reported very frequent contacts with environmental administrators in other municipalities. These contacts were even more frequent than those with their local politicians or with local action groups, local media, and local associations. CEI contacts with environmental officers at the county level are almost as lively as the contacts with municipal politicians. There is thus a very specific *professional* network on environmental and resource management at the local and regional levels (CEIS 1991).

The impact of such professional networks on the effectiveness of ecological governance (see further ch. 6) very much depends on the position of ecological competence within local government. The new Municipal Act of 1991 gave Swedish municipalities wide-ranging autonomy on how to organise local government. Except for a Municipal Board of Directors (elected from the polit-ical majority on the Municipal Council) and an Election Committee, earlier mandatory boards and committees can be substituted by an organisation tailored to the needs and political will of the individual municipality.

Within a year after this reform, 57 Swedish municipalities (or 20 per cent) had abandoned their EHPCs in favour of other organisational solutions (SOU 1993:19, p. 41 f.). The amalgama-tion of traditional, mandatory environment and health protection tasks with other local government activities continued during the 1990s. One line is *legal-administrative*; as many as 105 out of Sweden's 288 municipalities had merged all decision-making on activities needing permits in Environmental and Building Permit Committees after the 1998 local elections. Another is *environmentalist*; traditional EHPCs existed in 83 municipalities, and 35 local governments had Environment Committees. A *resource management* perspective can also be discerned; 19 local governments had integrated Environmental and Planning Committees. Finally, there is a *risk management* view; 16 municipalities had joint Environmental and Rescue Committees. It is further notable that nearly 10 per cent of Sweden's local governments did not have a politically appointed Committee with the word 'environment' in its name in 1998 (Hagevi 1999).

There seems to be no necessary link between a politically appointed Committee dealing with environmental issues and an independent Environmental Administration. Soon after the 1991 reform, 25 per cent of all local governments had integrated environmental protection officers within other municipal administrations, like the Real Estate and/or Building or the Technical and Infrastructure. This trend towards integration of environmental issues into other parts of the local governmental organisation was particularly visible in smaller municipalities (SOU 1993:19, p. 43). All in all, the organisational changes in local government during the 1990s seem to have weakened the possibilities for ecological governance both politically and administratively.

*Agenda 21 and local measures for sustainable development*
As an outflow of the Rio Conference on Agenda 21, the Swedish Cabinet in early 1994 proposed that all Swedish municipalities should formulate their own Agenda 21, based on local problems and alternatives for local solutions. The process should encourage local groups and interests to engage in a discourse to find alternative, less resource-demanding and less environmentally disturbing ways to conduct their daily activities, and integrate sustainability concerns into every branch of the local government itself. The municipal Local Agenda 21 documents were expected to contain a comprehensive sustainable development programme for the municipality (Cabinet Bill 1993/94:111, pp 63 ff.). The

Cabinet's Environmental Advisory Board (situated in the Environment Ministry) distributed a handbook to guide the municipalities in their LA 21 process with an emphasis on *ecologically* sustainable development (see SOU 1994:128). Money from employment support programmes was allocated to local governments for hiring Agenda 21 co-ordinators. Most municipalities came to make use of this support.

Literally interpreted, the 1994 bill implied wide-ranging autonomy for municipal governments. Local action programmes for sustainable development should be drawn up without interference from higher governmental levels. A lively activity unfolded at the local level. By the end of 1996, more than half of Sweden's local governments had appointed LA 21 co-ordinators. Municipalities arranged seminars and courses, and gave practical advice on how to proceed to different target groups as well as to the general public. The Swedish report to the UN follow-up conference on Agenda 21 in 1997 stated that 'all' Swedish municipalities had started work on Local Agenda 21 (SOU 1997:105).

By spring 1998, 56 per cent of Swedish local governments had adopted an LA 21 action plan. The political centrality is revealed by the fact that (a) over three quarters of the municipalities set aside a special LA 21 budget, and (b) over 90 per cent of the plans were adopted by the highest political bodies, i.e., the Municipal Council or the Council's Board of Directors. Around 70 per cent of the adopted action plans were furthermore co-ordinated and implemented by either the Board of Directors or a specially appointed LA 21 Committee or Delegation. Only 12 per cent were under the ægis of the Environmental and Health Protection Committees. This implies that most municipalities viewed sustainable development as involving a broader resource management perspective than that of traditional environmental policy (Brundin and Eckerberg 1999).

The municipal LA 21 activities scored high in terms of autonomy and democracy. Most local governments took active steps to involve their citizens in the process, and three quarters launched multi-faceted campaigns, including public meetings, educational activities, study circles, and direct information to the households. As many as 40 per cent reported that the local civil society initiated, or played an important role, in the LA 21 process. General interest was reported as increasing, or at least not changing, in about 75 per cent of the municipalities in spring 1998 (Brundin and Eckerberg 1999).

At issue, then, is how Sweden's LA 21 activity scores in terms of effects on sustainable development. Are the LA 21 action plans actually integrated into the daily activities of local government, and if so, to what extent? Except for traditional environmental tasks, integration is slow. The 1996 changes in planning and building legislation directed local governments to strengthen citizen involvement in detailed planning and to integrate the LA 21 and regular planning processes (Cabinet Bill 1994/95:230). However, just over 50 per cent of the municipalities had formally decided to join these two processes at the turn of the century, and half of the LA co-ordinators reported that there had been little or no practical integration by 1998. Municipal finance, budget and accounting processes are, by far, the municipal sectors least integrated in the LA 21 activities (Brundin and Eckerberg 1999).

There are doubts about the prospects of LA 21 as a vehicle for ecologically rational local governance. The Cabinet's 1998 decision to provide SEK 50,000 to each of the 70 smallest municipalities (see Parliament Housing Committee 1998/99, p. 18) may not suffice to help economically hard-pressed local governments. As one close observer puts it: 'It is clear that that the gap between pioneer and laggard municipalities is increasing.' This implies that 'those municipalities that have few staff and little resources to manage comprehensive LA 21 programmes' will not live up to the original 1994 expectations of comprehensive sustainable development plans (Eckerberg 2001:35).

*Between resource mobilisation and sustainable resource governance: a continuing local dilemma*
Local governments are encountering three different logics in relation to resource management, all affecting the possibilities of establishing an ecologically rational system of governance. To mobilise resources, i.e., to increase the tax base and induce local growth, they see merit in going alone. To use available resources efficiently, there are strong incentives in favour of co-operation to gain economics of scale in, e.g., large infrastructure investments. To achieve resource sustainability, dependence on other local governments may be quite obvious – like the case of communities downstream from polluting industries – or less distinguishable,

like acidification caused by long range transports of air pollutants (Lundqvist 1998:95 f.).

The main feature of the decentralisation measures just described is that they have vested more legal and administrative competence in local governments for decisions that bind actors *within* the spatial unit of the municipality. The changes in planning and environmental legislation up to the Environmental Code of 1999 have this spatial implication. In particular, the powers inherent in the local governments' planning monopoly are crucial. The Master Plans (*översiktsplaner*) are a rolling, more or less continuous exercise in which municipalities lay out visions and plans for the use of land, eco-services, and the built environment. Such exercises clearly invite local governments to work within the logic of resource mobilisation, i.e., to adopt an exclusively intra-municipal perspective to maximise the developmental potential and thus, hopefully, the attractiveness of the municipality. In fact, very few inter-municipal co-operative arrangements are found in planning (Lundqvist 1998:100).

It is indeed somewhat of a spatial irony that the Local Agenda 21 process has been organised along these traditional jurisdictional lines, despite the central government's emphasis on *ecological* sustainability as the core of that process. The local government initiates the process *within* the borders of the municipality. Co-operation among municipalities to make action plans for common pool resources is at best an added bonus, not something set out as a precondition for the process.

Informal co-operation among environmental and planning professionals across municipal borders may be a way of addressing the spatial problem of ecosystem management in a decentralised system of government. But the extent to which ecological rationality prevails in local decision-making is then dependent on the political and administrative strength of the proponents of the precautionary principle. The reorganisation of local government taking place in the wake of the 1991 reform implies that both the political and the professional strength in municipal government may have become weaker with the diffusion of the environmental functions into several other, and structurally stronger, local administrations.

The developments in local government during the 1990s as a result of decentralisation and municipal reorganisation, and even more as a result of the financial squeeze prevailing for most of the decade, seem to point in the direction of a continuous dilemma for ecological governance. Admittedly, the Regional Administrations have some possibilities to block ecologically questionable local actions and to initiate regional co-ordination of resource management. However, the dominant strategy of vesting authority in the hands of local governments provides few incentives and possibilities of a spatially rational system of ecological governance where decision-making capacity transcends administrative borders to follow ecosystem boundaries.

## 'Working sideways': local and regional governmental co-operation

*Water catchments – from mutual monitoring to actual management?*
If Sweden were to be divided politically and administratively on the basis of main water catchments, there would be 119 units of governance. The history of co-operation in water catchments dates back to the 1950s, when Swedish municipalities initiated and organised joint water quality management associations and boards. By 1993, there were over 50 catchment-wide associations in operation, varying in size from water management associations of the big lakes *Vänern, Vättern, Mälaren,* and the large rivers, e.g., *Dalälven,* and *Göta älv,* to water management committees in the small catchments in the Skåne region. Membership consists of municipal governments, local business, farming and forestry organisations, and others. The average size of membership was 25, varying from 52 in the water associations to 12 in the water committees. The catchment organisations do indeed transcend municipal and regional boundaries. When controlling for multiple drainage basin memberships, a 1988 study found that as many as 178 of the then 284 Swedish municipalities participated in organised co-operation on water quality management. At least one dozen were members of three such organisations. About half of the basin-wide organisations involved municipalities in at least two counties (Enell et al. 1988).

However, their authority and responsibilities do not correspond fully with the criteria for ecosystem *management* formulated earlier. The core activity is monitoring; the so-called 'recipient control program' involves the municipalities and stake-holder members in continuous, joint monitoring of water quality. The associations have only to a limited extent been involved in local resource planning. This holds both for setting up specific water planning documents and for active participation in the process of developing municipal master plans (*översiktsplaner*). It is worth noting that the 1977 Act regulating Water Associations (*vattenförbund*) explicitly aims at enabling joint municipal and stakeholder *management* of common water resources (Edenman 1990). Still, these water associations did not report any more extensive activity on water planning and resource management than other types of associations. They were only consulted, and did not play an active role in the municipal master planning process around 1990 (Gustafsson 1995). This pattern is further evidenced in an inventory made by the Swedish Environmental Protection Agency in late 1996. Half of the catchments are subject to no further joint activity than monitoring water quality. In terms of our previous criteria for ecosystem management, only three (3) per cent of the catchments reported having active cross-boundary municipal water planning including stakeholder participation (Norman 1997).

Why this pattern? Apart from the obvious lack of money and manpower, representatives of water catchment organisations point to the problem of credible commitment from local politi-cians, as well as to legislative and administrative hindrances (Gustafsson 1995). In fact, none of the municipal powers in land use and resource planning provided to local governments under the Planning and Building Act have been transferred from local governments to the catchment associations. They have thus not been nested firmly enough in the regular planning and manage-ment administration to play a significant role. Still, the principal view held by municipalities and regional administrations is that voluntary catchment co-operation would easily develop if local and regional levels were provided with more resources and better policy instruments (SOU 1997:99, p. 18).

Around the turn of the century, there was mounting domestic and international pressure to adopt a catchment perspective on water management. The 1997 proposals for a EU Water Directive explicitly built on this. Anticipating this Directive, the Swedish Government had already appointed a special commission on water management. Its October 1997 report recommended that Sweden be divided into ten 'Catchment Districts'. A special Catchment Authority would comprise two or three regional administrations and all local governments within the district area. Within the Catchment District, this Authority should (a) decide on collectively binding management plans to reach ambient water quality norms for catchments, (b) be solely responsible for environmental permit decisions under the Environmental Code, and (c) be responsible for monitoring and for liming of acidified waters. Within the District's major catchments, local governments should consolidate permit decisions into one permit decision-making unit per catchment (SOU 1997:99, pp. 49 ff., 69 ff.).

While these recommendations were geared towards sustainable management, the commission also addressed the issue of autonomy. It thus suggested that binding plans and norms should be worked out in close co-operation among regional administrations, local governments, existing water catchment associations, and all relevant stakeholders. Farmers and local governments should be allowed to 'swap' management actions in order to establish the most cost-effective ways to reach the water quality norms for their sub-catchment. Subsidies, polluter fees and other means could be used to encourage this form of ecosystem management co-operation (SOU 1997:99, pp. 75 ff.). However, collectively binding decision-making capacity could be delegated from the Catchment Authority to such 'local environmental management co-operatives' only if they fulfil certain criteria for joint associations laid down in the Swedish Constitution (SOU 1997:155, p. 81 ff.).

Anticipating the entering into force of the EU Water Directive, the Swedish Government in early 2001 mandated the Environmental Code Committee to work out suggestions of how to adapt the Swedish Code to the Directive's clauses on water action plans. The Cabinet also indicated that a special commissioner would be appointed to work out recommendations for the administration of the water catchment districts required under the EU Directive (Dir. 2001:25). Meanwhile, there has been substantive work done on water management scenarios within the Swedish Environmental Protection Agency. These scenarios range from very centralised action in particularly 'troubled' waters, over a 'strong district' model with popularly elected water district parliaments deciding on action plans, to a model of 'local participation', with an emphasis on new forms of co-operation, diffusion of information, and local stakeholder participation. The latter would include delegation of authority to existing water catchment associations (SEPA 2000a).

There are as yet (spring 2003) no concrete proposals to be finally acted upon by the Swedish Government. From the view-point of ecosystem management adopted here, a few comments are in order. First of all, most discussion seeks to incorporate a spatial ecosystem view – the water catchment – into the tradi-tional administrative system. But regional boundaries rather than catchments determine the width of the Catchment Districts. There is a firm view on nestedness; ecologically determined organisa-tions such as existing catchment associations and the proposed 'environmental co-operative groups' are to be bound by centrally and regionally determined water quality norms. Autonomy, i.e., 'freedom to organise' and to distribute costs and benefits among relevant stakeholders is so grudgingly recognised that it might detract from stakeholders' already low willingness to participate in management activities that cost money (SOU 1997:155, p. 54).

## Coastal zones – from water quality monitoring to ecosystem management?

If anything, the coastal zone outside the land area of a state is a common property resource. It is possible to detract individual resource units from that zone, but no one could claim total control of the stock. Water is running, and schools of fish and other species are moving. To achieve rational ecological gover-nance, it would thus seem logical to develop a spatially integrated coastal zone management.

However, Swedish coastal zone management in the mid-1990s was more like a patchwork (see Engen 1996). The environmental decentralisation in the late 1980s among other things involved the so-called 'recipient control programmes'. It was thus the bound-aries of the municipalities that determined the surveillance and monitoring of water quality in coastal and marine areas. The 1987 planning legislation furthermore made local governments responsible for physical planning out to 12 nautical miles from the territorial base line. This process of decentralisation meant

that the commons of the Swedish coastline and marine environment was administratively divided into 15 regional and 85
municipal administrative enclosures of planning and resource
management. At the same time, there was an ecological division
into 55 'coastal water areas', linked to the 119 major water catchments in Sweden (SOU 1997:99, p. 50).

In terms of spatially rational ecological governance, municipalities were given an order they could neither refuse nor deliver.
No local government can fully control marine waters within their
boundaries. What evolved of coastal zone management after
1990 reflected the narrow pattern of monitoring and measurement that prevailed in inland catchment areas. By 1993, the entire
western coastline from the Norwegian border to the Strait
between Sweden and Denmark, the coastal waters around Skåne
and along the Baltic Sea coastline up through the Blekinge and
Kalmar counties, was subject to inter-municipal co-operation in
coastal water associations (see Gustafsson 1995). The most striking discrepancy from the spatially rational model of ecological
governance outlined earlier is that the coastal water associations
emerging in the 1990s were confined to running commonly
financed monitoring stations along the coastline. Nowhere did
there develop any co-ordinated coastal *management* crossing
existing regional boundaries.

Why this spatial pattern? First of all, the initiative to set up co-
operative coastal monitoring schemes was top-down, from the
Environmental Units of the Regional Administrations. As arms of
the state, these Administrations and Units have the authority to
survey and co-ordinate actions on environmental and resource
issues crossing municipal borders. However, municipal planners
and officials were sceptical of 'planning in water'. Co-operation
across municipal borders seldom went beyond the mandatory
consultation procedures prescribed by law; no municipal authority to decide on land use and resource planning was transferred to
coastal water associations (Engen 1996). Thus, only one fjord
area on the West Coast had co-ordinated planning and environmental control policies involving all the littoral municipalities in
the mid-1990s, and this was furthermore the result of state
economic support directed to that particularly 'threatened'
marine environment.

The remedy to this situation may be coming from central

government. Following reports and recommendations of its Environmental Advisory Board (EAB), the Cabinet in December 1997 directed seven Regional Administrations to develop action programs for 'Sustainable Development in Sweden's Archipelagos'. The areas concerned are the Stockholm archipelago (with three Regional Administrations involved), the coastal areas of southern Östergötland and northern Kalmar regions, the archipelago of the Blekinge region, and the coastal areas of the new Västra Götaland region. The action programmes are to be worked out in co-operation among the Cabinet's Environmental Advisory Board, the municipalities and interested stakeholders with the Regional Administrations as the central co-ordinating actors (Environmental Advisory Board 1998:5 f.).

The action programmes for the four coastal regions are to cover both environmental management and economic and social development. They are to rest on four pillars, namely (a) Sweden's national environmental objectives (see below, pp. 64–9), (b) 'vital' environmental and resource interests as defined by earlier processes of national physical planning, (c) the Strategies for the Regional Environment (STRAMs) worked out by the Regional Administrations, and (d) the Local Agenda 21 documents worked out by the municipalities concerned. The objective is to establish coherent management programmes for the four coastal regions that are 'environmentally satisfactory and compatible with the need for [sustainable] socio-economic development' (Environmental Advisory Board 1998:6).

An EAB evaluation of the regional environment and resource management programmes worked out for the above-mentioned four archipelago areas came in 2000. The Board recommended that the municipalities in these areas should produce in-depth master plans for their coastal zones and marine waters by 2005. The Regional Administrations in these areas should very actively follow up municipal implementation and report to central government in both 2003 and 2005. For the remainder of Sweden's coastal areas, concerned Regional Administrations and local governments should produce such master plans by 2009. Regional Administrations and relevant central authorities are to have special responsibilities for providing local governments with the necessary knowledge base. Furthermore, they are to suggest what resources and measures should be given priority in local planning for sustainable coastal zone development (SOU 2000:67, pp. 37 ff.).

The Archipelago Management Programmes are still (spring 2003) at the planning stage. There are, however, aspects of sustainability that imply a development towards spatially rational ecological governance. The archipelagos are delineated as ecologically relevant planning areas. Several Regional Administrations are mandatorily linked in the formation and implementation process. They are to provide a firm basis of ecologically relevant knowledge to local planners. There are also recommendations for integration with the EU International Coastal Zone Management initiatives. With such a strong emphasis of co-ordination from above, what then about local and stakeholder autonomy? First of all, the explicit linking of environmental protection to sustainable resource use and socio-economic development of the regions points towards the kind of involvement from local stakeholders typical of ecosystem management. Second, the active interaction with the local population during the formation process is strongly emphasised as a necessary ingredient for successful implementation of coastal zone management (SOU 2000:67, p. 45).

*Air quality co-operation – the land is the limit, not the sky*
Air quality is both influenced diffusely over large areas, and locally affected by agglomerations of population, buildings, industries, and transportation. While the former implies a commons of vast dimensions, the latter indicates a more limited spatial perspective, such as metropolitan areas or main traffic arteries. And how should the relevant spatial unit be defined if the local problem is caused by mobile sources? Furthermore, global climate change problems imply that air quality management is not easily defined in terms of 'natural' spatial boundaries.

Actors may thus be tempted to define air quality problems along established boundaries. Indeed, Swedish co-operative efforts in air quality management are predominantly organised within the borders of the Regional Administrations. Just before the turn of the century, there were air quality associations in all except the northernmost of the 24 counties. Most of those associations were founded just before 1990, after initiatives from the Regional Administrations' Environmental Units. The statutes, organisation and activities of the associations are almost identical. They (1) initiate measurements and monitoring of air quality within the county borders; (2) provide support and assistance to investigations of the environmental and health effects of air pollution; (3) inform members and other interested parties about monitoring results and air quality developments within the county, and (4) pledge to 'work for' co-ordinated action to abate air pollution (see e.g., Kalmar, Kronoberg, and Östergötland Counties, 1997–99).

There are three membership categories, i.e., all the municipalities within the county, the main industrial polluters, and regional non-industrial organisations. Members pay an annual 'service' or 'monitoring fee' to finance measurement activities. Some of the administrative functions are carried out by the Regional Administrations' Environmental Units. The actual measurements are contracted out to the Swedish Environmental Research Institute, (IVL, see www.ivl.se). There are a few cases of inter-regional co-operation on the basis of some air shed models. The six southernmost counties run co-ordinated air quality monitoring throughout that part of Sweden (Kronoberg County 1996). Most inter-regional co-operation occurs in metropolitan areas with substantial air pollution problems. The Stockholm project on air quality measurement involved six Stockholm area municipalities. The Municipal Association of the Gothenburg Region comprises Gothenburg City and ten surrounding municipalities in three counties.

The Swedish air quality associations are examples of how an external actor moves in to bring about spatial co-operation on a problem that the concerned actors – municipalities and polluters – may not even recognise they have in common. The main activity of the associations is limited to monitoring. Individual municipalities may hesitate to commit resources to joint air quality management since the possible gains may literally be gone with the wind. In areas dominated by mobile sources and differing meteorological conditions for individual local governments, it is furthermore quite difficult to define the common interest. We are thus justified in concluding that in the field of air quality and management, the land rather than the sky is the limit.

*From monitoring to management; a small step for central
government or a giant leap for local actors?*
The planning powers enjoyed by Swedish local governments
provide them with a spatial monopoly that becomes a formidable
factor in hedging the focus and interests of local governments
within the borders of the municipality. The description of inter-
municipal environmental and natural resource-related activities in
Sweden confirms this view. While local governments *do* acknowl-
edge the necessity to co-operate on managing environmental and
natural resources held in common, they do not seem overly enthusiastic to transfer some of their authority. There are few, if any,
examples of inter-municipal, ecosystem-based *management* units
having the power to plan for, and much less to decide and distribute the use of natural resources and eco-services common to two
or more municipalities. The monitoring activities of water, air or
coastal zone associations are thus not firmly nested within the
traditional political and administrative structure. To provide for
a spatially rational perspective would thus involve a giant leap for
local governments in terms of restructuring power relations and
organisational patterns.

At the same time, we have seen that central government, sometimes with pushing from the European Union, is taking some
steps in this direction. The on-going design of co-ordinated
coastal zone management institutions for the main archipelagos,
and the proposed Water Districts and Authorities, are prime
examples. The former seems directed towards ecosystem management in that it is to deal also with the social and economic claims
and use of resources and eco-services. The latter are so far more
exclusively geared toward the ecological sustainability of water
resources, albeit on a catchment scale. Common to both is that
the central government is trying to design, from above, management units that are spatially rational in an ecological sense, as
well as nested within the traditional political and administrative
chain of command. What remains to be seen is whether and to
what extent these movements will lead to a spatial redistribution
of power that reflects the natural scales of relevant ecosystems
and if so, to what extent they will be combined with features that
secure values of local autonomy.

## 'Scaling up' – centralisation to and within the national government

*Implementation from above: local investments for an 'ecologically sustainable society'*

Accepting the leadership of the Swedish Social Democratic Party in March 1996, the then Minister of Finance Göran Persson proclaimed the achievement of an 'ecologically sustainable society' as a new, 'noble mission' for his party. Presenting the Cabinet Policy Platform as the new Prime Minister two weeks later, he envisioned Sweden as 'an internationally driving force and a forerunner in the endeavours to create an ecologically sustainable development' (Parliamentary Record, March 22, 1996).

Several programmes and measures were launched to implement this vision. At the core, however, was massive central government support to investment programmes for local sustainable development (Environment Minister Anna Lindh 1997; DESD 1997:2; Prime Minister Göran Persson 1997; SAP 1997). In January 1997, a *Delegation for Ecologically Sustainable Development* (DESD) was formed within the Cabinet, consisting of the Ministers of Environment, Agriculture, Taxation, Basic Education, and the Junior Minister of Labour. The Delegation's first assignment was to 'develop a platform for the Cabinet's comprehensive policy for an ecologically sustainable society' (Prime Minister Göran Persson, Parliamentary Record January 22, 1997).

The DESD proposal for *A Sustainable Sweden* came in March 1997. The proposed Sustainability Investment Programme included (1) one billion SEK to eco-cycle adjustment of built environments and infrastructure, (2) nine billion SEK to eco-cycle transformation of the Swedish energy system, and (3) six billion SEK to local sustainability investments by municipal governments (DESD 1997). In its April 1997 Economic Bill to the Parliament, the Cabinet proposed 12,6 billion SEK for the period 1998–2000 to local investment programmes (LIPs), and infrastructure and energy conversion projects. The bill was subsequently passed by the Parliament (Cabinet Bill 1996/97:150, pp. 87 ff.). In spring 1998 the Parliament decided to spend a further two billion SEK for the year 2001 (Cabinet Bill 1997/98:150, Spending Area 18, item E1).

The drive for centralised implementation was in clear evidence. The Cabinet – not any central agency – should set criteria for and make decisions on applications from local governments (DESD 1997). The DESD even specified the demands that the Cabinet should make on LIPs receiving support. It was not until amidst the decision-making process that the government issued the statute regulating the LIP application and grant process. The statute described in great detail what municipal applications should contain, but there were no explicit rules or criteria for how the Cabinet should go about determining which municipal LIPs would be worthy of state support (SFS 1998:23).

In fact, the granting process for the first programme year had begun already in the autumn of 1997. All except two of Sweden's 288 municipalities sent in notifications of interest by mid-October. Within the Environment Ministry, a Preparatory Working Group consisting of 12 members together with the ministers in DESD selected 40 of these as particular municipalities for a dialogue on how to proceed with applications. 115 municipalities sent in full applications for state LIP grants. Very few of the applications were sent for consultation to expert central agencies. The *Riksdag's* Housing Committee evaluation states that the process with its 'unclear structures of decision-making within the Cabinet's Office and the unclear administrative practice within the Environment Ministry's Preparatory Working Group ... raised doubts about the continuity, predictability and equal treatment of applicants' (Parliament Housing Committee 1998/99:20 ff.).

During spring 1998, 42 municipalities were given a total of 2.3 billion SEK in state grants for their LIPs, with an average state subsidy rate of 30 per cent. The government's view of the *political* centrality of the LIP grant programme is shown by the fact that whenever a grant decision was taken, one of the five Ministers in the Delegation for Ecologically Sustainable Development went to the municipality in question. There, they announced the granting decision at well-organised press conferences, particularly pointing to the number of jobs resulting from the local 'green' investment programme (see Environment Ministry Press Releases spring 1998).

What then about the implications for sustainability of the supported programmes? First of all, it is clear that the programme did not adopt a spatially rational perspective; municipal bound-aries were the criteria of 'sustainable' investments. The Swedish Nature Conservancy Association (SNF) stated that the supported LIPs were not directed towards more than three out of the 14 serious environmental threats identified by the Swedish Environmental Protection Agency (Kågesson and Lidmark 1998, ch. 9). The Auditors of Parliament concluded that meaningful evaluations of environmental effects could only be made relative to such quantified objectives that existed *before* the establishment of Sweden's National Environmental Objectives and subsequent targets and sub-goals. For the seven comparisons thus possible, the measures taken through LIPs granted in the first programme year were estimated to contribute between 0.029 and 3.6 per cent to the actual achievement of national objectives (Auditors of Parliament 1998/99:94).

In terms of autonomy, municipal work on preparing the noti-fication of interest and the final application was hard pressed by the narrow time limits set by central government. Many munici-palities thus could not find time to incorporate new ideas that came up during the LIPs' write up phase. Neither were the LIPs fully anchored within the different branches of local government. In particular, the local financing part, averaging 70 per cent, seems to have caused internal political problems for some local governments (Parliament Housing Committee 1998/99:30 ff.).

As shown earlier, the Swedish government in effect launched *two* programmes for sustainable development in the mid 1990s. The Agenda 21 process spanned all levels of government, but the *local* governments and the grassroots were given a most crucial role (Cabinet Bill 1993/94:111, p. 63). The programme for 'A Sustainable Sweden' was a *central* governmental initiative, launched amidst the build-up of the Local Agenda 21 processes, and in fact run by a specially designated Working Group within the Environmental Ministry that could bypass most of the tradi-tional lines of Swedish public decision-making (see Lundqvist 2001a). The three different investment programmes forming the economic core of the programme would each in its own way have important consequences for the Swedish municipalities. Official statements contended that the LIPs would be 'directly linked to the Local Agenda 21 process. This also means an established linkage from the local level to the central decision-making within the Cabinet and the Parliament' (SOU 1997:105, p. 11).

If the autonomy criterion for ecologically rational governance is met, this should mean that local investment plans supported by central government money are congruent with or compatible to the Local Agenda 21 action plans. However, evidence shows that citizen involvement in LIP preparation processes was lower and local business involvement much higher than their respective involvement rates in the Local Agenda 21 processes in general in the first LIP year (Brundin and Eckerberg 1999). One report concludes that the sheer size of the LIP grant programme and the economic pressure on poorer municipalities may together create preconditions that will change 'the direction of their Local Agenda 21' (Brundin and Eckerberg 1999).

The forms of the LIP process have changed somewhat since the first programme year. Still, it seems fair to say that when finished in 2004, this state-supported programme is a prime example of disguising centralised 'implementation from above' as a demo- cratically anchored process of ecologically oriented governance (see Lundqvist 2001a).

*Beyond the fence: international conventions for trans-boundary ecosystem management*

Sweden is a contracting party to conventions aiming at joint management of trans-boundary common pool resources. Two of the most important ones cover the marine environments of sea areas adjacent to Sweden. The 1992 Convention on the Protection of the Marine Environment of the Baltic Sea Area is a revised and updated version of an earlier 1974 convention. Administered by the Baltic Marine Environment Protection Commission in Helsinki (HELCOM), the 1992 convention covers the Baltic Sea and the entrance to the Baltic Sea up through the Kattegat to the parallel of the Skaw in the Skagerrak (http://helcom.fi/). It thus overlaps somewhat with the 1992 Convention for the Protection of the North East Atlantic Marine Environment (OSPAR). The OSPAR convention combines the earlier 1972 Oslo Convention for the prevention of marine pollu- tion by dumping from ships and aircraft and the 1974 Paris Convention for the prevention of marine pollution from land- based sources, and covers the North East Atlantic including Skagerrak and Kattegat (www.ospar.org/).

These two international conventions oblige each of the signatory states to implement the provisions for prevention of marine pollution from land-based sources and sea vessels within their territorial sea all the way to the base line. The Baltic convention also applies to a country's internal waters, i.e., the landward side from the baseline to the coastal line as defined by each littoral state. In substantial management terms, it is the states that are responsible for implementing common decisions. The contracting states pledge to adopt the precautionary principle to avoid the introduction into the marine environment of substances and energy that may bring about hazards to human health, harm living resources and marine ecosystems. They agree that costs of pollution prevention, control and reduction measures are to be borne by the polluter. The countries set out to apply best available techniques and best environmental practice including, where appropriate, clean technology (www.ospar.org/). The Baltic Sea convention spells out that the states should use Best Environmental Practice for all sources and Best Available Technology for point sources. Both conventions oblige the member states to take relevant measures also on land without prejudice to their sovereignty to prevent marine pollution (http://helcom.fi/).

Special Commissions supervise the implementation of the Conventions and review the condition of the maritime areas and the effectiveness of the measures being adopted. They may also engage in developing further programmes and measures for the prevention of pollution and for the control of activities that may adversely affect the maritime area, including economic instruments. Each of the littoral states has one vote in the Commissions of the respective convention, and the Commissions' decisions should be taken unanimously. A decision, but not a recommendation, becomes binding on member states that voted for it after 200 days, provided that three quarters of the member states have shown that they accept the decision (www.ospar.org/).

These two conventions provide examples of how spatial arrangements can be made to manage vast ecosystems. In a formal sense, Sweden and other contracting states oblige themselves to take jointly decided measures to protect the common marine resources of the Baltic and North Seas. At the same time, however, decision-making rules place final power in the hands of sovereign member states. In the OSPAR case, a contracting state may vote against a decision in the Commission, and thus not be legally bound by it. On the other hand, participation in these marine environment conventions also carries political implications. By engaging in such conventions, states actually commit themselves to participate constructively in the governing of the commons of the high seas. As it turns out, the work in these conventions has been paralleled by ministerial and prime ministerial conferences, where obligations have been made to undertake measures more far-reaching than those stipulated in the conventions (see, e.g., SOU 1996:153, pp. 47 ff.).

**'Nested enterprises' and compatible scales?**

*Ecological governance and the problem of fit; seventeenth-century fences are still crossing the commons*
This chapter has dealt with the problem of spatially rational ecological governance, i.e., how to solve the problem of fit between naturally bounded eco-systems and man-made systems of government. The premise is that the solution could be provided through a system of interlinked jurisdictions proceeding from naturally distinguishable, but socio-economically and culturally meaningful ecosystems as the basic units. For such a system to become functional, three criteria should be fulfilled: (1) the resource regime must have *clearly defined boundaries*; (2) the resource users/dependants must have a *recognised right to organise and participate* at the relevant spatial scale, and (3) the complexity of society-environment relationships should be addressed through *nested enterprises*. The basic units of governance are successively linked with local, regional and national jurisdictions in order to solve problems of scale and achieve sustainable environmental and resource use and management.

Admittedly, there are problems with and conflicts among these principles. First of all, there are problems of defining ecologically proper boundaries. These are most pronounced for air quality management, but more easily dealt with for the management of water catchment areas. Coastal zones and marine environments are somewhere in between, open-ended but still possible to define in an ecologically and even socio-economically meaningful way. Second, there is potential conflict between autonomy, i.e., the right to organise for the resource appropriators and dependants, and sustainability, i.e., the need for effective co-ordination of overall and long-term resource planning and use through inter-linked local, regional and national jurisdictions. Existing scales and units of government may prove a strong fence against trans-ferring autonomy to new scales and units of governance.

The empirical evidence provided here corroborates this propo-sition. Although there are many examples of new strategies to solve the problem of fit between natural and societal scales, they do not yet fully live up to the three conditions of boundaries, recognition and nestedness. First of all, we have found that the strategy of *scaling down* is fundamentally one of decentralising to the traditional local unit of government, i.e., to the municipalities. There are few, if any, examples of power being delegated further down to users and dependants on ecosystem resources on a smaller scale. (It should, however, be noted that some limited experiments with local water management co-operation among farmers on a sub-catchment level have been carried out; see SOU 1997:155). With regard to the Local Agenda 21 process, it seems as if the original design of municipal autonomy and bottom-up linking of plans was disturbed, and even overrun, by the centrally initiated and managed programmes for local investments in sustainable development.

Secondly, the strategy of *working sideways* to establish inter-municipal co-operation around common ecosystems like water catchments has so far not involved any delegation of autonomy and authority to catchment associations to allow them to actually manage the resource. These associations are not yet firmly nested within the system of political and administrative governance. They have very little if any influence over the planning process that determines much of the land and resource use at the local level. Whether and to what extent the implementation of the EU Water Directive will involve a stronger role for these ecosystem-based associations is still (spring 2003) an open question. Air quality associations reveal a similar non-nested pattern. Since they have been initiated within and downwards from the Regional Administrations, their scale of operation does not seem adapted to geographically more relevant scales of air pollution.

Third, *scaling up* to achieve a co-ordinated response to the challenge of sustainable development has in one case meant super-centralisation. The national government's 1998–2004 grants to local investment programmes for sustainable development placed decisive powers at the Cabinet level. This is contrary to the traditional Swedish system of managing such programmes through central agencies that are constitutionally independent of the Ministries when deciding on individual cases of implementation. The autonomously developed Local Agendas did not become firmly integrated in the process. By making the municipalities the prime targets for support, the central government furthermore directed this huge effort to achieve 'A Sustainable Sweden' to traditional administrative rather than ecologically relevant natural scales. The international conventions in which Sweden participates to achieve sustainable development of adjacent marine environments are built on the states' sovereignty to adopt or reject common management measures.

Traditional political and administrative scales and units thus make their presence felt throughout the land. Common pool resources and coherent ecosystems have yet to become accepted as legitimate spatial units of governance. Indeed, the boundaries of local governments and regional administrations existing at the threshold of the twenty-first century enclose and fence off the commons in much the same way as they did in the seventeenth, when the present borders of the Regional Administrations, now crucial actors in the Water District, Archipelago Management and Air Quality Monitoring schemes, were once drawn.

### Straddling the fence; moves toward spatially rational ecological governance

'*É por ce muove!*' Galilei is (falsely) said to have exclaimed when receiving his verdict from the inquisition. So is Sweden; there *are* moves to get over old fences to make man-made jurisdictional scales more compatible with ecologically rational governance for sustainable development. The most evident signs are the recent proposals for new systems of governance for water catchments and the environments of Sweden's larger archipelagos. Water catchments are recognised as proper units for organising activities to achieve sustainable development. Given traditional identities in the archipelago areas, the delineations are most probably culturally and socio-economically meaningful enough to appeal to affected actors and interests.

Admittedly, there is still a lot of ground to cover to reach spatially rational ecological governance. The issue of autonomy is still clouded. There are yet (spring 2003) no concrete proposals to delegate authority and responsibility to ecosystem-linked actors for decision-making and management of resources *within* the ecosystem boundaries, but *across* political borders. Discussing in more vague terms of information, participation and consensus building, recent proposals seem intent on striking a balance between nestedness and co-ordination on the one hand, and user influence over management on the other. The archipelago proposal places the programme development and goal setting in the hands of Regional Administrations, while the *central* Environmental Advisory Board is to lay out how different local and regional actors and interests should be involved in the implementation of those action programmes (see SOU 2000:67). Different alternatives for stakeholder involvement in developing and implementing Water Catchment Action Plans have been suggested in scenarios worked out by the Swedish Environmental Protection Agency (see SEPA 2000a).

On balance, then, Sweden finds itself straddling old fences in efforts to negotiate a better spatial fit between natural and societal scales, i.e., to reach a spatially rational system of ecological governance.

# 3
# Up or down with the ecology cycle? Strategies for temporally rational ecological governance

## Political terms and ecological cycles

*Next budget and next election; dominant time spans in politics*
From the early nineteenth century onwards, the dominant political cal view of time was one of continuous 'progress' with the state at the centre of change (Ekengren 1998:30). This *linear* conception of time is, however, just one possible view. Political time can also be seen as (series of) distinct *events* or as connected *points* that have special meaning or importance. One can furthermore view political time as *cyclical*, with events recurring in a predictable fashion. The budgetary process is a prime example. Governments set strict timetables that bind the procedure step by step, and the organisation level by level, in a predetermined, annually repeated cycle (see Brunsson 1995:12 ff., 182 f.).

Elections are crucial political *events* reoccurring at predetermined intervals. They determine the views and uses of time among political representatives. Elected representatives then have two to five years before they face the verdict of the electorate at the next election. A major motivation for their actions and standpoints thus is how these influence the chances to become re-elected. Consequently, the immediate questions of here and now tend to take precedence over longer-term issues. The *timing* of a political initiative is often a strategic consideration by politicians bent on political gains (Edelman 1988). In combination with the constant pressure from the media, such strategic considerations may lead to extremely short term political horizons.

There are, however, also other conceptions of political time.

Efforts are made to break the one-year cycle of the budgetary process by introducing three- to four-year budget cycles for certain policy fields. Perspectives of up to 15 years have been used in infrastructure planning and development. Defence policy works with 30- to 40-year perspectives when deciding on major air or naval systems of warfare. Politicians thus face a *multitemporal* situation, where they take part in an increasing number of interactions with different social and political time scales (Ekengren 1998:26).

Still, time perceptions in politics are predominantly geared towards the 'next budget' and the 'next election'. These cycles and predetermined points in time converge to instil into political and administrative life a bias in favour of the immediate scheduled tasks, and the wishes and reactions of the present electorate. The dramatic growth of information and communication technology enhances further this predominance for the 'here' and 'now' at the expense of the historic and well as future 'then'. Rapid and dramatic moves in global financial markets can – so is the lesson driven home by the 1992 economic turmoil in Sweden – put pressure on politicians to provide decisions literally 'within the hour' to avert a major national crisis.

*Doing time on earth; politics as ultimately fenced by natural ecocycles*
This institutionalised political shortsightedness is increasingly challenged. The long-term trends of population growth, water and air pollution, and possibly irrevocable climate change, have created doubts about the sustainability and productivity of the planet's ecosystems. The picture of 'Spaceship Earth' as a finite entity with finite resources has driven home the lesson, sometimes forgotten in the era of linear 'progress', that man – also *political man* – is ultimately fenced within nature and the productivity of its ecosystems. Nobody can escape from doing his or her time here. Furthermore, this recognition draws attention to the generational cycles of reproduction. If we are fenced in now, so will be our descendants, one generation after the other.

The emphasis on lifecycles and their importance for long-term productivity show that natural time can be seen as a *circular* phenomenon. Water circulates between the ground and the atmosphere. Plants and species come to life, mature, reproduce and die. A smooth and balanced functioning of the seasonal and other short-term patterns is the necessary basis for the systems' longer-term health and productivity. Just like politics, the natural environment thus exhibits a plurality of times, reaching from millennial geological changes to seasonal and even shorter cycles (see Adam 1994).

There is, however, an important difference between political cycles and ecological lifecycles. Short-term tactics and strategic *timing* may lead to a smoother functioning of the political processes of the day, but may detract from the longer-term viability and productivity of the political system as a whole by diminishing popular support and democratic legitimacy. While it may take only one line in a budget or bill to save a government coalition, that single line may devastate an ecosystem to the extent that it will take decades to restore it.

In the broadest sense then, political time is ultimately bound by the life cycles of ecosystems that produce and reproduce resources necessary for human life. Political actors can not escape from this basic relationship when they mobilise resources for collective endeavours by way of their democratically legitimated use of power in society. They are forced to find ways to achieve temporally rational ecological governance. Above all, they have to adopt an inter-generational time horizon. Present actions should be judged in the light of long-term ecological sustainability as well as autonomy for future generations.

*From here to sustainability; ways of reconciling political and ecological time scales*
There are several alternative ways of reconciling political and ecological time cycles. The most long-term binding perspectives have historically been found in physical *planning*, i.e., the process of directing, restricting, or even forbidding certain uses of land and resources. Planning regulations and processes infringe on present resource use to an extent that makes it perhaps the most authoritative way of reconciling political and ecological time perspectives. To pass the autonomy test, systems of comprehensive planning in ecological governance should thus exhibit participatory mechanisms that allow present stakeholders and the general public a meaningful say in the process before binding decisions are taken.

Another alternative is to adapt more fully to the circular processes in nature by closing as much as possible the flows of goods, materials, energy and resources through society. Such *eco-cycle adaptation* is fully achieved when 'the handling of the flows of material and other resources, like land, is such that natural ecocycles can absorb rest products and renew the resources for future generations, and does so with preserved biodiversity' (Ecocycle Commission 1997:16 f.). While leaving much room for autonomous choice to present generations, eco-cycle adaptation may create a temporal illusion if it does not fully achieve this ideal. Leaks and loopholes in the cycle, huge inputs of energy needed to redirect flows of goods and materials through society, as well as new uses for the energy and materials saved, all detract from sustainability (see Jänicke et al. 1999:128).

The strategy of *increased resource use efficiency* is actually directed towards 'beating time' by decreasing the input of resources to provide the same or a larger output of goods and services. This would make possible the transfer to the next generation of a sustainable society with leeway for autonomous choice without sacrificing present welfare. Linked to this strategy is a specific view of the relationship between economic growth, social welfare, and ecological sustainability, viz. ecological modernisation. At its core is the view that building a sustainable society demands new, resource-saving and resource-efficient technologies, which provide a rapidly growing market and thus become an engine for growth and jobs (see Gouldson and Murphy 1997:74 f.). Ecological modernisation is said to dissolve the perceived conflict between economic growth and environmental protection (Cohen 1998:150). Environmental protection and economic growth are turned into a positive-sum game, where industry finds anticipatory development of green technology profitable, and politicians can preach 'green' growth (Hajer 1995:26 ff., 273).

This shift in outlook is accompanied by changes in policy principles, instruments and organisation. The emphasis is on early internalisation of ecological values and modes of thinking among all relevant actors. Stable and foreseeable regulations, and increased use of economic and monitoring instruments, are expected to provide a good climate for innovative eco-technology. This in turn increases resource and energy efficiency in the processes of production, consumption and recycling, and may give

forerunners comparative advantages in world markets (Stavins and
Whitehead 1997:112; see Dobers 1997:63 ff., 114 ff.).

With the possible exception of planning, these strategies imply
enormous problems of co-ordination and overview. The *timing* of
actions and events becomes increasingly important, as does the
question of what stage in the process of political and ecological
reconciliation is actually reached. The 'New Public Management'
focuses on goals and objectives as the most important aspect of
managing large systems, leaving those responsible for implementation to decide on the most effective mix of instruments to attain
these objectives. But might not this become an exercise in
symbolic politics? For *management by objectives* to actually take
on a self-binding character is crucially dependent on how the relationships between political orderers of action and administrative
and other performers of action are institutionalised and organised. Management by objectives consciously brings relevant
actors into the system of governance, in particular those
contributing to the non-sustainable patterns of environmental
and resource use. The translation of sustainability objectives to
targets and action plans takes place at lower levels and in co-operation with affected interests and stakeholders (Jänicke et al.
1999:111). Much effort is put into setting up specific timetables
for goal achievement. Comprehensive systems of monitoring in
the form of commonly accepted indicators and operationalised
measures are included. Together with specified target dates, this
is meant to enable actors in the system to get commonly understandable answers when 'checking time', i.e., assessing progress
(see Jänicke et al. 1999:68 ff.).

### Green and just in time; criteria for temporally rational ecological governance

The precautionary principle urges decision-makers at all levels to
take into account the future environmental and resource consequences of present action. But what is irreversible is uncertain,
and might not be distinguishable until way into the future. To
play it safe, decision-makers are thus pushed towards constraining present action beyond critical thresholds (see Barry 1999:225
f.). The institutional and procedural design is thus of utmost
importance to safeguard against both ecological irreversibility
and inter-generational injustice.

When analysing the Swedish strategies to achieve temporally rational governance, we first look for *specified target dates* for achieving objectives of sustainable development. Ecological governance is temporally rational when these time schedules are based on, or linked to, ecologically relevant characteristics, such as 'safe' levels or concentration of substances, lifecycles relevant to the health of ecosystems, as well as to the scope and pace of resource and materials flows through society and the economy.

However, targets and dates do not become binding on the present if they are not accompanied by a well-developed system of surveillance and monitoring, as well as statistical measures and indicators. We thus look for *premeditated ways of monitoring and evaluating goal achievement.* Temporally rational ecological governance distributes specific responsibility for achieving certain targets to specific units, thus binding their future activities to the overarching objective of sustainable development. These instruments do not only show the state of progress. They also show which processes and activities in society put pressure on environment and resources, and the results of measures taken to counter such pressures.

Such an environmental and resource information system provides not only experts and administrators with opportunities to make autonomous judgements over time about the progress towards sustainability. A transparent process of decision-making, implementation and feedback also makes this possible for the ordinary citizen. Temporally rational ecological governance is thus *democratic.* The participants in the process to reach decisions on objectives, binding target dates, and methods of goal achievement are defined on the grounds of their contribution to, as well as dependence on eco-cycles, energy and material flows. Specific mechanisms are built in to safeguard the value of autonomy for future generations.

## The 'telescopic state' – binding the present for the future

### Land use planning and restrictions on future resource use
The conditions for land use and resource utilisation can be manipulated through the structuring of physical space (Eckhoff 1983:29). Ever since the dawn of the twentieth century, 'allocation of special functions to areas' (Glasbergen 1992:197) has been

used in Sweden to set aside geographical areas as national parks, nature reserves, and nature conservation areas. By 1998, such areas reserved for future generations comprised over 38,000 square kilometres, equivalent to over eight (8) per cent of Sweden's total area (Statistics Sweden 2000:227 ff.). The 1968 *Sarek Agreement*, later ratified by Parliament, declared four major rivers in northern Sweden off limits for hydroelectric power exploitation. This binding decision was further confirmed in 1993, when the four rivers were labelled 'national rivers' (Cabinet Bill 1997/98:45, Part 1, p. 241).

The Planning and Building Act of 1947 made Sweden's local governments and their Building Committees responsible for all local planning. Geared towards housing and urban infrastructure, municipal *master plans* and *detail plans* provided general and specific guidelines for expected municipal expansion. Plans were made legally binding through ratification by Regional Administration Boards or, for larger and more important plans, by the national government (Lundqvist 1972, passim). The planning process did little to link local development to the scale and quality of natural resources. Increasingly frequent clashes among competitive demands for land and natural resources could not be resolved, and resource issues spanning many municipalities and whole regions were not properly addressed.

This led the national government to develop more comprehensive national *physical* planning. Surveys were made in the late 1960s of foreseeable demands for natural resources over the next 30 years for industrial production, urban development, outdoor recreation, and environmental quality. To this was linked an inventory of the location and amount of available resources. Areas where future clashes of interest might occur were then pointed out. Following simulations of alternative land use patterns, principles were established for an adequate location of different resource demanding activities. The system of *National Physical Planning* decided by Parliament in 1972 contained four elements:

- Guidelines for the planning of *activities* involving competing claims on land and natural resources.
- Guidelines for the planning of geographical *areas* with particularly intensive competition for land and natural resources.

- Processes for implementing these guidelines into a *national physical plan* covering all of Sweden.
- *Binding provisions* for cases of severe conflicts over resource use implying comprehensive cross-sectoral impacts.

Decisions on the location of nine types of industrial and other activities with heavy demands and impacts on Sweden's natural resources and energy supply now had to be made by the Cabinet. The Cabinet's decision would then bind subsequent planning and environmental assessments. Environmental permit authorities could not prohibit an activity allowed by the Cabinet and *vice versa*. A municipal *veto* meant that the Cabinet could grant a location permit to a large-scale, resource-demanding activity *only* if the Municipal Board of Councillors in question had approved of such a location (Lundqvist 1979:248 f.).

Only a decade later, a Governmental Commission reported that Sweden's land use and resource planning was not sufficiently geared towards long-term *sustainable* development. Planning for use and protection of natural resources should be guided by such concepts as the carrying capacity of ecosystems and biochemical cycles. In particular, the use of non-renewable resources should be put under much more stringent control (SOU 1983:56). However, to make sustainability the core criterion in land use and resource planning was an idea whose time had yet to come. A 1984 Cabinet memorandum pronounced it more 'reasonable' to proceed from the present National Physical Planning programme. The 1985/86 Cabinet proposal for a new Natural Resources Act explicitly stated that the resource management concept should have a relatively narrow content, linked to the use of man's physical environment (see SOU 1993:27, p. 280 f.).

However, some steps to incorporate emerging ideas on longer-term sustainable development were taken in the 1987 Natural Resources Act (NRA). This Act was an umbrella, covering and 'guiding' eight other acts relevant to natural resource use, among others the Planning and Building Act, also codified in 1987 (Cabinet Bill 1990/91:90, pp. 165 ff.; Michanek 1991:22 ff.). The NRA made Environmental Impact Statements (EIS) mandatory for all potentially harmful activities requiring a permit under any of these acts. The EIS requirement included location of large projects and facilities, environmental permit procedures, large-scale use of water and forest resources, as well as infrastructure developments (see Cabinet Bill 1990/91:90, pp. 169 ff.).

The Natural Resources Act and the acts covered by it are now incorporated under the comprehensive Environmental Code ratified in 1998. The inclusion of the NRA in the Environmental Code was seen as an instrument for comprehensive judgements in the planning process to secure 'an ecologically, socially, culturally and socio-economically sound resource management'. The Code enumerates those areas and natural resources in Sweden that are of 'national interest'. Such areas may be subject to industrial or other polluting activities only under very special circumstances. Further areas of 'national interest' can be designated through a process involving national agencies and Regional Administrations. However, these areas become fully accepted as of 'national interest', and thus binding on future activities, only after an explicit decision under any of the relevant acts within the NRA/EC umbrella (Cabinet Bill 1997/98:45, Part 1, pp. 242 ff.).

Under present (2003) planning legislation, municipalities establish an *overview plan* for their territory, describing future land and water use, and defining areas for infrastructure, commercial and housing developments. Overview plans are not binding; only the *detail plans* for particular areas are. Municipalities may issue *area regulations* for areas outside detail plans. Before the Municipal Board adopts an overview plan, the Regional Administration must issue a report asserting whether or not the plan is compatible with the NRA/EC definition of areas of 'national interests' (Michanek 1991:28 ff.; Cabinet Bill 1994/94:230).

Indeed, the 289 municipalities are issued a tall order to save areas for the future. By the turn of the century, the more than 2,200 areas declared of 'national interest' covered nearly 25 per cent of Sweden's total area (Statistics Sweden 2000:229). About one-quarter of these areas are physically protected as nature reserves, which means that industrial activities cannot be located there. The other 75 per cent may be secured for the future through municipal prohibitions, environmental permit decisions, or Regional Administrations' conditions for exploitation (Sveriges Nationalatlas 1991:164 ff.).

*Planning for the present, the future, or ... ?*

What then, does this planning process offer in terms of sustainability and autonomy? First of all, it is reiterative; local governments are expected to renew the overview plans by five-year intervals. In reality, however, the time perspective is often shorter. Plans are 'rolling', and quite often subject to negotiations between local governments and parties with relatively short-term interests in resource exploitation and commercial development. The National Audit Office contended in 1996 that the Swedish process of environmental impact assessment (EIA) exhibited several flaws. Environmental expert authorities had no regulated standing in the process. Long-term environmental effects went unattended, due to lack of necessary competence for the review of EIA documents. Usually, the alternative preferred by the exploiters was the only one being assessed in the process. All in all, Swedish EIA process was said to lack formal rules, standards of content, and allocation of rights and duties among actors (National Audit Office 1996: passim; see Kjellerup 1997).

Criticism also concerned the democratic aspect of planning. Formally, municipalities are required to arrange procedures of consultation and hearings with the citizens, firms, organisations and others concerned when they prepare detail plans. Changes in 1994 actually aimed at strengthening citizen participation (Michanek 1991:28 ff.; Cabinet Bill 1994/94:230). However, the National Audit Office concluded in 1996 that public involvement comes in too late, if at all (National Audit Office 1996: passim; see Kjellerup 1997).

The 1997/98 Cabinet Bill on National Environmental Objectives put much emphasis on the idea of *A Sustainable Sweden*. A broad conception of sustainable development is used. The Cabinet stated that the 15 long-term NEOs (see further below, pp. 65–7) should guide all physical planning. 'Through co-operation across sectoral lines, national and municipal authorities shall promote an ecologically sustainable development with a good living environment for all' (Cabinet Bill 1997/98:145, p. 321 ff.). New instruments were conceived. Regional environmental and resource management (ERM) programmes are to be developed for areas with such severe environmental and resource management problems that environmental quality norms may be imposed. These programmes are to be based on the NEOs, on the

'national interests' determined on the basis of NRA/EC regula-
tions, as well as on the regional environmental strategies
(STRAMs) worked out by the Regional Administrations (see
Arwidsson 1999:8 f.).

Planning is expected to integrate the precautionary principle
through the EIA process. The government claims that Swedish
EIAs reflect the integration of environmental concerns in a proac-
tive planning process. However, there is an 'integration
confusion' between a consensual planning *process* and an adver-
sarial examination at *one stage* in that process. There is no
screening of alternatives, no scoping of effects of interrelated decisions, no early public consultation, no requirements for
non-technical summaries, and no formal EIA decision. Long-term
binding effects of contextual decisions may thus still go unattended (Emmelin 1998:189, 205). The building of the railroad
tunnel through *Hallandsås* (to allow for a 12 minute gain in travel
time between Gothenburg and Copenhagen) caused an ecological
scandal affecting the sustainability of the region. It thus provides
a glaring example of deficiencies in the planning process that
detract from temporally rational ecological governance (SOU
1998:137, esp. pp. 91 ff., 123 f.).

*A silent revolution: self-binding for the future through
'management by objectives'*
An important distinction in the thinking on governance is
between 'policy' and 'management'. As mentioned, 'New Public
Management' points to *management by objectives* (MBO) as a
flexible way of moving towards commonly formulated and shared
views of a future state of affairs. As a temporal strategy of governance, MBO exhibits the following characteristics:

- Co-operative and consensual processes to formulate objectives,
  including (measurable) target levels and dates, and dominated
  by political decision-makers.
- Deliberate ways of internalising common problem views
  among implementers and target groups.
- Decentralised competence to use program resources for implementing common objectives, involving negotiation and
  agreements among programme administrators and (organised)
  target groups.

- Continuous monitoring and assessment of progress in relation to target levels and dates, with a strong role for political decision-makers.

The MBO strategy thus leaves much discretion and responsibility to administrators in the process of instrumentation and implementation. However, continuous political evaluation and goal (re)formulation together with conscious methods for internalisation of objectives and problem views are thought to lead to expected future outcomes (see Jänicke et al. 1999:68 ff.). Evidently, the possibility that the MBO strategy will take on a self-binding character is very much dependent on how the relationships between the political *principals* (the orderers of action) and the *agents* (the performers of action) are institutionalised and organised into a coherent system of governance. Clear objectives with explicit time limits, linked to specific responsibilities and resources provided to specified actors, would certainly add to its 'binding' nature.

The Swedish process of reorienting traditional environmental policy towards one of sustainable development began in the mid 1990s. In the spring 1997 Budget Bill, the Cabinet proposed a broad strategy for sustainable development, to be based on three overarching objectives; *protection of environmental quality, efficient use of resources,* and *sustainable ecosystem productivity* (Cabinet Bill 1996/97:150). An earlier report of the National Agenda 21 Committee had pointed to the incoherence among the numerous 'goal like' expressions in official policy statements. In September 1997, the Environmental Protection Agency proposed that those more than 170 'goals' be condensed into 18 environmental quality objectives (SEPA 1997).

In May 1998 the Cabinet presented a bill proposing 15 'national environmental objectives' (NEOs) to be achieved 'within one generation', i.e., by 2020–25:

- Reduced Climate Impact
- Clean Air
- Natural Acidification Only
- A Non-Toxic Environment
- A Protective Ozone Layer
- A Safe Radiation Environment

- Zero Eutrophication
- Flourishing Lakes and Streams
- Good-quality Groundwater
- A Balanced Marine Environment, Flourishing Coastal Areas and Archipelagos
- Thriving Wetlands
- Healthy Forests
- A Varied Agricultural Landscape
- A Magnificent Mountain Landscape
- A Good Built Environment

This was the starting point for 'a system of government by objectives and results' that – in the eyes of the Cabinet – presented the 'most effective way of governing a broadly conceived programme for sustainable development with participation from all sectors of society'. The NEOs would be broken down into further, more precise sectoral (and geographical) targets, to be decided upon by the Cabinet. Involved public agencies and municipalities would enjoy wide discretion in selecting instruments to achieve the goals, and voluntary action by firms and enterprises was welcomed (Cabinet Bill 1997/98:145, p. 38 f., esp. p. 41). The further content of the bill indicated that this new structure would not become another exercise in symbolic politics. It outlined a process for developing targets and action plans for different sectors, and distributed clear responsibilities for this process among agencies and authorities. Furthermore, the proposal envisaged a system of indicators and mechanisms for monitoring and surveying progress of the work towards the 15 objectives (Cabinet Bill 1997/98:145, pp. 169 ff.).

The MBO process for sustainable development started even before Parliament had voted on the NEO Bill. Already in June 1998, the Cabinet instructed 17 sectoral agencies and all the Regional Administrations to develop proposals for targets, sectoral goals and action plans necessary for reaching the NEOs within their area of competence and authority. The Swedish EPA was to provide co-ordination and support to sectoral agencies in their work on targets and action plans, and make sure all agencies reported back to the Cabinet by October 1999. The Cabinet furthermore appointed a Parliamentary Commission to review the agency reports and particularly evaluate the environmental, socio-economic, fiscal, and specific sectoral consequences of targets and action programmes. The Commission presented its final report to the Government in June 2000 (SOU 2000:52), and a Cabinet Bill was sent to Parliament in April 2001 (Cabinet Bill 2000/01:130).

The temporal perspective is evident and, to say the least, brave. The objective is 'to hand over to *the next generation* a society in which the major environmental problems have been solved' (italics added). The structure of this MBO system of ecological governance is as follows (Cabinet Bill 2000/01:130, pp. 11 ff.):

- The *15 NEOs* define the state of environmental quality to be achieved by 2025; one main definition of each 'generational' objective is further developed into sometimes as many as ten specific features of the environmental quality to be achieved.
- *Interim targets* state the direction and time scale for ongoing, concrete measures; most interim targets relate to what should be achieved by 2010 in terms of emission level reductions or specified levels of environmental quality.
- *Action strategies* to co-ordinate measures to achieve several NEOs at the same time, as well as other policy objectives:

    1. A strategy for more efficient energy use and transport
    2. A strategy for non-toxic and resource-efficient cyclical systems, including an integrated product policy
    3. A strategy for management of land, water and the built environment.

For each of these strategies, an orchestrated set of policy instruments is envisaged. The 'energy and transport' strategy builds, among other things, on a 'green' tax shift in the range of SEK 30 billion (€3.3 billion) up to 2010. The 'eco cycle' strategy envisages more 'green' tender and procurement in addition to an integrated product policy. Finally, the 'resource management' strategy rests on regulatory measures and procedural safeguards to strengthen protection of valuable nature and water resources, and a revision of the physical planning process (Cabinet Bill 2000/01:130, pp. 196 ff.).

Three modes of implementation are pointed out as crucial to the success of these strategies. One is the integration of responsibility for an ecologically sustainable development into the mandates of public agencies and the activities of enterprises and other organisations in various social sectors. As for the 24 public agencies specifically pointed out, this mandate includes identifying their 'ecological' roles, formulating action programmes with specified sectoral objectives and measures, assessing the effects of these measures on the public economy, and making sure that sectoral action programmes are implemented by making them part of all their decision–making. To ease this ecological administrative reform, public agencies are to make Environmental Management Systems (EMS) an integrated part of their processes. Another mode of implementation is to complement legal and economic instruments with voluntary agreements with industry and business. These agreements can be based on existing regulation, or form the basis for action instead of regulations. The argument for such agreements is that they may lead to more cost-efficient methods of achieving sustainable development (Cabinet Bill 2000/01:130, pp. 17 ff.).

The third mode is a comprehensive system of monitoring and evaluation, based on a system of statistics that comprises the state of the environment, reflects the development of factors affecting environmental quality, and points to measures needed to counter negative trends. This will include data from the National Environmental Surveillance Network, as well as statistics on the use, accumulation, recirculation and productivity of materials and energy in society. A system of indicators of sustainable development (*gröna nyckeltal*) is to be developed to furnish decision-makers and the general public with information on Sweden's progress towards sustainable development. An Environmental Objectives Board (EOB) was established under the SEPA in 2002 to co-ordinate the efforts of the national and regional authorities with specific sectoral responsibilities for sustainable development. The Council will report directly to the Cabinet to provide the basis for the Cabinet's annual report on progress towards achievement of NEOs. A more in-depth report on the progress towards 'Sustainable Sweden' is to be delivered to Parliament every four years (Cabinet Bill 2000/01:130, pp. 223 ff.).

If this MBO process continues according to plan, Sweden will in a few years have a coherent plan of national, sectoral, and regional action, complete with time-tables for achievement of sustainable development. Sweden will also have a system for continuous review and measurement of trends and developments indicating whether and to what extent achievement of the national environmental goals and interim targets is actually forth-coming. This gives an impression of Swedish environmental and resource management as an example of democratic self-binding. The formal procedure of ratifying objectives through parliamen-tary vote fulfils the democratic criterion. There is an easily understood temporal goal; an environmentally sound society is to be achieved 'within one generation'. The elaboration of interim targets and operationalisation of sectoral goals means that agen-cies become bound to programmes and time-tables they have helped design and have come to internalise as 'feasible' to them-selves as well as to affected sectoral actors and interests along the way. The democratic self-binding is further strengthened by the elaborate system of monitoring and evaluation. Built as it is on extensive statistics and understandable indicators, it enables the general public to make autonomous judgements about progress towards sustainability, and thus to hold political and administra-tive decision-makers accountable for the success or failure of the MBO strategy.

**Towards the 'ecocycle society'? Closing the loops of goods and materials**

*Ecocycle adaptation; policy action from the 1992 Recycling Bill to the present*
The Bourgeois Government labelled its Ecocycle Bill of 1993 as a first step towards 'a society based on the principle of ecocycles' (Ministry of the Environment 1993:3). The bill introduced specific *demands* and *targets* to reduce solid waste and adapt products for reuse and recycling. Demands were defined as specific percentages to be reached by 1997 for reuse or recycling of packaging materials that were already then recycled to a large extent (SFS 1994:1235). Targets concerned packaging materials that were only recycled by small factions of the total volume (Cabinet Bill 1992/93:180, p. 78 f.). The Government introduced the principle of *producer liability,* comprising the whole life cycle of the package or material, and including responsibility to take care of the waste in an 'environmentally acceptable' way (Cabinet

Bill 1992/93:180, pp. 53 ff.). A special Ecocycle Commission was appointed in 1993 to 'develop a strategy for eco-cycle adaptation of the commodities sector and propose successive extensions of the producer liability' (Ecocycle Commission 1997:3).

Apart from some general remarks on the necessity for adequate separation and collection systems, and of the need to inform consumers, the 1993 Cabinet Bill left the manufacturers to decide on the 'how' of this eco-cycle adaptation. The largest manufacturers in branches affected by the liability regulations swiftly formed a self-regulatory organisation. Special 'materials companies' were established for cardboard, corrugated paper, plastics and metals, as well as a special recycling company for glass. These companies are run as 'not-for-profit companies', contracting out the actual collection and recycling. The materials companies control the reuse and recycling activities of their member producers, while producers outside the companies account for their reuse and recycling to the SEPA (Statistics Sweden 2000:114). Combined, they form the service organisation that disseminates information on collection and recycling, and how and where to deposit packaging (www.repa.se).

What have been the Government's activities after the 1993 Bill? A 1996 bill passed by Parliament mandated the Cabinet to prohibit the dumping of burnable and organic waste by 2002 and 2005, respectively (Cabinet Bill 1996/97:172). The 1997 strategy report from the Ecocycle Commission suggested quite ambitious objectives for infrastructural change, adaptation of new goods and commodities, and waste products (Ecocycle Commission 1997:28). The 1998 Bill on National Environmental Objectives extended the list of goods and commodities subject to producer liability, and linked this to target levels and dates. Up to 80 per cent of worn out tyres were to be recycled or taken care of in an environmentally friendly way by manufacturers and dealers after 1998. Car manufacturers must take care of cars registered 1997 and later left for scrapping after 1998, and to make 85 per cent of each individual post-1997 model car recyclable or reusable by 2002. This share is to reach 95 per cent by 2015. For electric and electronic products, regulatory changes concerning the producer liability were put on the books (Cabinet Bill 1997/98:145, pp. 201 ff.)

The 1998 bill also addressed the eco-cycle adaptation of large-scale systems in the society's infrastructure, such as waste dumping and water and sewage. The prohibitions against dumping burnable and organic waste by 2002 and 2005, the pending permit regulations for waste transportation, and the pending proposal to introduce a tax on all dumped waste would, in the Cabinet's view, increase the assortment of waste at the source and its use for recycling or energy production. The objective was to reduce, by 2005, the total volume of dumped waste by 50 to 70 per cent in relation to 1995 volumes (Cabinet Bill 1997/98:145, p. 146, 205 f.). As for the closing of nutrient cycles between urban and rural areas, the 2005 prohibition against dumping of organic waste would also concern sludge from sewage treatment plants (Cabinet Bill 1997/98:145, p. 207 f.).

A Cabinet Communication to Parliament in May 2000 reported on a strategy for a sustainable products policy. Working closely with the EU, and adopting a life-cycle perspective, the Swedish Government and its agencies will continue to work towards decreasing the negative impact on human health and the environment of commercial products. Measures comprise information, EMAS, green tender and procurement, green labelling and standardisation, as well as widened producer liability (Cabinet Communication 1999/2000:114, passim). Elaborating on the strategy for non-toxic and resource-efficient cyclical systems in its NEO bill of 2001, the Cabinet pointed to several new initiatives that are to be taken on issues such as an environmentally adapted products policy, international co-ordination, a programme for the production, use and retrieval of chemicals, reduction of the dumping of waste, and others (Cabinet Bill 2000/01:130, pp. 209 ff.). A special Commission was set up to report during 2001 on further concrete measures to extend producer liability to other product areas (Dir. 2000:28).

*Ecocycle adaptation in practice; leaks, loopholes, and full circles*
How far, then, have Sweden's efforts towards eco-cycle adaptation progressed in practice? Five years after the producer liability regulations came into force, annual recycling had increased by 130,000 tons for packaging materials, by 10,000 tons for paper, and by 10,000 tons for tyres. Of the 20,000 companies and firms affected by producer liability for packaging materials, producers accountable for 90 per cent of all packaging materials in Sweden

had joined the materials company in question (http://environ.se as of June 15, 1999).

As shown in Table 3.1., there are several examples of relative 'success' in the Swedish process. The most obvious closing of life cycles concerns products that actively involve consumers. Glass and PET bottles, and aluminium cans, are reused and recycled to the extent that targets are already reached. So is the case for recycling of paper from newspapers and journals. A contributing factor to this achievement is most probably that price conscious consumers make use of the system of repayment for old bottles and cans in force at grocery stores throughout the country. Furthermore, local governments have arranged recycling stations in most neighbourhoods, where individuals and households can deliver paper, cardboard, bottles and cans, as well as batteries and old clothes. It is also notable that several of the targets for more 'industrial' recycling and reuse are close to being reached.

However, these examples of relative success in closing cycles of goods and materials comprise only those areas subjected to producer liability. A system for collection, transport and reuse by manufacturers can be built up by reversing the flows from consumers to producers. A spring 1998 survey of nine industrial branches showed that car manufacturers, producers of electric and electronic products, tyre companies and the packaging industry all use several ecocycle adaptation criteria throughout the production phase. However, only a few areas report on prolonged product life cycles. Even fewer engage in making their products upgradeable (Ecocycle Commission 1998: 165 ff.). Far greater challenges to eco-cycle adaptation are raised by the large-scale systems in the society's infrastructure. With lifecycles of up to 150 years, most were built up long before the (re)discovery of the problems of the commons. The effect is a locking in of flows of nutrients, energy, materials, and waste in technologies and structures (Ecocycle Commission 1997, ch. 7).

In terms of sustainability, the strategy of eco-cycle adaptation thus still has a long way to go. The 'direct material input' (DMI) into the Swedish economy was close to 25 tons per capita in 1998. Input of fossil fuels seems to have stabilised during the 1990s, while that from other non-renewable materials oscillates. There is, however, a steady increase in the input of renewable resources. About 10 per cent of the DMI becomes waste, and half

**Table 3.1** *Demanded and estimated actual levels of recycling and reuse for different goods and commodities subjected to producer liability in Sweden.*

| Good or commodity | Demanded level of recycling or reuse, and year of attainment | | Actually attained levels 1999 in % |
|---|---|---|---|
| | Up to June 2001 | After June 2001 | |
| **Packages** | | | |
| Glass containers | 70% recycling or reuse of material | 70% recycling | 84 |
| Corrugated cardboard | 65% recycling or reuse of material | 65% recycling | 84 |
| Cardboard, cartons | 30% recycling or reuse of material | 70% (40% reuse of material) | 40 |
| Steel sheets | 50% recycling or reuse of material | 70% recycling | 62 |
| Aluminium, (except beverage containers) | 50% recycling or reuse of material | 70% (40% reuse of material) | 33 |
| Aluminium, beverage containers | 90% recycling | 90% reuse of material | 84 |
| Plastics (not PET bottles) | 30% recycling or reuse of material | 70% (30% reuse of material) | 34 |
| Wooden packages | | 70% (15% reuse of material) | |
| Packages, other material | | 30% (15% reuse of material) | |
| PET bottles | 90% recycling or reuse of material | 90% reuse of material | 91 (refill), 73 (reuse of material) |
| Returnable glass bottles | 95% recycling | | 98 |
| **Other Products** | | | |
| Cars | | 85% reuse of material (from 2002) | |
| Tyres | 80% reuse of material (from 1999) | | 92 |
| Newspapers and recyclable paper | 75% (from 2000) | | 79 |

*Source:* www.environ.se/index.php3?main=/dokument/teknik/avfall/avfall1.htm (as of September 2001)

of this waste is recycled into the economy. It should also be noted that about 20 per cent of the annual DMI is hazardous to human health and the environment (Statistics Sweden 2000:108).

The eco-cycle adaptation strategy shows some interesting features in terms of autonomy. The Social Democratic government has stated that a 'Sustainable Sweden' should be achieved 'without disturbing effects on market competition', and as far as possible through voluntary action and negotiated solutions, also involving consumers (Cabinet Bill 1997/98:145, pp. 196 ff.). While providing consumers and citizens with incentives for 'good environmental conduct', the markets for recycling and reuse established in sectors subjected to producer liability, and the continuous information campaigns leave the choice of conduct to the individual. The implementation of the producer liability concept through branch agreements is seen as a model for the future widening of that concept.

## Changing gears – policies for resource efficiency

*Factor Ten and the quest for efficiency in energy and transport*
In its September 1997 report to the Parliament on 'Ecological Sustainability', the Social-Democratic Cabinet pointed to the need to make energy and material flows compatible with sustainable development. It would be necessary to achieve 'a manifold decrease in the demand for energy and materials'. The Cabinet explicitly pointed to the 'Factor Ten' concept, i.e., a tenfold effectivisation of resource use over the next two generations as 'a signal of the necessary level of effectivisation ... [and] ... a compass to stimulate new ideas' (Cabinet Communication 1997/98:13, p. 9). The Cabinet thus seemed to have accepted the thinking of its Ecocycle Commission: 'factor ten can be used as a benchmark for the need to dematerialise' production and consumption in a highly industrialised country like Sweden (Ecocycle Commission 1997:60).

Seven months earlier, in February 1997, the Social-Democratic Cabinet had reached an agreement with the Left Party and the Greens on a programme for 'sustainable' energy provision. In the March 1997 Energy Bill, the Cabinet stated that the exodus from the nuclear energy society agreed upon by the three parties opened up for a cost-effective energy provision with an emphasis on renewable energy sources, and with low future impacts on health, environment, and climate. Electric energy should be provided through a system of domestic, renewable and sustainable energy sources, and combined with efficient energy use and low use of fossil fuels. Not only would this ease the transformation into an ecologically sustainable society, but it would also stimulate Sweden's economic and social development. As much as SEK 8 billion would be allocated to support investments in already functioning energy-efficient technology and in renewable energy sources and to stimulate the development and use of competitive, efficient, environment-friendly energy technologies based on renewable sources (Cabinet Bill 1996/97:84, p. 28 f.).

The efficiency drive in the Energy Bill was clearly anchored within the Cabinet's by then emerging strategy of 'ecological modernisation' (see below, pp. 77–81). At the core of the arguments of the Minister of Industry and Trade was the traditional Social-Democratic view that increased production and economic growth is decisive for employment and thus welfare. A basic favourable element in this respect, argued the Minister, is the secure provision of inexpensive electric energy to industrial production. The new 'non-nuclear' energy policy built on the premise that industrial use of electric energy should be allowed to increase – but must also become more efficient – over the next decade (Cabinet Bill 1996/97:84, p. 7).

In the 2001 Cabinet Bill on National Environmental Objectives, the strategy for more efficient energy use and transportation is particularly tied in with the following NEOs: Clean Air, Reduced Climate Impact, Natural Acidification Only, No Eutrophication, and A Good Built Environment. The quite ambitious 2010 interim targets for these NEOs would seem to require very tough measures, impinging on individual autonomy. The Bill foresees an increased use of economic instruments to make the environmental costs explicit and to stimulate energy effectivisation and further development of performance standards for vehicles, machines and other moving equipment. Green tax reforms in the vicinity of SEK 30 billion were indicated for the period up to 2010, including increased $CO_2$ and energy taxes. There will also be a programme for infrastructural changes to achieve a sustainable transportation system (Cabinet Bill 2000/01:130, pp. 198 ff.).

What then are the implications for sustainability from recent patterns of efficiency and productivity in energy and transportation? Final energy use decreased in industry and the built environment in the latter half of the 1990s. Energy use per SEK of product value sank by one-third from 1980 to the end of the century. Energy productivity rose steadily by about 1½ per cent annually (SOU 2001:2, pp. 141 ff.). The pattern is not that positive for the transport sector. Final energy use rose steadily in the 1990s. The amount of gasoline per vehicle kilometre decreased by 12 per cent in the 1980s, but has since levelled out. The shift in demand towards heavier vehicles, and the lower number of passengers per vehicle together contribute to higher use of gasoline per passenger kilometre in 1998 than in 1970 (SOU 2001:2, pp. 147 ff.).

*Sweden and the middle way: seeking consensual ecological modernisation*
When the then Minister of Finance Göran Persson assumed leadership of the Swedish Social Democratic Party in March 1996, he surprised many observers by proclaiming the achievement of an 'ecologically sustainable society' as a new, 'noble mission' for his party. Presenting his Cabinet Policy Platform two weeks later, Prime Minister Persson stated that Sweden should be 'an internationally driving force and a forerunner in the endeavours to create an ecologically sustainable development' (Parliamentary Record, March 22, 1996). The *temporal* aspect was of central concern. The present pattern of continued economic growth would – so argued the Ministers and the party elite – overtax natural resources and leave future generations disinherited (Prime Minister Göran Persson 1997; Environmental Minister Anna Lindh 1997; DESD 1997:1; SAP 1997).

However, the transformation of the country into 'A Sustainable Sweden' should not mean draconian measures towards present generations. The ruling Swedish Social Democrats put a strong emphasis on the *social* and *economic* aspects of sustainable development. Allusions were made to the glorious past, when the party ruled over the transformation of Sweden into a modern welfare state, *folkhemmet* (the 'People's Home'; see Tilton 1990:125 ff.): 'Now, we have a similar mission. We will realise the vision of a *green* welfare state, and bring about a thorough *ecological modernisation* of Sweden' (SAP 1997; italics added). In its Finance Plan for 1997, the Social Democratic Cabinet stated that the transformation of Sweden into a 'green people's home'

> means an increased demand for investments and development of modern technology. Energy is a case in point. If Sweden is a forerunner in developing new technology, new markets are created for Swedish business and many new firms will be established in the energy sector. (Cabinet Bill 1996/97:150, p. 22)

Said the Prime Minister: '[W]e will all gain from ... the marriage of ecology, economy and employment'. (Cabinet Policy Platform, September 17, 1996; Environmental Minister Anna Lindh 1997; DESD 1997:2; Prime Minister Göran Persson 1997; SAP 1997; see Edman 1998)

This policy shift indicated a wholesale acceptance of the strategy of *ecological modernisation* (see Jänicke 1985, Hajer 1995, Gouldson and Murphy 1997, Lundqvist 2000). This strategy is founded on a combination of regulatory and economic policy instruments to propel the growth of new, green technologies and production/consumption processes in society (see Murphy 2000:3). This way of promoting *economic* growth is in fact a long-term hallmark of Sweden's Social Democrats; it seemed only 'natural' to extend it to promote 'green' growth in consensus with broad socio-economic interests. Ministers pointed to the fact that Swedish public sector annually purchases goods and services for nearly 300 billion SEK (about €33 billion). The government could thus 'directly create a market' for green goods and services through an active 'green procurement' policy for public agencies at all levels. The tax system should be subjected to successive changes to promote both eco-sustainability and the competitiveness of Swedish firms and enterprises. Massive government support of eco-investment programmes would also be forthcoming to stimulate the ecological modernisation – read greening – of the 'People's Home' (Environmental Minister Anna Lindh 1997; Prime Minister Göran Persson 1997; SAP 1997).

The *Delegation for Ecologically Sustainable Development* (DESD) formed in January 1997 within the Cabinet became the vehicle for this strategy. The Delegation's first, explicitly short-term assignment was to 'develop a platform for the Cabinet's comprehensive policy for an ecologically sustainable society.' (Parliamentary Record January 22, 1997, Prime Minister Göran Persson). The Delegation's March 1997 report on *A Sustainable Sweden* called for a *Sustainability Investment Programme* to run from 1998 to 2004. It included

- one billion SEK to eco-cycle adjustment of built environments and infrastructure;
- nine billion SEK to eco-cycle transformation of the Swedish energy system, and;
- six billion SEK to local investment programs (LIPs) for sustainability by municipal governments (DESD 1997).

Not only was such a programme important for the possibilities of future generations to lead a good life, argued the Delegation. The 'most thrilling aspect' of the work towards sustainable development was to 'be able to utilise the markets to open up for environmentally adapted products and services', thus stimulating growth and competitiveness, and creating new jobs. The Cabinet's spring 1997 Economic Bill allocated 12,6 billion SEK for the period 1998–2000 to the Sustainable Sweden programme as a whole. Of this, 5,4 billion SEK was specifically destined to support the Local Investment Programmes (LIPs) (Cabinet Bill 1996/97:150, pp. 87 ff.).

### 'Beating time'? The record of future-oriented ecological modernisation

The policy statements of leading Social Democrats indicated that they wanted to achieve the ecological modernisation of the 'People's Home' through consensus. The view of the economy-ecology relationship as a positive-sum game was clearly meant to imply that the road to sustainability is one where present generations would gain as much as those of the future. What, then, is the record so far of the LIPs in terms of autonomy and sustainability?

The political centrality attributed by the Cabinet to the Sustainability Investment Programme is clearly shown in the implementation process. Contrary to usual procedures of distributing grants through formally independent agencies, the Cabinet formed a Special Unit within the Environment Ministry for this purpose. The statute regulating the process and establishing the criteria for grants affords wide leeway and discretion to this Unit

(SFS 1998:23). Local governments send 'notifications of interest', outlining investment ideas. From these, the Special Unit selects a number of local governments for 'dialogue', during which the investment ideas are further developed. After receiving the final applications, the Special Unit scrutinises them, and may then seek counsel from relevant national agencies and the Regional Administrations. Early assessments of the process pointed to several problems. The criteria for decisions on grants were not clear and transparent. Agency experts were not consulted to an extent that would guarantee the cost-effectiveness of supported investments in relation to environmental objectives (Standing Committee on Housing 1998/99, pp. 25 ff; see Auditors of Parliament 1998/99:97). A survey to the municipal Local Agenda co-ordinators at the end of 1998 revealed that LIPs were seldom anchored within the Local Agenda 21 processes and the sustainability ideas developed in discussions among citizen groups and local politicians and administrators. The indication was rather that administrative and business elites within the municipalities dusted off old pet projects (Brundin and Eckerberg 1999).

The 'consensus' was thus very much one promoted by the activities and views of the Environment Ministry's special unit. This in turn implies that the autonomy of present local citizens – expressed, e.g., in Local Agenda 21 plans – was somewhat compromised. But was not this in their long-term interest, as the programme promoted sustainability and thus autonomy for future generations? Under the statute, municipalities applying for LIP grants were required to describe how the proposed measures *might* stimulate the development of new technology (italics mine). The statute 'demands' that grants to 'sustainability' investments by industry or business *must* promote such development (SFS 1998:23). However, the technology-*driving* grants were never more than a tiny part of the whole programme (see Auditors of Parliament 1998/99:87). Even with a very generous interpretation of 'new' technology, only about one (1) per cent of the 2.3 billion SEK granted in the first year were of this kind (Kågesson and Lidmark 1998).

Against this background, it only seems logical that the Swedish government notified the EU of changes in the 1998 statute to the effect that the technology-development conditions for grants to competitive industries and firms is withdrawn from autumn

1999. Furthermore, Internet information to applicants emphasises that LIP grants are different from other state grants. There is
'no technology driving conditionality, i.e., the Cabinet does not
point out which technological solutions should be supported.
Instead, the ecological and employment effects are in focus'. The
Ecocycle Billion, explicitly designed to stimulate development of
technologies for ecologically sustainable development, was taken
out of the state budget in April 1999. Only one-fifth was ever
used for project grants, and only a few of the supported projects
were technology-driving (National Audit Office 1999a:passim.
See www.hallbarasverige.gov.se as of June 1999). With the basic
element of the ecological modernisation strategy withdrawn, the
Prime Minister's vision of the LIP programme as a promoter of
green technology and new 'niches' of sustainable growth for
Swedish industry thus in effect came to nought.

But could not the programme have employment and environmental effects that would in the longer term justify the
Social-Democratic strategy of ecological modernisation?
According to the latest available official figures, 141 municipalities (just under half of Sweden's 289 local governments) were
granted a total of SEK 5.6 billion to LIPs up to the autumn of
2001. Out of the total investments of SEK 21,5 billion, directly
environment-related investments totalled SEK 17 billion. The
employment impact estimated by the municipalities comes to
about 15,600 'green jobs' up to 2002. There are, however, only
about 1,800 permanent new jobs created through LIPs
(Government Communication 2000/01:38, p. 24; see
http://miljo.regeringen.se/M-dep_fragor/hallbar utveckling/LIP).
As for environmental effects of the LIPs, the only base for judgement comes from the estimates made in the municipal application
for grants. The funds invested up to 2001 'are expected' to
produce the following results:

- Energy consumption down by 2.1 TWh per year.
- Fossil fuels equivalent to 2.3 TWh per year replaced by renewable energy sources.
- Carbon dioxide emissions down by 1.57 million tonnes or 2.8
  per cent of all Sweden's emissions.
- Nutrient and phosphorous discharges down by 2 and 4 per
  cent respectively of the current discharges into water.

- The amount of waste going to landfill down by 500,000 tonnes, which is the equivalent of 10 per cent of present volumes (Cabinet Communication 2000/01:38, p. 58 f.).

In their assessment of the first two programme years, the Auditors of Parliament stated that meaningful judgements on environmental effects could only be made relative to such quantified objectives that existed *before* the establishment of National Environmental Objectives and subsequent interim targets (see above, pp. 65–8). For the seven comparisons thus possible, the measures resulting from LIPs granted state support in 1998 contributed only infinitesimally to the actual achievement of these quantified objectives. The Auditors could not judge the LIPs' cost effectiveness, since the Environment Ministry's database did not classify the grants according to estimated environmental effects. Seen from the sustainability perspective, the Auditors' conclusion on the LIPs' contribution to 'A Sustainable Sweden' is worth quoting. The Auditors found it

> questionable whether the Cabinet – by using other policy instruments – can stimulate activities that make sure the other 95 per cent of the effects necessary for goal achievement will actually materialise. (Auditors of Parliament 1998/99:97)

## Ecological self-binding in Sweden: up or down with the ecocycle?

### *'Saving' time: are physical planning and ecocycle adaptation closing in on the future?*

Temporally rational ecological governance means that societal and economic processes are made compatible with underlying, and ultimately binding, ecological and natural resource cycles. The precautionary principle demands that decision-makers at all levels avoid actions that may have irreversible effects on these cycles. But what is irreversible is surrounded by great uncertainty, and may not be discovered until way into the future. The precautionary principle thus forces decision-makers to play it safe by constraining present action through 'self-binding' measures. For such binding to count as temporally rational ecological governance, we defined three constitutive elements: (1) *defined target dates* when specific sustainability objectives are to be achieved, (2) *clearly outlined processes of monitoring and evaluation* of actual goal achievement, and (3) *democratic procedures* for decision-making and implementation, regardless of the self-binding strategies used.

Four major Swedish strategies of constraining present action in favour of future sustainability and autonomy have been studied, i.e., *physical planning* and *management by objectives, eco-cycle adaptation,* and *resource efficiency.*

Physical planning exhibits a peculiar relationship to temporally rational ecological governance. The time frames of present physical planning provide a temporal context for environmental and resource management, but do not in and of themselves define targets or dates of their achievement. Defined from political and economic rather than natural cycles, the temporal frames of planning differ among sectors. The problems with physical planning as a means of binding us now for future sustainable development also come out clearly in the quite limited and indecisive role of Environmental Impact Assessments. Physical planning processes have proven unable to block certain large-scale developments with possibly irreversible environmental and resource consequences, with the Hallandsås railroad tunnel as a case in point (see below, pp. 109–11). In terms of autonomy, present planning procedures exhibit a gap between formal and real opportunities for public participation and influence. To what extent resource and environmental considerations emanating from public involvement actually find their way into local master plans is presently unknown.

Having said this, one should however not forget that Sweden's national physical planning has been instrumental in 'preserving' time by defining and defending areas and specific resources of 'national interest'. Almost one quarter of Sweden's area is under such constraints that activities detrimental to sustainable development and environmental quality cannot take place there. The regional Strategic Environmental Guidelines (STRAMs) are a major source of identification and prevention of such areas. Finally, the future linking of all sectoral planning to the 15 National Environmental Objectives and their interim targets, indicates a longer time perspective and a more co-ordinated process. This linkage holds the promise of making the planning process more binding on resource-related decision, and thus more instrumental to sustainability.

The eco-cycle adaptation strategy is essentially one of 'saving' time and resources for the future. An increased recycling and reuse of materials and products now leads to lower pressure on the resource base and environmental quality in the future. A clear streak of autonomy is visible. The most remarkable progress has been made in fields where individuals – as consumers and as citizens – have access to markets as well as infrastructural arrangements aimed at easing individual choice of this strategy. Packaging materials, newspapers, as well as glass, aluminium and PET beverage containers are examples of recycling and reuse where achievements are even ahead of projected targets. In terms of sustainability, the fully eco-cycle adapted society is a long way off. Comprehensive infrastructural socio-economic processes – such as those of sewage and transportation – will not be adapted for some time to come, because of the 'lock in' effects of present technologies.

What is important to note, however, is that eco-cycle adaptation has become a constituent part of Sweden's environmental and resource policy. Decisions are taken, and moves are made to push further with this strategy. Regulations of material cycles in key industrial and other branches, and explicit timetables for the recyclability/reusability/upgradeability of several products and materials are projected to take effect over the first decade of this millennium.

### *'Beating time': does ecological modernisation have a future?*

In essence, ecological modernisation holds the promise of 'beating' time. By making energy and resource use more and more efficient, the intergenerational conflict can be avoided (for a glowing Swedish 'homage', see Edman 1998). Efficiency hikes in line with 'Factor 10' will allow present generations to uphold their living standard but still leave future generations with enough resources to allow for autonomous choices of ways of life. Much of this strategy's credibility thus hinges on the actual effectiveness of programmes launched to stimulate the growth of 'green' and 'lean' technology. While it is too early for final judgements on programmes with a temporal scope of generations, the results of presently available evaluations may give indications of where these programmes are heading.

When announcing the ecological modernisation strategy in 1996, the Social Democrats said it would build a future, 'green' People's Home, saving environment and resources for future generations. After a flying start there are, however, strong indications that the programme is turning away from this central idea. The technology-driving element, so central to the strategy, has become subdued in the LIPs. The 'Ecocycle Billion' grants to stimulating new resource- and energy-efficient technologies were even abandoned.

The discretionary decision-making process, with lack of strict criteria, little if any analysis of longer-term strategic effects, seemingly no cost-effectiveness analyses, and an almost programmatic non-involvement of expert authorities, seems to have compromised both the sustainability and autonomy elements of temporally rational ecological governance. The programme of subsidies for long-term conversion of Sweden's energy provision and distribution systems is split between authorities and sub-programmes, and thus is difficult to assess in terms of its contribution to sustainable energy provision. All in all, however, the effects on environmental quality and energy conversion from the 'eco-efficiency' strategy seem quite marginal. The Auditors of Parliament even called for a reconsideration of national environmental quality and resource management objectives should this strategy continue.

The 'efficiency' strategy has had a special impact on autonomy and democracy. The LIP grant programme is characterised by a very high degree of centralised decision-making. Traditional ways of implementing decisions through independent expert authorities have been bypassed (see Lundqvist 2001a). Most of the grants to local investment programmes for sustainable development were decided by just a dozen officers within the Ministry of Environment's special LIP unit. Ideas emanating from municipal Local Agenda 21 processes, and anchored within discussions among local citizens, have not found their way into LIP grant applications to an extent compatible with the criterion of autonomy (see Kågesson and Lidmark 1998; Brundin and Eckerberg 1999).

This leads us to an intricate question: Will ecological modernisation – and the 'efficient use' strategies based on it – really 'beat' time by bridging us over to affluence for future generations without detriment to the present? Given the record so far, one is forced to answer in the negative. For the ecological modernisation's 'positive-sum-game' to materialise, more resource-efficient and environment-friendly technologies must develop, and provide new opportunities of socio-economic development also for the present generation. When that element is compromised, as seems to be the case for Sweden, the auspices for autonomy and sustainability held out by ecological modernisers certainly seem clouded.

*An idea just in time? The prospects of ecological management by objectives*
Still, temporal aspects are integrated parts of Sweden's environmental and resource policies. Planning regulations, programmes for ecocycle adaptation, and even efficient use strategies *do* address the longer-term aspects of sustainable development, and *are* binding – with different strengths – on future decisions. But if there is not enough of 'saving' and 'reserving' time, and if the prospects of 'beating' time are not all that clear, is there really a future for temporally rational ecological governance?

Perhaps the most interesting answer to this question is provided by an idea whose time has just come, i.e., ecological *management by objectives (MBO)*. The three overarching objectives of *protection of environmental quality, efficient use of resources,* and *sustainable ecosystem productivity* formulated in 1997, explicitly lifted the perspective to one generation from now to around 2020–25. With the 15 National Environmental Objectives and the specification of interim targets, ratified by Parliament in 1999 and 2001 respectively, all societal sectors will have explicit goals and target dates for sustainable resource use and environmental management by the middle of the first decade of the third millennium.

The reader may argue that this is just some rattling at the fences, and not a binding pledge to attack problems of sustainable development. Admittedly, management by objectives *is* a loosely structured process in classic political and administrative terms. But the interim targets are there, binding agencies and actors involved in the process of developing sub-goals and targets further down the line. They will most probably come to feel formally, but above all mentally, bound to these objectives and targets. Another crucial aspect of the MBO strategy is that the choice of methods of goal achievement is left with the responsible agents and their client groups. The agencies and the politically responsible elites must bring responsible sectoral actors into consensus around the objectives and constructive decisions as to proper measures for goal achievement, something that implies a considerable degree of autonomy in the process.

However, temporally rational ecological governance is not just about how to arrange political institutions to take account of different life cycles and time scales important to the balance of ecosystems. To the aspect of becoming 'green in time' is thus added the aspect of being politically accountable and 'just in time'. A most interesting aspect of the MBO strategy is its entrenchment in central bureaucracy. In effect, present bureaucrats function as 'ombudsmen' for future generations. If the subgoals and targets come to reflect judgements of administrative feasibility as much as considerations of levels necessary for sustainable development, this may affect the autonomy of future generations. It should, however, be noted that an elaborate structure of political, and thus open, review of progress towards goals and targets is envisaged with annual reports to Parliament, and a broad State of the Environment report every mandate period. Together with the explicit linking of the MBO strategy to a supportive context of monitoring, evaluation, and new statistical accounts, this means that the development towards goals and targets can be closely scrutinised and the adequacy of goals and targets challenged by the interested citizen.

# 4

# The commons of governing: the knowledge base of ecological governance

## Science, politics and sustainable resource management

*Between knowledge and power; scientific research and ecological politics*

Yesterday's environmental problems were rather tangible in spatial and temporal terms. Often easily detectable causes and effects made them relatively simple to manage. The up-stream polluter could be forced to compensate the down-stream victim. However, the causes and effects of modern environmental problems are increasingly difficult to delimit in time and space. Catchment eutrophication, long-range transport of air pollution, thinning of the ozone layer, and global warming are examples of this growing diffuseness of environmental problems. Resource use decisions are increasingly made under conditions of uncertainty. There is thus a growing need to ground rational ecological governance in scientific knowledge of ecosystems and of the effects of resource use (see Berkes and Folke 2000).

This means that scientific expertise comes to hold a key position in governance for sustainable development. Scientists are called upon to assess the spatial and temporal scale of environmental problems, as well as to define the range of technically, economically and socially possible solutions. We approach a 'scientisation' of ecological politics. Participants in the debates over ecological governance are keen to use scientific arguments to justify their positions. The turns of the debate over global warming provide a clear example of how experts and counter-experts are brought in to support differing standpoints. Scientists who want *their* findings accepted as the proper basis for policy measures engage in a lot of lobbying-like footwork in the corridors of political power. All this also means a 'politicisation' of science. The importance of finding a 'valid' scientific base for action propels political actors to seek ways of 'steering' scientific research towards valued political ends (see, e.g., Jasanoff 1990; Lee 1993). As a consequence, the boundaries between scientifically validated facts and politically accepted opinions are blurred.

Research on the role of scientists and of knowledge in environmental and resource management has produced two lines of argument. Institutionalists view policy-makers as rational actors involved in political bargaining to further their interests and objectives. Knowledge is just one among other inputs into the bargain, providing supportive arguments to political actors with rather stable interests. Institutional factors that promote or block the choice of knowledge to support certain alternative courses of action are particularly important. Others argue that consensual knowledge is what actually shapes the environmental and resource management 'regime' and its patterns of action by moulding the interests of the actors (Haas 1993:183 ff.). Epistemic communities, i.e., networks of researchers and experts are able to wield political power by cognitive authority based on commonly accepted knowledge. These communities become vehicles for institutional learning that, in turn, influences the content of ecological governance (Haas 1997:200, 205 f.).

*Speaking truth to power; access, validation and acceptance of scientific arguments*
These two views of the relationship between science and politics point out several aspects influencing the possibilities of ecologically rational governance to achieve both sustainability and autonomy. Scientifically validated knowledge about what promotes sustainability is increasingly crucial to such governance. But the growing complexity of environmental problems means that the process of obtaining knowledge, and of processing and validating it, creates a need to organise knowledge production, assessment and diffusion.

First, *by whom* should this knowledge be generated and validated, i.e., accepted as common ground for ecological politics? Most often, developed industrial nations see this as a matter for scientists and experts, working in research institutions, and not a task for lay people relying on practical experience (see however, Olsson and Folke 2001). The underlying idea is that specialisation and professional skill will lead to a reliable and valid base for policy measures. Second, *how* should knowledge be produced and evaluated? Ideally, the research process should not be directed by politics or special interests. Researchers should be unhindered to seek results in scientifically accepted ways. Otherwise, science might not be speaking truth reliably to power.

But even if science speaks the truth, *what* knowledge should be produced and validated? At one stage in the process, the answer may be that we need validated knowledge on the actual relationships between causes and effects of specific environmental problems. This presumes that there is some consensus as to which environmental problems are the most critical ones. At a later stage, priority may have to be given to specific courses of action, i.e., practicable solutions to environmental problems. Ideally, this prioritisation should have access to scientific evidence about the scope and seriousness of specific environmental problems and their effects, in order to widen political judgement and make it more probable that political action is directed towards the most relevant targets. Obviously, different kinds of knowledge are required to solve problems of sustainable development. The argument that research on sustainability should be less curiosity-driven and more problem-driven leads to a re-evaluation of scientific standards with respect to 'tolerable' uncertainties (see, e.g., Board for Sustainable Development of the National Research Council 1999).

Ideals are one thing, however, and reality another. On all these three aspects, the lines between science and politics do get blurred, with quite distinctive consequences for the possibilities of achieving both sustainability and autonomy. Scientists fight publicly over method; the *how* of knowledge production and assessment is judged by criteria that differ among disciplines or schools. They proceed from differing assumptions and perspectives, which makes the prioritisation about *what* and *by whom* even more complicated for political decision-makers (see Holling et al. 2000:344 ff.). Since scientific arguments are not always transparent to policy-makers, this increases the possibility of influence from science over decisions about research priorities.

Problems of scale also come in here. Sustainable development largely focuses on global issues and global problems whereas political decision-making structures and the systems of knowledge generation are nationally organised.

*Ecocracy vs. democracy; the normative dimension*
We thus end up with starkly normative questions about the proper role of science in the policy process. Too much science tends to withdraw policy-making from popular control, thus blurring the lines of accountability. Too much politics in science may threaten the validity of research results, as the research process becomes impregnated with assumptions not derivable from theoretically defendable premises. Thus, while the need to achieve sustainable development makes it necessary to base political decisions on the best possible scientific knowledge, democratic norms force us to find ways of balancing politics and science. How should a system of ecological governance be designed to make sure that ecologically relevant *scientific* knowledge is brought to bear on issues related to sustainability, and still allow for *democratic* accountability of public decision-makers?

Some are clearly in favour of tipping the balance towards the scientific end of the scale. Eco-authoritarians contend that the pace of ecological degradation is rapidly threatening the ecological survival of society. This leads them to argue that democracy may be counterproductive to securing that objective. Invoking the authority of science, they claim this to be an 'objective' definition of the sustainability problem. Science *can* provide the appropriate technical solutions. The resolution to the overriding problem of scarcity is an oligarchic system '... with only those possessing the ecological and other competencies necessary to make prudent decisions allowed full participation in the political process.' (Ophuls 1977:163).

However, decisions on the best way to reach an ecologically rational relation between society and the natural environment 'will affect more lives (private and collective, present and future), and to a greater extent than, arguably, any other policy area', with the exception of war (Barry 1999:199). Those tipping the scale towards the democratic side argue that scientific knowledge *is* necessary and useful. However, the scale and possible consequences of ecological governance are so comprehensive as to demand that the demos as a whole, or its representatives, must have the last word. Democratic politics should determine what are the problems involved in sustainability, and decide on the appropriate solutions: 'Once these major issues have been demo-cratically decided, then technical considerations may be appropriate. Experts ought to be "on tap, not on top" ...' (Barry 1999:199 ff.).

### Criteria for knowledge-based and democratic ecological governance

But how should that tap be construed to ascertain that 'the appli-cation of science is *within* rather than *beyond* democratic regulation' (Barry 1999:203)? How are we to make sure that the answers to *what*, *how* and *by whom* are based on the best possible knowledge available and, as far as possible, on comple-mentary and competing views on problems and solutions? First of all, it seems important that the question of *what* should be subjected to scientific research and production of knowledge is answered through an intricate balancing of scientific, political and social aspects. Scientific discoveries and findings concerning the society-environment metabolism can be used to address issues of the scope, intensity and direction of 'problems' related to sustainability. An institutionalised dialogue between science and politics can then guide political decisions on how to allocate public funding for future research. This is particularly important for a small country like Sweden with limited resources in terms of both money and manpower.

However, both second-generation environmental and – in particular – sustainability issues involve uncertainties and risks of an unprecedented order. Citizens and actors in civil society can never fully avoid being exposed to these uncertainties and risks. On grounds of autonomy, the evaluation of risks and uncertain-ties should *not* be left to policy-makers and scientists alone. This 'post-normal' situation has been used to argue for a more conscious involvement of citizens and a different role for civil society in the production of *problem*-oriented knowledge (Funtowicz and Ravetz 1993).

Thus, the issues of *how* and *by whom what* knowledge should be generated and assessed ought to be addressed by securing a structure of autonomous and semi-autonomous institutions that gather, assess and then disseminate knowledge on sustainable resource management to political decision-making bodies and to the general public. This may involve university departments, independent research and monitoring institutes. It may also involve agencies that work much like the semi-autonomous institutions presently found in the judicial and – to an increasing extent – financial spheres. For such a pluralistic structure of scientific activity to provide complementary and competing knowledge, it is of course necessary that the answers to the question of *what* are such that competition is enhanced by the system of funding. Norms of democracy and autonomy mean that there should also be institutions where scientific knowledge on the state of the environment, and on resource use alternatives and their effects, can be politically evaluated and judged. Such institutions, be they parliamentary commissions, judicial boards of appeal, public hearings or other devices for participation, must be easily accessible for the actors and interests wanting to influence or challenge resource-related decisions.

With regard to the knowledge aspect, the following criteria for ecologically rational governance may thus be formulated:

- Governance is ecologically rational to the extent that the structures built up to develop, assess and disseminate science-based knowledge allow for free exchange of complementary and competing views.
- Governance is ecologically rational when competing knowledge is made accessible to public debate and scrutiny in the policy process.
- Governance is ecologically rational to the extent that scientific knowledge is brought to bear on, and to interact with, political judgement to arrive at democratically legitimate decisions on how to use and manage natural resources to achieve sustainable development.

**Organising knowledge for sustainable resource governance**

*Science for governmental policy: agency-sponsored research for policy implementation*
From the outset, the what, how and by whom of Swedish environmental research was intimately linked to the implementation

of governmental policy. An Environmental Research Board within the Swedish Environmental Policy Administration decided on the allocation of research grants. The SEPA Director General also chaired that Board. A number of specialised Research Committees examined applications for grants. These committees consisted of active researchers as well as representatives of sectoral agencies, municipalities, and sometimes industry, with officers from the SEPA Research Department working as secretaries to the committees. Now and then, specific environmental problems were singled out as 'Programme Areas'. A Programme Area Officer from SEPA's Research Department co-ordinated research within a designated area, and was ultimately responsible to report the results to the Research Board.

The environmental research budget was decided upon together with all other state-supported research in the Cabinet's Omnibus Research Bill sent to Parliament every third year (see Cabinet Bill 1990/91:90, p. 459 f.). The allocations grew from about SEK 20 million in the early 1970s to around SEK 150 million in the mid 1990s, constituting about one-tenth of total state expenditures on environmental policy. Besides the objective of building competence in Swedish environmental science, SEPA and its Research Board emphasised direct practical applicability of research results when awarding grants. Information and reports about Board-sponsored research results were made easily available through several series of SEPA research reports. The objectives of SEPA Action Plans during the 1980s and 1990s were to a large extent based on the results from agency-sponsored research (Lundqvist 1996:285 ff.).

This linkage between policy and science corresponded to the then dominant view of the society-environment relationship. Environmental problems were seen as linked to media (air, water, soil), and/or to their sectors 'of origin' (agriculture, transport, large resource-based industry, etc.). They were mainly discussed in natural science and technical terms, and could be 'solved' one by one with the right facts and the right techniques. A broader view, including perspectives on the society-environment relationship prevalent in social science and the humanities, was mainly missing. Not until the late 1980s was a specific Research Committee on Society and the Environment set up within the SEPA research structure. Its share of the environment research budget remained infinitesimal, however, and the committee was early on restructured to reflect the views of different organised interests.

The problems inherent in this organisation of the science-policy relationship became increasingly apparent by the 1990s, as the broader views of sustainable development and the more diffuse character of second-generation problems got to the top of the environmental agenda. A special environmental research commission recommended a broader, more problem-oriented perspective and more co-ordination among different users of research than the prevailing 'environmental' and 'cause-effect' research structure dominated by the SEPA (SOU 1992:68, pp. 108 ff.; Cabinet Bill 1992/93:170, p. 513).

*Science for markets; solution-oriented research to develop green technology*

By then, environmental research was drawn into political turmoil. Upon winning the 1991 elections, one of new Bourgeois Government's first, and certainly most well advertised priorities was to dissolve the so-called Wage Earners' Funds (Cabinet Bill 1991/92:92). Somewhat reluctantly, the Social-Democratic Government established these funds within a year after regaining power in 1982, after years of intensive ideological debate. Part of the profit generated by Swedish business was to be placed in these employee-controlled funds. Over the years, the share of employee ownership and control over Swedish business would thus gradually increase. In its 1993 Cabinet Bill on 'frontline research' the Centre-Right Coalition proposed that part of the funds should be used for long-term knowledge expansion though basic research and recruitment of scholars in areas of crucial importance to Sweden's future competitiveness in a global economy. This included, among other things, strategic environmental research. The strategic component meant that there should be more research on new solutions, such as resource-lean technologies (Cabinet Bill 1992/93:171, passim).

The 1992/93 Research Bill developed these ideas further. The Bourgeois Government then in power proposed that the SEK 20 billion to be released for research through the dissolution of Wage Earners' Funds should be given to a few large 'research foundations'. Working for a period of about 15 years, these foundations should provide the best possible conditions for strong research *milieus* by concentrating their funding to broad but well-defined programmes. The drive for research to provide new solutions is evident. Said the Minister: 'It is of national importance to ensure that Swedish industry has access to an infrastructure of basic and applied research that enables it to conquer new markets.' (Cabinet Bill 1992/93:170, p. 35).

One of the new foundations would address strategic environmental research. This foundation, called MISTRA, was charged with using the interest on SEK 2.5 billion to support research that 'can be swiftly developed into practices of importance to the environment'. The MISTRA Board should be 'clearly anchored' in both the scientific community and Swedish industry (Cabinet Bill 1992/93:170, p. 38). Evidently, the Cabinet had in mind to break new paths for Swedish environmental research. What this meant to the traditional, discipline-bound cause-effect research is discussed below (see pp. 97–9).

MISTRA's historic record and present activities reveal a deliberate and continuous effort to bridge the gap between the scientific community and a broad spectrum of potential users of research results. To receive MISTRA funding, environmental research programmes must be driven not only by the scientific community's urge to be 'at the cutting edge of knowledge'. They must address the need to solve real world environmental problems. Such solutions should include environmentally sound products, services and processes that can make it in a market, as well as new judicial, administrative and other political measures. Fundable MISTRA programs should

- provide users in enterprises, authorities and organisations, as well as international negotiators, decision-makers on different levels and interest groups, with the latest scientific findings, irrespective of sectoral boundaries;
- provide the research community with problems as they have been formulated by the problem owners/users, irrespective of its disciplinary boundaries.

Also the enumeration of the different actors and interests that might get funded through MISTRA evidences this drive to bring scientific research and socio-economic practice together, in order both to solve environmental problems *and* bring about new technological development. The foundation's homepage states that 'MISTRA is for

- *researchers* who want to tackle problems, the solutions to which can forward the development towards a sustainable society;
- *Swedish companies* who want to be at the cutting edge when it comes to developing environmentally sound products, services or production processes. Scientific and commercial perspectives must be combined;
- *authorities* and legislators who wish to tighten the requirements on activities that may harm the environment. Tougher requirements must be based on solid scientific foundations;
- *international negotiators* charged with the task of drawing up international agreements on more stringent environmental requirements. A MISTRA programme must be able to meet both the demands of the international research community for quality and the need of negotiators for accurate information;
- *non-governmental organisations* and others striving for sustainable development.' (www.mistra-research.se/).

Programmes that fulfil these requirements, and pass the needle's eye of an extensive international peer review of scientific quality, usually get funded for two consecutive three to four year periods. Executive committees lead the programmes and are mandated to keep the programme's focus on problem solving and the practical implementation of research. The MISTRA secretariat is also quite active, checking each programme throughout its duration, e.g., by meeting representatives of each programme several times a year. About 20 programmes were running by the end of 2001, and the sum available for annual funding from MISTRA amounts to SEK 250 million (www.mistra-research.se/).

Since the mid-1990s, MISTRA has provided grants to Swedish environment- and resource-related research in the neighbourhood of SEK 1.2 billion (about €130 million). What has this comparatively rich funding meant so far for the role of knowledge in ecological governance? First of all, it has profoundly influenced the *how* and *by whom* of Swedish environmental research. Due to the thorough review of programme proposals, and the continuous evaluation of programme performance, scientific quality is kept at a high level. The MISTRA approach has also caused a dramatic increase in cross-disciplinary environment-related research; natural sciences, technology, and the social sciences have been forced to team up to get funded for research on different aspects of a common problem.

At issue, however, is the question of *what* is affected (and, one might add, the question of *for whom*). The MISTRA Board of Governors decides which programmes should be funded, often after active scanning and development of ideas through the MISTRA staff. The MISTRA and other strategic research foundations are deliberately made constitutionally sovereign in interpreting their statutes on how to spend their funds. The large sums allocated to research might thus not necessarily be in tandem with the priorities made in the Parliament's research policy decisions. The mandate to promote eco-technological developments in Swedish industry may further accentuate this. Another issue concerns who should own the research results. Should it be MISTRA as a foundation under private law? Or should it be those exploiting research results by developing new technologies, or other groups involved in the practical solution of environmental problems? The issue of government's role in ecological governance with respect to the knowledge dimension soon came to occupy centre stage in the political debate.

*For government's sake; the political fight to control strategic environmental research*
To the Social-Democratic government returning to power after the 1994 elections, the strategic research foundations were an aberration in research policy. The foundations' voluminous budgets, their independent status relative to the government, and their strategies for research and development had drawn heavy criticism. The Social Democrats were furthermore haunted by the repercussions of the acute economic crisis of 1992, and the continuously huge budget deficit. All this combined to promote an orchestrated attack on the strategic foundations, where environmental research in particular came to occupy centre stage.

In its drive to balance the state budget, the Social-Democratic Government in September 1996 ordered the SEPA to cut its budget by SEK 230 million in 1998–99. Searching for alternatives, the SEPA leadership suggested taking away the agency's whole research budget. This alternative was put forward because

the SEPA leadership seemingly nursed the view that MISTRA
would open its chest and fully compensate the SEPA for the cuts
in the research budget. However, it was not clear whether the
Social-Democratic Government and the Environment Minister
actually shared this view (Esselin and Arvidsson 1998:12 ff.).

The SEPA Director General (who incidentally was at the same
time Chairman of the MISTRA Board of Directors) counted on
the Cabinet to gain a political majority for opening the strategic
research foundations to governmental influence and control. A
1996 bill proposed that the Cabinet should have the right to
change the statutes of the foundations from 1997. This would
circumvent earlier regulations demanding that such changes be
preceded by a formal request from the foundation board (Cabinet
Bill 1996/97:22, p. 4). Furthermore, the Cabinet's research bill
proposed that the Cabinet should have the prerogative to appoint
and fire the members of the foundation boards. This would also
concern members representing the scientific community, who
should no longer be voted in by a special electoral collegium. The
Cabinet argued that this was motivated by the need to co-ordinate
scientific activities to research policy objectives, to free resources
for use elsewhere, and simply to cut the budget deficit (Cabinet
Bill 1996/97:5, p. 45 f.) Obviously, the Social-Democratic cabinet
saw these proposals as a way of getting the foundation boards to
allocate money not just to peer-reviewed research programmes
but also to state agencies and councils supporting environmental
research.

The changes in the statutes and the processes of appointing
board members were accepted by the Parliament after intense
debate (Esselin and Arvidsson 1998:15 f.). The 1997 Budget Bill
cut the SEPA's research budget for 1997 by one third, and allocated no research money for 1998 and 1999. There was a clear
ambition to compensate SEPA with money from MISTRA, so that
SEPA could fulfil its responsibility for co-ordinating and evaluating Swedish environmental research (Cabinet Bills 1996/97:1/20,
pp. 5, 22; 1996/97:5, p. 303 f.). However, the Social-Democratic
victory turned out to be of no consequence. The MISTRA Board's
Position Paper presented by mid-1997 made it strikingly clear
that the foundation would *not* grant money to the research traditionally supported by the SEPA. Indeed, MISTRA emphasised
that it would continue to concentrate on broad, interdisciplinary,

and above all, *solution-oriented* programmes to enhance Sweden's possibilities to capture greater shares of the growing eco-technology market (MISTRA 1997:16 ff.).

The efforts to gain governmental control over appointments to the boards of strategic research foundations were thus parliamentarily successful. However, the formal changes did not translate into changes in the directions of funding. The MISTRA board rejected state involvement in decisions on *what* research should be sponsored by MISTRA. Given the bleak prospects for future funding of SEPA-sponsored research, it thus seemed as if the SEPA had lost most of its former control of the research agenda and access to research results. Furthermore, the question of *what* environment-related research to support seemed to be tipping towards an emphasis on 'marketable' technological solutions to sustainability problems.

*Balancing the scale: towards a multi-faceted relationship between science, politics and market actors*

Soon, however, proposals for comprehensive changes in the system of research funding were put on the agenda. The 'Research 2000' Commission report released in October 1998 proposed to co-ordinate and consolidate the funding of basic, applied and sectoral research into four research councils. The final proposal presented in the Social-Democratic Cabinet Bill on research in March 2000 contained a mix of funding bodies and some interesting arguments for such a mix.

The purpose was to create a new funding organisation to enable 'concentrated efforts in important fields of scientific research, promote co-operation between research and development, and improve the diffusion of scientific knowledge'. This organisation should make it possible for Cabinet and Parliament to answer the question of *what* by directing research to 'important' fields of both basic and applied research, and to stimulate high quality research co-operation across disciplines. One large national Science Council, established through a conglomeration of the earlier, more specialised councils would now fund basic research. With respect to applied research, two new research councils would be set up, also on the basis of existing units. To secure a proper answer to the question of *how*, the scientific community would be provided with a legally guaranteed majority on the boards of the new funding councils. Furthermore, a special funding agency would be established to help develop research results into inventions and new technologies (Cabinet Bill 1999/ 2000:81, p. 9).

What, then, about research for an *ecologically* sustainable development? The Cabinet saw this as a highly prioritised field, in need of a strong base for concentrated, long-term research efforts involving not only research in natural science and technology, but also on social, cultural and economic aspects. One of the proposed new research councils should therefore fund research in the fields of environment, agriculture and forestry, as well as planning, building and housing. This meant taking over responsibilities from four earlier Research Councils and most of the traditional environmental research earlier funded by the SEPA. In one stroke, the Cabinet thus put an enormously broad spectrum of ecologically relevant research within one administrative framework. It funds research spanning all the way from molecular biology to comprehensive infra-structural planning. The Cabinet's major argument for this reorganisation was that since 'the organisation of society and our lifestyles are the ultimate causes of environmental problems, we must understand and change the underlying economic, political and social mechanisms in order to solve these problems' (Cabinet Bill 1999/2000:81, p. 28 f.).

The new Research Council for Environment, Agricultural Sciences and Spatial Planning – (FORMAS) – began its activities in the second half of the year 2000. The Cabinet's priorities as to the *what* and *how* of research within FORMAS's area of responsibility reflect efforts to carefully balance all the multi-faceted demands made on research for sustainable development. Charged with initiating and co-ordinating research of importance to the society's transition to 'Sustainable Sweden', FORMAS is to give priority to research on positive and negative relations among ecologically, economically and socially sustainable development. But it should also fund research that contributes to the achievement of sectoral development goals, and leads to increased competitiveness in agriculture and forestry and industries within those sectors, particularly the development of agricultural products not harmful to consumers.

The same concern for an appropriate balance of competing

demands is evident with respect to *how* research should be carried out. FORMAS should spur multi- and cross-disciplinary research for sustainable development by supporting concentrated Swedish activities in prioritised areas and by enhancing international research co-operation. FORMAS is also expected to support critical and independent research providing scientifically valid alternatives of action for Swedish agricultural and forestry policies. The new council is to co-operate with other research-funding bodies to make sure crucial problems related to sustainable development do not go unattended. Finally, FORMAS is charged with actively assembling and disseminating research results and accumulated knowledge to different groups and actors in society (Cabinet Bill 2000/01:3, pp. 116 ff.).

The division of labour determined by Parliament mandates FORMAS to secure a 'long-term build-up of knowledge' in all the areas within its responsibility, while the SEPA is responsible 'for research directly supporting its own activities.' (Cabinet Bill 1999/2000:81, p.30). The SEPA has since embarked upon a strategy of concentrating its research support to so-called 'initiative' areas. The themes are elaborated within the Agency, and then opened up for competition among groups of researchers. The final programme is worked out in co-operation between the researchers, potential users interested in the research, and SEPA officers, to secure quality, relevance and applicability of results (see, e.g., SEPA 2000b). The FORMAS budget for 2002 amounted to SEK 435 million, of which SEK 180 million were 'mortgaged' to already granted research (FORMAS 2001). SEPA returned as an actor with monetary capacities to provide grants to environmental research in the year 2000. The sum allocated to the SEPA is expected to increase from SEK 50 million in that year to SEK 80 million in 2003 (Cabinet Bill 2000/01:1/20, p. 35).

The reforms in the last decade of the twentieth century resulted in a quite multi-faceted structure for funding research to sustainable development. At one end, MISTRA can use its annually available SEK 250 million for grants to large-scale programmes involving primarily applied research aimed at solving particular environmental and sustainability problems, all in accordance with priorities made by its Board of Governors and staff. There is little, if any, government intervention with respect to the content of supported programmes. At the other end, the SEPA uses its funds of up to SEK 80 million to support research serving the Agency's mandate to implement policy measures for sustainable development. In the middle, we find the new FORMAS with its scientist-dominated board. FORMAS is expected to use its SEK 400 to 500 million to support not only basic research over the whole spectrum of sustainable development problems, but also research that could support public policy measures as well as strengthen the future competitiveness of sectors dependent on renewable natural resources.

There have been signs that the new research council FORMAS has tried to co-ordinate answers the questions of *what* knowledge should be sought, particularly in the field of climate change (www.formas.se). At the same time, MISTRA's strong financial independence means that the MISTRA Board can determine much of the answer simply by announcing new priorities for funding (MISTRA did so by the end of 2002 in the field of climate change. Research; see http://www.mistra-research.se). That came one year after the SEPA was funding a large research programme on the same topic (www.naturvardsverket.se). By the end of 2002, Sweden thus had three research funding bodies all giving attention to and spending money on climate-related research, each from their particular vantage point. This indicates that the two first criteria set up for the knowledge dimension of ecologically rational governance criterion – scientific competition and accessibility of results for public debate and scrutiny – are now closer to being met than they were before the big organisational shuffle of the 1990s.

*Monitoring – providing common knowledge for policy-making and evaluation*
A functioning system for continuous monitoring and evaluation is obviously a necessary means to gather knowledge about the state and trends of ecological systems. SEPA became responsible for the programme on measurement and control of environmental quality as early as 1978. Regional and local programmes were set up for water recipient control, covering most of Sweden's freshwater bodies and streams. Regional air quality measurement programmes were established around the largest urban conglomerations (see Lundqvist 1994:1739 ff.). Problems of co-ordination, dissemination and irretrievability soon developed. A 1994

commission report found that more than a dozen public agencies were engaged in data collection, with little exchange of information. Field studies made data collection very costly. Measurement stations were not co-ordinated with one another. No common central environmental database existed. The report emphasised that remote sensing methods should come into more intensive use, and be closely co-ordinated and integrated with the net of data-collecting ground-stations. It suggested a new, more co-ordinated environmental data system to provide the basis for environmental indices (SOU 1994:125, pp. 91 ff., 161 ff.).

Much of the data collected from national, regional, and to some extent local monitoring activities functioned as a database available to all and everyone interested in the environment. The SEPA ran a series called *Monitor* reporting trends in different environmental pollutants or different parts of the environment. Statistics Sweden and SEPA published (and still do) *The Natural Environment in Figures,* which gives an overview of global and regional environmental problems, reports on factors influencing the national environment, and contains a lengthy statistical description of the state of the environment in Sweden. Statistics Sweden also runs an information bulletin, presenting annual trends of different pollutants, hazardous products etc.

Later developments reveal an increasing concern with the connection between environmental monitoring and actual decision-making. A 1997 Commission report suggested that the monitoring programme areas set up by the SEPA and its Environment Monitoring Board, and the regional programmes, should in the future be closely connected to the environmental quality norms of the Environmental Code and the coming National Environmental Objectives. Furthermore, future EU directives might call for reconsidering 'relevant' spatial scales of monitoring. The increased costs of expanding monitoring and surveillance should be at least partly covered through payments from sector agencies with explicit NEO responsibilities (SOU 1997:34, pp. 131 ff.). The NEO Commission suggested an elaborate system of nearly 160 indices for the 15 NEOs. The eight national agencies assigned with realising these objectives should have explicitly defined monitoring responsibilities. The Environmental Objectives Board (EOB) established within the SEPA in 2002 is charged with co-ordinating monitoring and evaluation of NEO progress (SOU 2000:52, Part 2, pp. 723 ff.; see below, part 5.3.2). As passed by Parliament, the 2001 Bill on NEOs stated that the number of indices should be limited to allow for overview. The importance of monitoring and evaluation to provide commonly shared knowledge of the state of ten environments can be seen in the 70 per cent increase in budget allocations to monitoring and evaluation (Cabinet Bill 2000/01:130, pp. 223 ff.).

## Knowledge at bay – the role of science in key processes of ecological governance

*Taking the heat; science, politics and the issue of climate change*
I said above that governance is ecologically rational when its structures allow for scientific research results and expertise to make complementary and competing knowledge accessible to public debate and judgement in the policy process. The organisation of the science-policy relationship developing in Sweden at the turn of the century covers some distance in satisfying this criterion. Furthermore, I stated that for governance to be ecologically rational, scientific and expert knowledge must be brought to bear on and interact with actual decision-making related to the objective of sustainable development. To shed some light on this aspect, let us look at the actual role of science and expertise in processes of key importance to the achievement of 'Sustainable Sweden'. This will be done by looking at critical cases in three stages of ecological governance; policy formation, policy implementation, and one case of large-scale infra-structural development involving valuable natural resources.

First is the formation of Sweden's policy on climate change. There is profound uncertainty about whether and, if so, when crucial limits will be reached. There are no end-of-pipe solutions. This together with the complex relation between climate change and the energy and transportation systems on which modern societies depend means that climate change really highlights the precarious dependency of politics on science. In 1993, the Centre-Right Cabinet then in power appointed a special Climate Change Commission (CCC) under the Ministry of Environment. The CCC consisted of active climate researchers, representatives of agencies and councils supporting climate-related research, as well as officers from central agencies and representatives from Swedish industry. Its mandate was to co-ordinate Swedish climate-related research, give advice to the Cabinet on how to utilise research results in national policy-making and international climate negotiations, co-ordinate Sweden's activities within IPCC, and provide co-ordinated and continuous reporting on climate research (SOU 1994:138, foreword).

The CCC early on presented overviews of Swedish climate research and its funding. It set about organising national workshops on issues of climate change, and on how to come to grips with the emissions of greenhouse gases. Its 1994 report contains a comprehensive overview of the causes and present trends of global and regional climate change, as well as on the counter-strategies that might be deployed (SOU 1994:138, passim). The 1995 report developed these themes further, and more specifically concentrated on the global level and the international climate negotiations. The Swedish situation and options in the future negotiations were outlined (SOU 1995:96, passim).

It seems quite clear that the CCC during its first years enjoyed a highly regarded position within Swedish policy-making on climate change issues. This is to a large degree due to the fact that the CCC chairman was at the same time chairman of the IPCC. He could thus provide Swedish key policy-makers with comprehensive and valuable insights into the ongoing IPCC process, and offer advice on how Sweden should formulate its strategies in the continued negotiations. His international status both as a scholar and as a central IPCC actor furthermore gave him credibility within the Swedish climate research community. From this base, he used the CCC to bring both believers and sceptics among climate-related researchers into the Swedish debate. In the organisational and inter-agency linkages emerging in Sweden 'after the Rio Conference and on the road to Kyoto', the CCC came to be seen as the most important science-related institution (Elzinga and Nolin 1998:22, 53 f.).

In early 1996, the CCC was reorganised and thereafter located within the SEPA. The following year, the CCC chairman retired from his post in the IPCC. The initiative in Swedish climate policy now shifted from the CCC to the more policy-oriented 'Kyoto group', consisting of climate-specialised representatives of ministries, SEPA and the National Board for Industrial and

Technological Development. Meeting twice a month, this group became the focal point of Swedish policy-making on climate change. Whenever there were conflicting views within the group, the issue was moved directly to the Cabinet level for settlement. Scientific and expert knowledge had several inroads to this highly political group. In-house consultation was a way to get updates of knowledge, used particularly by the Ministry for Foreign Affairs. Use of outside expertise was made frequently by actively seeking out Swedish experts who had done research on specific climate-related issues. The former CCC chairman was consulted on issues confronting Sweden's negotiating team. Reviewers of the process argue that the focus was all the time on Swedish research; international knowledge came in mainly via Swedish scientists (Elzinga and Nolin 1998:62).

The *inter*-organisational structure of the Kyoto group was thus quite different from the highly *intra*-ministerial one found in the issue of allocating LIP funds (see above, pp. 77–81). The difference in relation to science and expertise is also striking. Admittedly, the climate issue is comprehensive, and has broad implications for Sweden's efforts to achieve sustainable development. But one could easily argue that this is the case also for the LIP programme. And yet, we find that the climate issue seemed to call for close interaction with the scientific community, whereas the sustainability issues involved in the LIPs did not (see below, pp. 107–9).

The CCC was dissolved in 1998. Work on Sweden's future policy towards climate change was then concentrated in the 1998 Climate Commission, a body of politicians and experts charged with developing strategies for achieving the NEO of *Limited climate impact*. This commission particularly emphasised the need to increase public knowledge on the greenhouse effect and the risks of global warming. However, the basis recommended for better knowledge primarily consisted of improved monitoring and evaluation of policy effects and general climate trends. Nothing in the 'basic action package' explicitly refers to continued or intensified climate research to widen the knowledge base (SOU 2000:23, pp. 272 ff., 597 ff.).

Meanwhile, the funding of climate-related research turned more action-oriented. As pointed out already (see above, part 4.2.4), the MISTRA foundation by the end of 2002 increased its activities in this field, actively seeking cross-disciplinary programmes involving also the social sciences. With research money again flowing in, the SEPA initiated a specific research initiative on climate policy instrumentation in 2001. Furthermore, the new FORMAS research council is developing further climate-related research activities funded by its predecessors. Finally, Swedish climate researchers have long been actively engaged in co-operative programmes at the European level (see Elzinga and Nolin 1998:27 ff.).

Thus, the Swedish research community and funding agencies seem to be taking the issue of global warming and its threat to sustainability quite seriously. What remains to be seen, however, is the extent to which Sweden's future climate policy will rely on such knowledge. Since the release of its report, the Climate Commission has taken much heated criticism for its views on what constitutes the proper basis for elevating citizen knowledge and awareness, and on the role of citizens as passive receivers of information.

*Paying LIP service to knowledge; the limited role of expertise in Local Investment Plans for sustainable development*
Let us then turn to the implementation of what I above labelled a flagship of Sweden's efforts to achieve a 'sustainable society', i.e., the large 1998–2004 programme of subsidies to local investment programmes for sustainable development (see above, pp. 78–81). The Cabinet put much political prestige into the LIP programme and thus set up a new, quite unorthodox structure and process for handling the LIPs. The Ministry of Environment established a *Unit for Ecological Transformation and Development* (here called MENUET) to process LIP applications. The Unit consisted of a dozen officials and was mandated to use 'whatever sectoral agency competence and expertise was needed' (Cabinet Budget Bill 1997/98:1, Spending Area 18, p. 46).

Central and regional expert agencies implementing environmental and natural resource policies were told by the Environment Minister that they would have a prominent role in the LIP process (Auditors of Parliament 1998/99:37). However, the Cabinet's designation of expert agencies to assist the MENUET and the municipalities in evaluating the sustainability aspects of locally suggested measures came only just before the deadline for final applications. The Regional Administrations (RA, *länsstyrelserna*) were linked to the process by a rule making it mandatory for local governments to seek RA counsel when applying for LIP grants (Auditors of Parliament 1998/99:38, 45).

The actual decision-making process differed very much from formal regulations. The application and evaluation process in the first programme year stretched over a period of only six months. During the first four months, 286 municipal notifications of interest were processed, and about 40 municipalities were selected for further dialogue with the MENUET. In the last two months, the 12 MENUET officials took decisions on 115 final applications and selected 42 municipalities. The designated expert agencies never really became part of the innermost network of actors. They were asked only to comment on individual 'measures' in the municipal notifications of interest according to a MENUET checklist, and could thus never provide overall expert assessments on the applications. Indeed, very few expert comments were sought. The three most knowledgeable expert agencies commented on no more than 26 of the 460 'measures' in the 42 LIPs finally receiving grants (Standing Committee on Housing 1998/99:URD1, p. 23 ff.).

The usual procedures for expert consultation thus did not work in this process. Very few measures were ever remitted to the expert agencies, and their comments were mostly not considered by the MENUET. The very limited role for the SEPA further reflects this demise of knowledge and expertise. Its so-called 'favourable' position only meant that a SEPA official could 'sit in' to provide support during the MENUET's initial scanning of municipal notifications selected for further dialogue (Auditors of Parliament 1998/99:37 ff., 77).

The expert role of Regional Administrations in the LIP process became totally blurred. Because the LIP Ordinance was too unclear, they could not provide answers to municipalities about which measures might be eligible for grants. Furthermore, they were unable to give adequate advice to the MENUET, because they were not let into the crucial 'dialogue' between the MENUET and selected municipalities. Neither could they assist municipalities not receiving grants, since they had no insight into the Unit's criteria, priorities and arguments (Standing Committee on Housing 1998/99:URD1, pp. 26 ff.). A majority of the 115 local governments making final applications in the first programme year said they met with changing or contradictory demands and guidelines from the MENUET on the proper content of the application. One third of the 115 MGs finally applying for grants actually doubted whether MENUET had enough competence or knowledge of the functioning of local government to really understand their problems with LIP applications.

The massive critique against this process did lead to some changes in the second LIP round of 1998–99. The agencies now had experts sitting in with the MENUET once or several times a week. Furthermore, some agencies' views were now sought both before and after the final applications were in. However, there remained a crucial question: Were the officials individually knowledgeable experts or representatives of their agencies (Auditors of Parliament 1998/99:40 f.)? Some agencies expressed fears about what might happen to the authority of agencies and RAs in ordinary planning and regulation, if or when municipal governments found that the MENUET was playing *political* games by 'facilitating or accommodating' municipal measures deemed inappropriate by professional expert standards (Auditors of Parliament 1998/99:42).

Expert knowledge was thus given secondary importance in the LIP process. By defining sustainable development as a cross-sectoral issue, the Cabinet downplayed the role of expert knowledge and obfuscated the status of the agencies representing such knowledge. The vagueness of the Ordinance's criteria for judgement on what measures in the LIPs were sustainability-oriented enough to be eligible for grants added to the uncertainty about the role of expert knowledge. As one evaluation puts it, the Unit 'did not satisfactorily assess the quality of the information provided in the municipal applications' (National Audit Office 1999b:41 f.).

*Tunnelled vision; the role of science and expertise in large-scale infrastructure investments*
During the ending decades of the twentieth century, the paradigm of centralised large-scale social engineering came under fire in Sweden. In particular, large-scale infra-structural projects such as nuclear power plants, highways and other facilities to be located

in local environments drew fire from ordinary citizens. Increasingly, such development projects were seen as threats to the local environment, local identity, and the continuity of preferred ways of life. A case in point is the renewal of the railroad on the Swedish west coast. Originally a vision promoted by the business elite in the European Round Table, the new double-track railway would provide a high-speed link, all the way from Oslo over Gothenburg and Malmö, and then via the new Öresund Bridge to Denmark connecting this region with the European continent. As much as SEK 8 billion would be invested. The Swedish Parliament allocated money for the project in 1991, and construction work began soon thereafter under the auspices of the National Rail Administration (NRA).

In ecological terms, the most crucial part concerned construction of two parallel 8.6 km railway tunnels through the Hallandsås, a rock-sand-clay ridge running between the Halland and Skåne regions. With several features judged of utmost national environmental concern, the area was subjected to severe constraints – protected areas, prohibited resource-related activities – under Swedish natural resource and environmental legislation. This was to be weighted against the economic gain from the tunnel; it would cut 10 to 15 minutes off the travel time between Gothenburg and Malmö, and would cost only about SEK one billion to complete. Most environmental concerns were, however, given less consideration, although the Water Court set some strict conditions concerning the allowable impact on groundwater resources in the ridge (SOU 1998:60, passim).

It soon turned out, however, that these conditions could not be met. The water leakage in the tunnel widely exceeded all limits, and groundwater levels on the ridge plummeted far below the levels allowed. Evidently, the geological characteristics of the ridge had not been given enough attention. In fact, the NRA flatly neglected already available geo-technical knowledge offered by geological expertise in an energy company that had built a fresh-water provision tunnel through the ridge a decade earlier (Falkemark 1998:16). Looking for methods of stemming this self-inflicted tide, the NRA first wanted the contractors to widen the tunnel to allow for lining. This would, however, lead to forbidding cost increases. Another solution was now sought in the form of some chemical sealant that could be injected into the tunnel to prevent leakage. The alternative chosen was Rhoca-Gil. After some initial investigations and trial injections of this sealant in early 1997, the NRA ordered 360 tons in late June. Injections with Rhoca-Gil were then made until early October 1997, totalling 1,400 tons for 550 metres. By then, several dramatic instances had occurred. Construction workers became severely ill, with symptoms of disturbances in their nervous system. Cattle had to be slaughtered when they became paralysed after drinking from water in the creeks into which excess tunnel water was being pumped.

At this stage, the local government – backed by the National Chemicals Inspectorate and the regional Labour Inspectorate – stopped the tunnel work. The toxic effects of Rhoca-Gil – caused by the ingredient acrylamide – were such that all activities must be abandoned. The most interesting thing here is that there existed both knowledge and information about this aspect of the Rhoca-Gil sealant when it was first tried out in the tunnel. Japanese experience indicated toxic effects on those handling the product, and the toxicity was clearly pointed out in the first trials and analyses by the contractor and then conveyed to the NRA. However, this was then tuned down and later evidently more or less neglected in the further handling (Falkemark 1998:36 ff.). By early summer 2003 the construction of the tunnel was still suspended.

It is evident from the many evaluations made of the tunnel case that the role of expert knowledge was consistently downplayed. This was true for the legal environmental constraints on large-scale construction in the ridge area. It was furthermore true for the assessment of the geological characteristics of the ridge. And finally, knowledge seems to have been consciously neglected or downplayed when it came to the possible negative effects on environment and health of the chemical sealant chosen to tighten the tunnel. The explanation offered by the evaluators is simple, and has far-reaching implications for the possibilities of establishing a relation between knowledge and decision-making that is rational in ecological terms. The vision among those responsible for the construction was tunnelled; the economic gains from the high-speed track and the tunnel obviously justified all the environmental and health costs incurred during the construction phase (Falkemark 1998:46 f.; see also Hydén and Baier 1998:36 f.).

**Knowledge matters, but politics (and money) counts**

*Knowledge and sustainability – the volatile role of science in ecological governance*
The degree of uncertainty surrounding *what* is sustainable and *how* to get onto a path towards sustainable development makes scientifically validated knowledge a necessary part of rational ecological governance. At the same time, the demand for effective decision-making makes for an unclear or uneasy role of scientific knowledge within ecological governance. The quest for reducing uncertainty implies that research results validated by the scientific community should provide the basis for decisions. But since scientific debate often concerns problems of validation, this puts scientific knowledge in somewhat of a veto position *vis-á-vis* political decision-makers in need of clear cut and reliable recommendations for action. On the other hand, the political demand for effective decision-making may push scientists to come forward with results and recommendations not yet fully meeting the criteria for scientific validation. Policy-makers eager to take action may neglect or downplay scholarly differences of opinion, or lend their ears to certain 'schools' of science, who may then come to dominate in 'speaking truth to power'. In the end, policy-makers then receive advice that is less instrumental for the effective implementation of rational ecological governance.

At least two of the three criteria formulated at the outset of this chapter address this precarious balance between validated scientific knowledge and effective decision-making in ecological governance for sustainability. We consider governance ecologically rational to the extent that the structures for developing, assessing and disseminating science-based knowledge allow for the build-up and exchange of complementary and competing views and arguments, and different bodies of knowledge. Furthermore, governance is ecologically rational when competing knowledge is made accessible to public debate and scrutiny in the policy process.

To what extent does the Swedish science-policy relationship in the realm of sustainable development live up to these criteria? The relationship prevailing in Swedish environmental politics up to the 1990s could be labeled monopsonistic. The Environment Protection Agency was in essence the only funding body, and thus 'buyer', of research related to environmental policy-making. A large part of the SEPA research budget went to areas or themes elaborated and decided upon within the agency itself. Consequently, the major part of environmental research was directed towards helping policy implementation in fields defined by the agency as most in need of improved knowledge.

While such an order of things could be seen as positive in relation to policy- and decision-making within the agency's area of responsibility, it is problematic in three interrelated aspects. First, the concentration of funding to research on narrowly specified environmental problems meant that broader interactive problems went mostly unattended. Given their dependency on one source of grants, the members of the comparatively small environmental research community in Sweden became highly specialised on specific issues. This in turn meant that science-based recommendations for how to tackle the broader issues of sustainable development were difficult to obtain from the research community. The efforts made in the 1990s to bring about broad-based 'Research Programmes for A Better Environment' show that this problem was increasingly realised by SEPA and other research-funding bodies (see, e.g., SEPA 1996).

By then, however, the situation for environment-related research had become even more volatile. A new and formidable player was moving to centre stage. With its large funds and its mandate to sponsor solution-oriented research and development, MISTRA has the power to bring about cross-disciplinary programmes that address issues crucial to the broader perspectives of governance for sustainable development. Undoubtedly, this has led to a widening of research perspectives and to a more inter-disciplinary profile of Swedish environment-related research. Furthermore, the exchange of differing views on problems, solutions and research priorities is provided with a new arena. On the other hand, while the links between research and governmental policy were quite obvious when SEPA dominated the funding landscape, they now became more obscure. When MISTRA – a private law foundation – makes its research priorities, how do they relate to govern*mental* strategies for sustainable development?

Given that the SEPA was bereft of its research funds while MISTRA flourished, it seemed for a while as if Swedish environment-related research was thrown from one monopsonist situation to another. However, the emergence of the new scientist-dominated FORMAS research council, and the revival of SEPA as a research-funding body clearly point towards a more pluralistic situation. More funds are now available for research on issues crucial to ecologically rational governance than ever before. As shown earlier, these three bodies represent a broad spectrum in terms of science/policy dominance. There are now funds available from bodies with different mandates and objectives. The development of large cross-disciplinary programmes means there will be more competing and complementary knowledge, and thus more open scientific exchange on alternatives for ecological governance. One should also take into account the increasing Swedish participation in European research programmes. Circumstances thus seem favourable for both competitive knowledge formation and broader scientific exchange.

*When the votes are all in; science, democracy and ecological politics*

But a most crucial issue remains. Are scientific knowledge and expert advice actually used, and expert advice actually heeded to the extent implied by our criteria for rationally ecological governance? We earlier defined governance as ecologically rational when knowledge and expertise is brought to bear on, and to interact with, political judgement to arrive at democratically legitimate decisions on how to use and manage natural resources to achieve sustainable development. In these carefully balanced words lies a consideration for political autonomy. The collective of citizens in the democratic system should have the last word – through their representatives – on how to proceed towards the 'sustainable society', not the scientists or experts. At the same time, democratic representatives have a political responsibility to seek out and make use of the best possible knowledge for decisions on sustainable development.

The way science and expertise have fared in recent, and for the project of 'Sustainable Sweden' quite crucial, decision-making processes, makes the prospects for meeting this criterion seem rather mixed. When Social-Democrats wanted to make a show of their commitment to sustainable development, they seemed to look more to gaining politically from the first round of LIP programmes than to reducing uncertainty about the actual effectiveness and effects of the measures of implementation. The implementation of the first rounds of the LIP programme strongly supports this conclusion. On the very uncertainty-ridden problem of climate change, Swedish policy-makers and international negotiators from the outset worked quite closely with leading Swedish scientists and experts. Although this relationship may have weakened somewhat after 1998, as evidenced by the treatment of science in the Climate Commission's report on Sweden's future climate strategy, efforts are now (spring 2003) underway to strengthen Swedish climate research (see www.mistra-research.se). Finally, the spectacular tunnel case implies that even in areas strongly protected by environmental and resource legislation, exploitation for large-scale high-technology projects may proceed without due weight being given to knowledge about effects on sustainability.

One might argue that this picture is all too pessimistic. After all, Sweden has a well-established system of governmental commissions to investigate new policies and large-scale socio-economic and technological programmes. These commissions most often gather scientific and expert opinions on what to do and how to do it, and take scientific opinion into account when making recommendations in the SOU reports. Furthermore, one could point to the policy of sectoral responsibility (see below, pp. 128–32), which mandates central authorities to investigate and assess all their actions and programmes in relation to their effects on the achievement of the 15 NEOs (see above, pp. 65–7). Since these national environmental objectives are operationalised into interim targets and sectoral objectives, citizens and their representatives have a fair chance to judge scientific assessments and disputes over programme effects and goal achievement. Even where knowledge would really matter, money and prestige count.

This leads us to the so far less shown card in the science-policy game. The intensified programme of environmental and resource monitoring, and the envisaged system of 'green indicators' (see below, pp. 132–4) may well turn out a trump, both in terms of sustainability and autonomy. As for sustainability, the monitoring programme provides for a continuous and systematic build-up of ecological knowledge to be used in collective decision-making on environment and resource management. Knowledge gained from this programme will be published in annual governmental reports and used as the basis for quadrennial general debates in Parliament on the state of the environment. It will provide for continuous democratic discussion and debate, thus holding the promise of becoming a catalyst for future, more firmly knowledge-based and democratic ecological governance.

# 5
# Governing in common – integration and effectiveness in ecological governance

## Specialisation or integration. Organising principles of ecological governance for sustainability

*From environment to sustainable development; the quest for effectiveness and integration*
The first decades of environmental policy in Sweden were characterised by an amalgamation of different governmental units dealing with aspects of the environmental issue into a recognisable *sectoral* policy domain. This was how SEPA came to be a specialised agency, whose mission was to prevent or mitigate the effects on the environment of different socio-economic activities. Top priorities were to clean up and prevent pollution, and help in creating a system of constraints against undue exploitation of valuable natural environments. The guiding normative principle was one of 'balancing interests'; the environment was seen as one societal interest that should be weighted against others, and could sometimes lose out in the process (see Lundqvist 1971). Within this normative and administrative context, the strategy was for some time remarkably successful (Lundqvist 1995).

However, with growing evidence of the cross-sectoral and cross-temporal character of ecological and socio-economic relationships, as manifested in the 'diffuse source' problems of pollution, the need for more integrated modes of governance was increasingly realised in the 1980s. An important contribution no doubt came from the development of new ideas and thoughts at the international level. The Brundtland Commission's report explicitly stated that the 'standard agenda' of environmental

policy focusing on environmental effects would no longer do;
concentration must from now on be on the policies that cause
these effects. In the words of the Commission,

> Sustainable development objectives should be incorporated in the
> terms of reference of those cabinet and legislative committees
> dealing with national economic policy and planning as well as
> those dealing with key sectoral and international policies. As an
> extension of this, the major central economic and sectoral agencies
> of governments should now be made directly responsible and fully
> accountable for ensuring that their policies, programmes, and
> budgets support development that is ecologically as well as
> economically sustainable. (WCED 1987:314)

The Commission's words point towards two different but
interrelated problems of ecological governance. One problem
concerns *effectiveness* and *efficiency*. Ecologically rational governance for sustainable development is then seen as a conscious use
of strategies to achieve ambitious ecological objectives through
policy integration, striving for 'a lasting, systematic and innovative opening of the non-environmental policies towards ecological
policies in the comprehensive sense' (Knoepfel 1995:198). The
problem here is *how* to instil ecological concerns into the workings of traditionally non-environmental sectoral policies and
agencies to achieve not only effective goal achievement, but also
to do so in the most cost-effective way.

The other problem is related to the *strength* of ecological
concerns in such policy integration. Where the effectiveness/effi-
ciency problem concerns *how* to integrate and how to make that
integration work in a cost-effective way, the problem of strength
relates to *how much* weight environmental or ecological
concerns should carry in the decision-making process within and
across different policy fields. On the one hand, if objectives of
sustainability are put above other concerns in the hierarchy of
objectives of political governance, then liberal democratic
concerns for individual autonomy and equality of opportunity
may be jeopardised. On the other hand, if objectives of ecological sustainability continue to be dealt with in the way
environmental concerns were historically 'balanced' in Sweden's
environmental policy, the prospects for sustainable development
are dimmed.

*Ecologically sustainable development as an integrative criterion for rational governance*

What was just said about effectiveness/efficiency and strength indicates that policy integration has organisational as well as normative aspects. The organisational aspect of environmental policy integration could be taken to mean how environmental concerns are 'integrated into' different sectoral policies. In this respect integration includes, among other things,

- access for ecological governance to policy instruments used in sectoral policies;
- build-up and/or strengthening of institutional structures to bring attention to issues of sustainability and provide arenas for solution of conflicts;
- conscious strategies and means of monitoring ecological performance in terms of resources used and results achieved in relation to the sector's overarching objectives (see Knoepfel 1995).

Integration then becomes, in effect, similar to problems of coherence, co-ordination, conflict resolution, and effective performance found within most policy areas. But when is a policy fully integrated? It has been suggested that for this to be the case, three criteria should be satisfied, i.e., comprehensiveness, consistency and aggregation. The first refers to the inclusiveness in terms of space, time, actors and issues. Aggregation means that policies and policy measures are evaluated from some overarching criterion or principle, and consistency connotes that the components of the policy are in agreement. An integrated policy is thus one where 'all significant consequences of policy decisions are recognised as decision premises, where policy options are evaluated on the basis of their effects on some aggregate measure of utility, and where the different policy elements are in accord with each other' (Underdal, 1980:162).

The most important aspect of Underdal's definition is that of aggregation. It directs attention to the issue of what relative weights should be given to different objectives or standards existing alongside each other in policy-making both intra- and inter-sectorally. Noting that earlier discussions on environmental policy integration – (such as Collier 1994; Liberatore 1997) – assume a 'balance' or a possible resolution of goal conflicts among sectoral objectives, Lafferty argues that the core aim of such integration is, at the very least, to avoid situations where environmental objectives become subsidiary. It also means – in the broader purview of sustainable development – to ensure that they become principal or overarching societal objectives. This is, he contends, 'arguably *the* essential difference between *environmental* policy integration and policy integration in general' (Lafferty 2001:10). In his view, environmental policy integration implies:

- the incorporation of environmental objectives into all stages of policymaking in non-environmental policy sectors,
- a specific recognition of this goal as a guiding principle for the planning and execution of policy;
- an attempt to aggregate presumed environmental consequences into an overall evaluation of policy, and
- a commitment to minimise contradictions between environmental and sectoral policies by giving priority to the former over the latter (Lafferty 2001:10).

Lafferty's definition addresses the normative issue of prioritisation of environmental concerns. It pictures environmental objectives as fundamental premises throughout all policy processes. Furthermore, it breaks with the earlier assumptions of 'balancing' and 'conflict solvability' by explicitly making environmental concerns central in all policymaking. This is, argues Lafferty, motivated by the increasing recognition that there are environmental/ecological objectives 'which simply cannot be "balanced" with political goals that challenge the basis' for life-support systems (Lafferty 2001:11).

However, if such infusion of, and prerogative for, environmental concerns in all policy were taken to imply that environmental objectives should always come before other objectives of societal governance, then democratic norms and the value of autonomy would seem to be endangered. In particular, the effectiveness/efficiency argument for integration may find such norms and values burdensome. How the balance between democracy and autonomy on the one hand and an ecologically rational pursuit of sustainability on the other should be achieved is thus a most crucial issue for ecological governance.

*Common criteria for operational and effective integration*
The perspective of ecologically rational governance used here is
particularly concerned with the institutions, processes and policies of *government*. Historically, governments have developed
patterns of differentiated sectoral responsibility. To elaborate the
concept of environmental policy integration into operational
criteria for integrated ecological governance, one should thus
relate it to the structures and processes of government.

*Effective* integration means that environmental concerns are in
fact taken into account at all stages and levels of policy- and decision-making with as little sacrifice as possible in terms of time,
money and human input. To achieve this ecological efficiency in
a sector of government makes it necessary for the responsible
bodies to identify the sector's environmental problems as well as
the key actors and how to relate to them. Furthermore, there
should be a strategy for achieving sectoral environmental objectives with target levels and dates, as well as plans for sectoral
environmental action, linked to the sector's budgeted resources.
To enable judgements about impacts there should be arrangements and procedures through which the actual achievement of
environmental/ecological objectives can be monitored and meas-
ured. One should note, however, that this type of integration
could still be analysed as *intra*-sectoral. 'Effective environmental
policy can be realised only if infrastructure policies become "ecologised"' (Knoepfel 1995:214).

However, the extent to which sectoral agencies have been
internally ecologised 'does not presuppose an overarching
primacy for environmental goals at the cabinet level' (see Lafferty
2001:12). What one may call *inter*-sectoral integration comes
about only if and when the ecological concerns are given a
specific *weight* in relation to other sectoral objectives, all the way
from equal to 'more equal than others'. The analysis thus
concerns what is the 'basic mandate for environmental privilege',
and what are the measures for driving this home within and –
above all – across the different sectors. Central government – read
the Cabinet – has many regulatory, economic and informative
instruments to steer the sectoral agencies towards a preferred
balance among economic, social and ecological aspects of sustainable development. These include such features as special
constitutional provisions on environmental rights, Cabinet long-

term sustainable development strategies, the designation of a
specific body with cross-sectoral co-ordinating responsibilities,
monitoring feedback reporting arrangements, as well as specific
mechanisms for solving conflicts between ecological and sectoral
objectives (see Lafferty 2001:14).

To provide a baseline for analysing the effectiveness and integration aspects of rational ecological governance, we can now
formulate the following criteria:

- Ecological governance is effective in so far as 'ecological'
  values and norms, ecological capacities, and codes of ecologically good conduct are actually integrated into the political and
  administrative decision-making process of sectoral agencies
  and authorities.
- Ecological governance is integrated in so far as 'ecological
  concerns' are given specific weight or preference through political decisions at the highest level of authority, and when this is
  communicated and implemented into the political and administrative decision-making process of sectoral agencies and
  authorities.

## Providing the base for sectoral integration

*Early signs of policy co-ordination and sectoral environmental
responsibility*
A peculiar feature of the Swedish system of government is the
division between 'political' ministries and 'administrative' agencies at the central level. The Cabinet and the Ministries in Sweden
deal almost exclusively with policy *formulation*. The Cabinet, and
thus the Ministry of Environment, has access to the constitutionally 'independent' national agencies and boards and their
expertise when formulating new policies or revising old ones. The
Cabinet as a collective, not the individual minister, issues implementation directives to these central agencies, but Ministers
cannot decide on policy *implementation*, i.e., decisions on individual cases. This is, constitutionally, a matter for about 70
central national agencies, the nowadays 21 Regional
Administrations, and the 289 local governments, the latter also
enjoying a wide sphere of authority on local matters, such as
taxation and physical planning.

For more than two decades after the introduction of 'modern' environmental policy in the 1960s, environmental issues were the preserve of the Ministry of Agriculture. As the major governmental agency for environmental affairs, the SEPA was given the mandate to protect the environmental 'sector interest' against that of other sectors. The major 1987/88 Environmental Bill spoke of a new strategy: 'A successful environmental management presupposes that care for the environment is integrated into the development plans for different sectors of society ... [who have] ... a responsibility to prevent new environmental damage' (Cabinet Bill 1987/88:85, p. 35 f.). The Ministry for Energy and Environment established in 1987 was to have 'an offensive and co-ordinating role within the Cabinet'; it should instil environmental aspects into other policy sectors, and thus also into other Cabinet Ministries (Cabinet Bill 1987/88:85, p. 28). Energy issues were brought back into the Ministry for Industry in 1990, when the Ministry of Environment took over issues of national physical planning from the Ministry of Housing and Physical Planning. The new Ministry of Environmental Affairs was strengthened to fill the role as co-ordinator of environment-related issues at the Cabinet level (Loftsson et al. 1993:71).

The 1990/91 Environmental Bill acted further on the integration theme. The Cabinet stated that the 'mission of the 1990s is to readjust all societal activities in an ecological direction'. To this end, the Cabinet now proposed that the future environmental policy should include 'increased sectoral responsibilities and decentralisation to secure broad support for environmental management, including individual, business, and municipal action as well as participation by public agencies and units in all sectors of society. A stronger emphasis must be put on evaluating the results of policy measures and instruments' (Cabinet Bill 1990/91:90, pp. 11, 13). The bill strengthened the environmental responsibilities of the national agencies for road, air and railway traffic, agriculture, fisheries, and forestry. Their charters would from then on require them to 'elaborate sectoral plans and programmes with precise environmental objectives to bring about the implementation of nationally determined goals in the most cost efficient way'. The central environmental agencies – SEPA and the Chemicals Inspectorate (*Kemikalieinspektionen*) – should provide information and knowledge to the sectoral agencies, and actively co-operate with them to formulate, follow up and evaluate sectoral action plans (Cabinet Bill 1990/91:90, p. 66).

The sectoral perspective thus began to recede around 1990. It now gave way to a view that environmental concerns should be integrated into other policy areas as a 'sectoral responsibility', explicitly including not just government – all sectoral agencies and all levels – but also private economic and social actors. However, such integration was still more of an aspiration than an actual, effective change. There was no clear-cut weighting of this environmental responsibility relative to other sectoral objectives. This is revealed in the 1991–94 Right-Centre Coalition Government's discussion on long-term sustainable development: 'Concern for the environment must influence decision-making at all levels and in all sectors of society. This means giving prior consideration to the environmental impact of every decision that might have a major impact on the environment.' (Cabinet Bill 1992/93:100, Part 15, p. 2). But what would such 'prior consideration' actually entail in relation to other policy objectives and impacts?

### 'Common cause'? Integrating policy objectives for sustainable development

It is evident that the issue of integration was brought to the fore even more intensely as a result of the commitments made by Sweden at the UNCED conference in 1992. Sustainable development in the sense discussed in the Brundtland report, and laid down in Rio, now emerged as the point of departure for bills across the political agenda. A first answer to the question of relative weight came with the 1993 decision on forestry policy; the objective of environmental quality should have *equal weight* to the earlier one of durable, effective and gainful production (Cabinet Bill 1992/93:226, p. 26).

However, the role of environmental and sustainability concerns varied a lot in the wave of cabinet bills that followed particularly in the parliamentary year 1997/98. Bills on transportation and consumer policy gave the clearest indication. Transportation policy objectives should be *subordinate* to other comprehensive societal goals. With respect to the environment, the Swedish transport system should be developed to 'promote good environmental and resource management' (Cabinet Bill

1997/98:56, p. 16 f.). Long-term sustainable development should also have a clearer role in consumer policy. The Cabinet deemed it necessary to take action to give this objective the *'same weight as other objectives'* in this field (Cabinet Communication 1997/98:67, p. 2 f.; italics mine).

Other policy statements were not as distinctive. In an earlier bill to change planning regulations, the Cabinet stated that planning is 'part of a coherent policy for sustainable development', and local physical planning should be 'successively developed towards *increased attention* to environmental concerns' (Cabinet Bill 1994/95:230, pp. 30, 45 ff.; italics mine). The culture policy bill stated that nature and culture are intimately linked. Therefore, the 'culture sector' must spread information about the cultural-natural heritage and 'actively participate in the public debate to *promote* sustainable development' (Cabinet Bill 1996/97:3, pp. 126 ff.; italics mine). The 1997 sustainable energy bill was hammered out after tough negotiations to secure a parliamentary majority. The bill stated that one objective of future energy policy would be to *'ease the transformation* to an ecologically sustainable society', through increased energy efficiency and reliance on renewable energy sources (Cabinet Bill 1996/97:84, p. 7 f.; italics mine).

The bill on fisheries and agricultural policy contended that measures must be taken in 'all policy areas' to bring Sweden towards ecologically sustainable development. The formal 'sectoral responsibility' for central agencies means that they 'must actively work to *decrease the environmental burdens*' of their sectors and develop action plans for that purpose (Cabinet Bill 1997/98:2, pp. 5 ff.; italics mine). Both the 1992 UNCED and the 1996 Habitat conferences were seen as bringing new dimensions to housing policy. In addition to the historic 'social housing policy' objective, this policy should now *'create conditions'* for sustainable development, including its ecological dimension. The LIP programme would be a major measure in this respect (Cabinet Bill 1997/98:119, pp. 38 ff.; italics mine. See above, p. 78).

A stream of governmental policy proposals in the latter part of the 1990s thus infused ecological values and norms into sectors of crucial importance to the fate of the environment. This incorporation of sustainable development as a policy objective in key sectors of society was, however, at the level of intentions. It was furthermore done with differing clarity and determination. The integration of 'sustainable development' in the hierarchy of sectoral policy objectives would thus have to be backed by common rules, procedures and denominators to create a truly integrated and effective ecological governance.

*'Common rules'; a new, comprehensive environmental code*
In the 1980s, it became increasingly evident that existing Swedish legislation concerned with environmental quality and the management of natural resources was insufficient to come to grips with the new generation of diffuse pollution problems. The challenges posed by the quest for sustainable development, and the joining of the EU further accentuated the need for an integrated body of law to regulate the society-nature relationship. The 1989 Environmental Protection Commission's report of 1993 proposed an amalgamation of more than a dozen environment-related laws into one single Environmental Code, intended to 'protect human beings, nature and the environment generally', where the latter included 'land, water, air, biological life and also human settlement'. The Commission recommended a shift from control of individual pollution sources to legally binding 'environmental quality standards', to be issued by the 'Government or an authority empowered by the Government' (SOU 1993:27, Part I, pp. 49, 52, 58). The Right-Centre coalition hurried its Code bill to parliament in August 1994 but lost the September election. The incoming Social Democrats recalled the Bourgeois bill and issued new directives to the now renamed Environmental Code Commission, who presented its final report in summer 1996. Just before Christmas 1997, the Social-Democratic Government finally sent its proposal for a new Environmental Code to Parliament, who passed the bill the following year.

The objective of the 1998 Environmental Code is to 'promote a sustainable development to ensure that present and future generations have a good and healthy environment.' (SFS 1998:808, §1). The Code amalgamated no less than 15 different environment and natural resource-related Acts, and a special bill was passed to adjust all pertinent legislation to the Code (Cabinet Bill 1997/98:90). The Code contains 'general protection rules' with legally binding principles such as *Polluters' Pay, Best*

*Possible Technology, Least Harmful Product Substitution,* and *Least Harmful Location.* There is also a *Mandatory Duty to Collect Relevant Information and Knowledge* before taking any action potentially dangerous to human health, natural resources and the environment (SFS 1998:808, Ch. 2). Legally binding *Environmental Quality Standards* are introduced, together with a further widening of the area of mandatory *Environmental Impact Assessments.* All this reflects the Government's emphasis on integration and internalisation of the sustainability objective into all walks of life (Cabinet Bill 1997/98:45, p. 201 ff.; SFS 1998:808, Chapters 5 and 6).

Seeing the Environmental Code as a means of 'inspiring those actors to think and act in such a way that they anticipate the mandatory rules of the Code' (Cabinet Bill 1997/98:45, p. 161), the Government presented motivations that hint at a particular view of integrated and effective ecological governance. The legal framework of the Code would build a platform for 'decentralised and preventive environmental measures' from which 'different actors – business, central and local administrations, associations, households and others – can formulate their environmental strategies'. The Government thus saw the Code as a central means to 'promote the development towards a sustainable society' (Cabinet Bill 1997/98:45, p. 170).

Even if the new legislation turns out to be successful in inspiring such anticipatory and environmentally favourable behaviour, there might still be conflicts of interest over the use and management of natural resources, and over the necessity to protect the environment. A crucial test of the Code's integrative strength is thus whether it contains rules giving specific weight to environmental concerns in crucial decisions. The Cabinet stated that the Code is '*not* superior to other laws', and should be 'applied *in parallel* to other laws regulating such activities, measures, facilities and products covered by the Code but directed at other issues.' Insofar as there would be a conflict between the Code and other statutes and 'there is no prescription as to which rule should have precedence, such conflict should be resolved by applying general legal principles' (Cabinet Bill 1997/98:45, pp. 190 ff.; italics mine).

It is true that the Environmental Code incorporates some of the balancing sectoral perspective of the 1969 Environment Protection Act (SFS 1998:808, Ch. 2, §7). There are, however, some priority rules. A balancing of economic and ecological aspects must never violate an environmental quality standard (see Gipperth 1999:176 f.). There is a stop rule; an activity can be stopped or legally prohibited if it is judged as a threat to human health or environmental quality. Only the Cabinet may issue an exemption from this rule (SFS 1998:808, Chapter 2, §§ 9–10). In the case of conflicts over the use of natural resources or areas deemed of 'national interest', priority should be given to such use(s) that are most compatible with the promotion of long-term sustainable management (SFS 1998:808, Chapter 3, § 10).

## Making sectoral integration work

### *'Common responsibility' for sustainable development; the greening of agencies' programme*

Presenting his Social-Democratic Cabinet Policy Platform in March 1996, the new Prime Minister Göran Persson proclaimed the achievement of the 'ecologically sustainable society' as a new and 'noble' mission for Sweden's government. 'Environment must be an explicit and long-term priority', and Sweden should be 'an international driving force and a forerunner in the endeavours to create an ecologically sustainable development' (Parliamentary Record, March 22, 1996). That there was a determination to give ecological concerns greater emphasis was revealed in many ways in the months that followed. One sign was the swift change in content of the annual Cabinet Communication to the Parliament on the State of the Swedish Environment. Unlike earlier reports, the one from January 1997 (and those issued ever since) did not address individual environmental problems. Instead, it took as its point of departure the argument that the political objective of an ecologically sustainable society includes adjustments to both eco-system capacities and socio-economic growth and welfare, and requires integration of 'environmental care and resource management ... into all processes in society'. The report contended that 'different societal sectors must assume an increased responsibility' in this respect (Cabinet Communication 1996/97:50, p. 4).

This shift in *problem views* was accompanied by changes in *organisation*. Internalisation and anticipation would be promoted not only through common causes in general policy statements and common rules of the Environmental Code. Sectoral agencies would have explicit responsibilities to address ecological concerns. The formation in January 1997 of the *Delegation for Ecologically Sustainable Development* (DESD) within the Cabinet was a core element in the Social-Democratic strategy. Consisting of the Ministers of Environment, Agriculture, Taxation, Basic Education, and the Junior Minister of Labour, this group's first, and explicitly short-term, assignment was to 'develop a platform for the Cabinet's comprehensive policy for an ecologically sustainable society.' (Cf. Cabinet Bill 1997/98:150, Part 5).

Only two months later, in March 1997, the five Ministers presented their proposal for *'A Sustainable Sweden'*. Defining sustainable development in terms of protection of the environment, efficient resource use, and secured long-term eco-system capacity, the Ministerial Delegation emphasised the inter-relatedness of economic, social and ecological aspects of sustainability. To 'create the conditions' for ecologically sustainable development, there must be political measures to encourage new behavioural patterns, and to select the most resource efficient policy alternatives. The system of governance needed would go far beyond that of environmental policy, involving all levels of government from the international to the local, as well as target groups and individual citizens.

The Delegation proposed a host of mechanisms for sectoral integration and internalisation of the sustainability objective. One concerned *environmental objectives* for all relevant sectors in society (see above, pp. 64–7 on the NEOs). Another would consist of a *Greening of National Agencies Programme*. This involved a common responsibility to organise for and carry out ecological sustainability assessments of all major agency actions, as well as a 'greening' of public purchase tenders. An elaborated system of *Sustainable Development Reports* based on commonly developed indicators should be set up to allow for environmental auditing of sectoral development (Cabinet Bill 1996/97:150, Part 5).

In this programme of greening public agencies, the Cabinet could build on already initiated changes. Its Environment Advisory Board reported in 1996 and 1997 on the sectoral integration of ecological concerns, recommending both a general and a specific environmental and sustainability responsibility for sectoral agencies (SOU 1996:112 and 1997:145). The general sectoral responsibility meant that the Director-Generals of all governmental agencies would now have to 'take into account' the demands on the agency activities following on not just from environmental policy, but from the objective of ecologically sustainable development (SFS 1995:1322, § 7).

A 1998 Cabinet decision prescribed a specific sectoral responsibility for 24 national agencies. These agencies 'shall integrate environmental concerns and resource management in their activities and promote ecological sustainability within their sector' in line with the 'overarching objectives for ecologically sustainable development' (Cabinet Communication 1998/99:5, p. 13). First and foremost, sectoral agencies are required to identify their environmental roles in relation to their 'core' sectoral missions. They must furthermore assess how sectoral activities affect ecological aspects of sustainable development, and develop sectoral objectives and targets under the NEOs (see above, pp. 65–8). Some of them are specifically pointed out as 'responsible for the NEOs'; the SEPA accounts for eight of these objectives. Four central agencies are pointed out as particularly responsible for 'comprehensive' cross-sectoral NEO issues, connected to the environment, physical planning the cultural environment and human health (Cabinet Bill 2000/01:130, p. 226 f.).

All agencies and authorities covered by these aspects of sectoral responsibility for sustainable development are required to describe the socio-economic consequences of the objectives and targets to allow for cost-effective sectoral measures, and co-operate with sectoral actors as well as other agencies to promote sustainable development. Furthermore, they are expected to describe and evaluate progress and problems related to their ecological sector responsibility in their annual reports to the Cabinet (Cabinet Bill 1997/98:145, p. 173 f.). The SEPA and the National Audit Office were given mandates to develop generalised forms for such reports, which would contribute further to the internalisation of the agencies' ecological responsibilities (Cabinet Bill 1996/97:150, Part 5).

There has been a swift spread in the public sector of Environmental Management and Auditing Schemes (EMAS). This involves systematic environment-related work in accordance with 'greening' objectives and guidelines formulated in action plans, precise lines of environmental responsibility, as well as routines for monitoring and performance evaluation. The EMAS was introduced in 24 state agencies in 1997, and has been successively widened. By the end of 2001, nearly all of the totally 234 state agencies, authorities and administrative units ordered by the Government to introduce EMAS, were actually doing so (Cabinet Communications 1998/99:5, p. 12; 1999/2000:13, p. 10; 2000/01:38, p. 14; 2001/02:50, p. 17; see Table 5.1.).

**Table 5.1** *The Adoption and Development of Environmental Management and Auditing Schemes (EMAS) in Swedish National Governmental Agencies and Units 1997–2001*

| Year | 1997 | 1998 | 1999 | 2000 | 2001 |
|---|---|---|---|---|---|
| Swedish national govt. units beginning EMAS work | 24 | 38 | 35 | 38 | 96 |
| Cumulated number | 24 | 62 | 97 | 135 | 231 |

*Source:* www.environ.se, as of 2001–11–19

It is interesting to note the Cabinet's expectations as to what this infusion of common ecological responsibility would entail. 'Sweden's long-term and systematic transformation work will prove that it is possible to find ways of integrating objectives of ecological sustainability into different policy areas and make them co-operate with the development within those areas' (Cabinet Communication 2000/01:38, p. 11). This integration is seen as a means for systematically steering the policies for sustainable development, as well as a means for decentralising ecological governance to the agencies and to relevant target groups and actors. This in turn will allow for anticipation of environmental effects at an early stage, leading to cost-effective preventive action. But for this to materialise there must be mechanisms for decision-making in cases of conflicting objectives of sectoral development and environmental quality. There are now regulatory and administrative mechanisms and incentives for bringing attention to such conflicts early on in the planning and decision-making process (Cabinet Communication 2001/02:50, p. 18). Still, however, the final and authoritative balancing of policy and sectoral objectives should come through the overarching budgetary and regulatory decisions by the Parliament and the Cabinet (Cabinet Bill 2000/01:130, p. 23).

*'Common yardstick': a system of indicators to monitor (and evaluate?) sectoral ecological performance*
It is one thing to 'encourage internalisation of environmental values among economic actors, i.e., make them feel responsible for the environmental impact of their action'. It is another to assess the progress towards environmental and sustainability objectives. This necessitates 'reliable data on the state of the environment' related to production and consumption processes in the different sectors as well as for society as a whole. And it implies the importance of 'making such information part of the standard operating procedures of sectoral agencies and ministries' (Jansen et al. 1998:294 ff.). The major alternatives discussed have been those of *green indicators* and *State of the Environment reports* integrating physical, economic and environmental data. There are at least three alternative types of indicators in use. First, there are *descriptive* indicators in line with the European Environmental Agency's work on indicators according to a *Drivers-Pressures-State-Impacts-Response* (DPSIR) model (see SOU 1999:127, p. 27). *Performance* indicators compare actual conditions 'with a specific set of reference conditions'. *Efficiency* indicators aim at providing insight 'in terms of the efficiency of the resources used, the emissions and waste generated per unit of desired output' (Smeets and Weterings 1999:11 f., 14).

The process of developing the indicators followed two lines. In accordance with a 1997 Directive, the Cabinet's Environmental Advisory Board presented a series of proposals in 1998 and 1999 for a number of aggregated 'green' *key* indicators, eleven of which would be immediately put into use and six others projected for the not too distant future (see SOU 1998:170). This aggregate approach was influenced by the OECD work on indicators based on the Pressure-State-Response model (OECD 1993). The Board proposed aggregate green indicators as descriptive measures of *pressure* (the uses of energy, materials and chemicals), *state* (greenhouse effect, eutrophication, acidification, air quality in urban areas, and biological diversity), and *response* (environmentally adapted travel and transport, consumption, work processes, and changing nutrient cycles). As 'key' indicators they should, argued the Board, reflect ecologically strategic conditions. They should be measurable over long periods, and as far as possible be based on available data. Furthermore, they should provide for easy oversight, be few and easily understood by everyone. The 'key' indicators would thus provide a good base for public debate on sustainable development in Sweden (SOU 1999:127, pp. 7 f., 21 f.).

At the same time, a Swedish system of indicators would also have to be detailed enough to allow for monitoring the progress towards the 15 National Environmental Objectives and the many interim targets and sectoral goals formulated to operationalise these NEOs. The green key indicators should therefore be linked with the system of 210 very detailed indicators for monitoring NEO progress worked out by the SEPA. This disaggregated SEPA system of indicators and measures was developed on the European DPSIR model (see SEPA 1999). The purpose is mainly descriptive, i.e., to follow the development and see whether, and at what pace, the NEOs are approached. If the level of aspiration were increased to include also to what extent actions taken to make progress towards the NEOs are cost-effective, even more detailed information would be necessary. This would be provided by continuously updated knowledge from research, environmental monitoring, special commission reports, official statistics, etc. (SEPA 1999).

The Environmental Objectives Commission reporting in the year 2000 followed the same line of reasoning. The Commission stated that green key indicators provide a good oversight of the progress towards a sustainable society. However, they might give a too simplified picture in view of the many and complex demands for information among different target groups. The Commission thus suggested a total of 159 indicators to follow-up and evaluate progress, and pointed out 25 agencies and units as responsible for one or several indicators at the central governmental level. Out of these 25, the eight agencies with 'main responsibility' for the 15 NEOs should co-ordinate monitoring and 'evaluate the effectiveness of policy measures and actions within their target sectors' (SOU 2000:52, Part 2, pp. 726 f., 732 f.).

However, the NEO system's complex web of structures and processes obviously necessitates some sort of co-ordinating hub to sort out the mass of data and provide guidance, oversight and continuous refinement and evaluation of progress measurement. The NEO Commission thus argued that the since the SEPA is already designated as having an overarching responsibility to co-ordinate the environmental policy field, this responsibility should be extended also to the monitoring and evaluation of progress towards 'Sustainable Sweden'. To this end, the Commission proposed the establishment of an Environmental Objectives Board (EOB) within the SEPA. This Board would be charged with co-ordinating monitoring and evaluation of NEO progress, pointing out and suggesting necessary changes in policy to improve goal attainment, and with identifying needs to improve monitoring and evaluation. Although closely connected to the SEPA, the new Objectives Board should report directly to the Cabinet (SOU 2000:52, Part 2, pp. 723 ff.).

In its NEO Bill to Parliament, the Cabinet argued for a somewhat smaller number of indicators to monitor progress. At the same time, the Cabinet clarified and extended the responsibilities of the Environmental Objectives Board. The Board is charged with effecting a co-ordinated and unified system of monitoring and reporting on the progress from all agencies and authorities under the NEO system. To this end the Board is to suggest NEO indicators as well as 'green key' indicators, and to provide monitoring and reporting guidelines to all responsible agencies and authorities. Most interesting is that the new Objectives Board is charged with the task of '*illuminating possible conflicts* between the NEOs and other policy objectives set by the Parliament' (Cabinet Bill 2000/01:130, p. 229; italics mine). The composition of the Environmental Objectives Board appointed in December 2001 provides a hint of what the Cabinet included in its understanding of 'ecological governance'. Together with officers from the NEO agencies, there are representatives from other sectoral agencies, the Regional Administrations, local government, interest organisations and business (see www.environ.se). No doubt, the EOB's further work will be heavily influenced by the efforts to go beyond green 'key' indicators to provide a system of indicators covering *all* aspects of sustainable development. A first report on such an integrated system of indicators was published in May 2001 as part of Sweden's preparations for the Rio+10 conference in 2002 (SCB 2001).

*A 'common account': producing 'green' records and 'green' budgets for ecological governance*

Clearly the agencies' responsibility to assess the ecological consequences of their own actions and the sector's development in general will push decision-makers to integrate environmental concerns. The same is true for the obligation to keep numerical tabs on ecological key aspects of agency actions and sectoral developments. Not the least will the EOB efforts to provide sectoral agencies with standardised ways of reporting on NEO developments force the agencies to elaborate their 'ecological routines'. The ultimate purpose of this whole exercise of monitoring the NEO process is to provide the basis for a conscious and continuous move towards what is here called ecological governance. However, it is evident from the many reports and bills on this subject that developing this basis is not solely a matter of measuring developments toward sustainability. It is also meant to provide decision-makers, targets groups and the general public with means for meaningful participation in the debate over governance, and thus to promote individual autonomy.

The 'key' indicators are obviously meant to meet the need for easily understood, yet very meaningful information about the state and trends of Sweden's ecology ('ecology' here interpreted in the same way as 'economy' in, e.g., State of the Economy reports). The more elaborate system of NEO indicators provides decision-makers and sectoral interests with the means of assessing their actions. The NEO Commission proposed, and the Parliament confirmed, an elaborate system of reporting on the basis of indicators. Every year, the Cabinet is to provide Parliament with an account of how the NEO work progresses. This annual report is to be based on a selection of indicators, and is expected to give enough information for decisions to change or intensify action in areas where the process does not run on schedule (Cabinet Bill 2000/01:130, p. 230). There is already a tradition of how and when these reports are delivered to Parliament that reveals the degree of importance given to the indicators. Beginning in spring 1999, select green 'key' indicators are presented to Parliament in connection with the 'State of the Economy' reports and the Budget Bills (see Cabinet Communication 2000/01:38, p. 13).

However, even if monitoring and indicators are means to

136        *Sweden and ecological governance*

*describe* the direction, intensity and scope of change towards the goals of ecologically sustainable development in Sweden, this is not enough for meaningful political debate over ecological governance. There must also be some account that allows for *evaluating* whether the measures taken toward ecological sustainability are actually working and if so, whether and to what extent they are cost-effective or could be improved in that respect. This is achieved by integrating the descriptive indicator system based on data from environmental monitoring with economic and physical data to establish so-called *environmental accounts* (see EEA 1999). Following a 1992 Cabinet request, the National Institute for Economic Research (NIER, *Konjunkturinstitutet*) ran a five-year programme to develop *monetary environmental accounts* and environmental economic models to present and assess important connections between economy and environment in Sweden. The ultimate purpose is to systematise environmental and natural resource statistics and to integrate these data with economic statistics. In a parallel process, Statistics Sweden (SCB, *Statistiska centralbyrån*) has developed *physical environmental accounts*, i.e., a system of statistics where pressures on the environment and the use of physical natural resources are linked to economic statistical data on production and consumption (Konjunkturinstitutet 1998:3 f.).

By the end of the 1990s, these integrated *National Environmental Accounts* had been developed so far that they are in effect functioning as a 'satellite' to the National (Economy) Account. New areas are developed and included over time, such as the environmental impact of imported goods and services, environmental pressures from different categories of goods, water and forestry accounts, and the environmental impact of household behaviour (Cabinet Communication 2001/02:50, p. 27). The importance for environmental policy integration is shown by the fact that the 1999/2000 Commission on Sweden's Long-term Development extensively used environmental accounts to adjust the estimations of the prospects for long-term economic and social welfare sustainability in Sweden (SOU 2000:7, Ch. 5; see also Apps. 2 and 7). National environmental accounts also came to use in the proceedings of the Commissions on Climate and on NEOs (see SOU 2000:23, chs.12–13; SOU 2000:52, part 2, Chapters 24–25). The integrated economic and physical environmental accounts will – together with the elaborated system of descriptive indicators – provide the basis for the 'deeper evaluation' of progress towards ecologically sustainable development that the Cabinet is to present to Parliament every fourth year (Cabinet Bill 2000/01:130. p. 230).

## A 'common purse'; green procurement and green tenders throughout the public sector

One of the major points in the spring 1997 report from the Cabinet's Delegation for Sustasinable Development concerned the possibilities of making the public sector a 'forerunner' towards sustainable development by utilising its position as a strong market actor. The size of governmental final consumption ranges between nine and 25 per cent of total GDP expenditures in the OECD countries (14 per cent in Sweden). An average of three-quarters of public purchases are on current consumable goods and services. The greening of public procurement is viewed by the OECD as an 'innovative tool capable of providing cost-effective opportunities' and as having 'a crucial role in supporting innovation' of greener technologies and promoting greener production and consumption patterns (OECD 1999a:35; OECD1999b:4).

It goes without saying that the greening of public procurement and public tenders will also function as a strong mechanism for integrating environmental concerns into public agencies and authorities at all levels. Thus the Cabinet Delegation for Ecologically Sustainable Development recommended that the 1996 guidelines for 'environmentally adapted public procurement' developed by the SEPA and two other agencies should be successively updated by way of integrating experiences from the 'pilot' EMAS agencies as well as from local and regional levels and international developments (DESD 1997). The Social-Democratic Government's Policy Platform of 2000 further emphasised the will to integrate 'environmental demands into all public procurement' (Cabinet Communication 2001/02:50, p. 18).

By then, the Cabinet's Committee for Ecologically Sustainable Procurement (CESP) had been working since early 1998. Its mandate up to the end of 2001 was to promote ecologically sustainable procurement throughout the public sector. A central concern is with *effectiveness/efficiency*; the Delegation should

concentrate on such goods and services 'where the greatest benefits of applying requirements on ecologically sustainable
development can be achieved'. Other parts of the CESP's mandate
indicate that the development of green procurement routines is
expected to promote *integration* of environmental concerns. The
Committee should disseminate knowledge, experiences and best
practice knowledge, initiate training programmes and seminars
for purchasers, and not the least, develop a common, Internet-
based instrument/guide for green procurement for the entire
public sector. Through an extended mandate, the CESP should
furthermore analyse the need for a special produrement policy for
the entire public sector (CESP 2001:5 f.).

In its final September 2001 report, the Committee presented a
new Internet-based instrument intended to 'help public sector
organisations integrate environmental concerns into their
procurement of goods, services and contracts'. This joint mechanism to be used throughout the entire public sector originally
included environmental requirements and information for about
70 different product groups. The requirements range from
mandatory demands over evaluation criteria to information on
producer/seller qualifications (EMAS, ISO 14001 certifications),
and eco-labelling of the goods or services in question. Upon delivering its report, the Committee pointed out that its integrative
tool is quite far-reaching; the EU Commission's interpretative
document issued in summer 2001 on environmental concerns in
public procurement was more narrow. It meant that several of the
Swedish CESP's requirements must be lifted out, reformulated
and – perhaps – reintroduced at a later stage (CESP 2001:17, 45
ff., 62; see SOU 2001:31, pp. 176 ff.).

Furthermore, the Committee found a need for a more developed, common policy for green procurement in the public sector.
Existing policies are usually too general to provide enough guidance. Not only the regulations in the Environmental Code, but
also, and particularly, the demands stemming from the revised EU
rules on eco-labelling and on EMAS necessitate a common policy.
This should contain specifications of how the policy is integrated
within the organisation, what role it is expected to play in
achieving the objectives of green procurement, as well as how
principles of precaution and substitutability are integrated in
the policy. Naturally, procurement policies should also include

the environmental requirements on sellers, goods and services, as well as mechanisms for monitoring and feedback on the greening of agency procurement (CESP 2001:53 f.). The government has yet (end of 2001) to act on the CESP's recommendations.

## Towards an effective and integrated organisation for ecologically sustainable development?

*'An offer they can't resist'? The mix of instruments to bring about effective ecological governance*

It was stated at the outset of this chapter that there are two different but interrelated problems with respect to integrated ecological governance. The *effectiveness/efficiency* problem has to do with how to achieve greater environmental effectiveness through cost-effective policy integration. The question is *how* to organise the structures and processes of governance so that ecological concerns are instilled into the workings of traditionally non-environmental sectoral policies and agencies in the most cost-effective way. This organisational aspect of environmental policy integration could be taken to include several measures. One concerns institutional structures to bring attention to issues of sustainability. Another is the conscious infusion into day-to-day decision-making processes of instruments that promote continuous attention to ecological concerns. Furthermore, there are strategies and means of monitoring ecological performance in terms of resources used and results achieved.

Quite clearly, the Swedish government has embarked on a conscious use of these strategies to promote an effective inclusion of environmental concerns at all stages and levels of governmental decision-making. It is also clear that these concerns have been widened to include the ecological aspects of sustainable development into the social, economic and cultural aspects traditionally pursued in the governance of the Swedish welfare state. Objectives related to ecologically sustainable development are explicitly inserted into all sectoral policies that have large actual and/or potential consequences for such development. All agencies, authorities and administrative units are now charged with a 'sectoral responsibility' for promoting ecologically sustainable development. Most of them experience this as a general duty on the leadership laid down in the General Agency Ordinance.

However, as many as 24 agencies have a *special* sectoral responsibility for the environment, with more far-reaching demands on
their performance.

The sectoral responsibility serves as a trigger to bring the
authorities' attention to environmental and ecological constraints
on, and effects of, their efforts to implement their traditional
sectoral objectives. Their attention to these constraints and effects
is furthermore triggered by the NEOs, since not only the ten agencies with particular NEO responsibilities, but also a host of other
sectoral agencies are expected to play important roles in developing further sectoral and regional sub-goals and interim targets.
Many of the acts regulating the use and management of natural
resources for different sectoral purposes are linked to and co-
ordinated with the Environmental Code. The principles contained
in the Code (see above, pp. 126 f.) thus also relate to public sector
actions potentially affecting environmental quality, as do the
binding principles of good husbandry laid out in the Code.
Agencies are also expected to carry out environmental impact
assessments of their major actions. The sectoral responsibility
also includes monitoring and evaluation of progress towards sub-
goals and interim targets. Furthermore, the policy for green
public procurement forces all agencies to look hard at their
routines and habits in terms of environmental standards, materials flows and resource efficiency. What all this means is that
Swedish public agencies find themselves obliged to integrate environmental concerns throughout the decision-making process.

The massive introduction of EMAS into more than 200 agencies and units is evidently a measure designed to provide for
effective environmental work throughout the public sector at the
national and regional levels. As noted earlier, the Social-
Democratic Government has seen this tool as a way of
decentralising ecological governance to the agencies, expecting
that it will lead to early and effective action: 'EMAS promotes
overview and efficiency in the work for ecologically sustainable
development' (Cabinet Communication 2001/02:50, 18).

The reader may interject that such utterances by government
are nothing but aspirations and expectations. Students of governance know that the implementation literature is replete with
accounts of great political expectations becoming ruins of hope
in the mazes of bureaucracy. Should we believe that all these

integrative measures and schemes will actually become effectively enforced and implemented throughout the public sector in Sweden because of a favourable administrative culture? Or must central government use much stronger mechanisms to make sure that the different units effectively integrate environmental concerns into their outward sectoral as well as inward administrative actions? And, most critically, will these mechanisms actually come to function as expected?

As to the first question, it is reasonable to judge Swedish bureaucracy as effective in carrying out mandates and missions. A glance at the annual reports to government from the NEO agencies reveals that they have taken their NEO responsibility quite seriously. Just as an example, the National Board for Housing and Planning (NBHP, *Boverket*) tripled its use of resources to processes for refining the relationship between planning regulations and guidelines and the NEO at the turn of the century (NBHP 2001:18). The Chemicals Inspectorate states that its activities in the year 2000 was characterised by 'active anticipation' of implementing the 'Non-toxic Environment' NEO once it is passed by Parliament (www.kemi.se). The SEPA set up a special NEO Agency Group to support the co-operation among agencies with specific sectoral NEO responsibilities in 2001 (www.environ.se).

Jumping directly to the third question, it must be kept in mind that both the integration of ecological concerns into decision-making processes, and the continuous monitoring, evaluation and feedback of information with regard to progress, put new and quite strenuous burdens on the agencies. It may therefore take some time before the agencies can meet these demands. A report from the National Audit Office (NAO) examines agency work on the NEO 'No Eutrophication' in the five central agencies concerned with that objective, as well as the Regional Administrations. Its conclusions provide for some guarded pessimism. The feedback information is diverse, not well co-ordinated, and in some areas totally void of systematic statistical data (National Audit Office 2000:90). The information in the agencies' Annual Reports on their own environmental work is 'fragmented' and presented in very general (non-measurable) terms. Activities are not properly related to costs and effects, thus not allowing for assessments of the cost-effectiveness of environmental integration. The report concludes that more precise government demands for feedback information in the annual Letters of Regulation (*regleringsbrev*) issued to governmental agencies just before the beginning of the new fiscal year would have positive repercussions throughout the administrative system. Through conditions laid down in those Letters, more streamlined measurement and reporting on progress closely linked to inputs, and more of co-operation on monitoring could be achieved (National Audit Office 2000:47 ff., 89 f.).

The report just mentioned refers to agency work in 1997, i.e., before the final formulation of the 15 NEOs. This brings us back to the second question. Yes, central government does have measures at its disposal to make sure integration of ecological concerns into policy implementation is an offer that sectoral agencies cannot resist. The budget allocations provide a crucial means in this respect. In the Letters of Regulation just mentioned, Cabinet Ministries can put forth very specific objectives and detailed conditions for how the agencies should allocate their funds. The agencies are forced to account for how they spent their budget allocations, and whether and to what extent they achieved the objectives. This they should do in their demands for budget allocations in the following years as well as in the annual reports. Whether or not in response to the critical assessments of the National Audit Office, this tool is increasingly sharpened to make agencies and units respond to the demands for integration of environmental concerns. Thus the Letters of Regulation issued by the Environment Ministry in December 2001 contain a considerable number of specifications for what the NEO responsible agencies within its domain are expected to perform and deliver as feedback information on the progress and effectiveness of ecological integration (see http://miljo.regeringen.se/index.htm). This provides the Cabinet with possibilities to follow up on environmental integration and to make changes for further effectivisation of the process.

With regard to the *effectiveness/efficiency* dimension of policy integration, we may thus draw a two-pronged conclusion. Sweden's approach to ecological governance contains several means and mechanisms to make integration *effective* in so far as 'ecological' values and norms, ecological capacities, and codes of ecologically good conduct are consciously and continuously brought into the political and administrative decision-making process of sectoral agencies and authorities. At the same time, there are still problems with respect to the (measurement of the) efficiency of actual performance, as well as with respect to co-operation and co-ordination among responsible agencies in reporting on the progress of integration.

### *Gaining weight? The role of ecology in integrated governance for sustainable development*

The most crucial question remains; are ecological concerns now *fully integrated* in Swedish policy-making, within as well as across sectors? In terms of the criteria for policy integration in general proposed by Underdal – (see above, p. 119) – there is *inclusiveness* in terms of space, time, actors and issues. All agencies in sectors with recognisable impacts on the environment, and indeed all other units of national government, have a statutory sectoral responsibility to take ecological concerns into account, and to evaluate their actions and performance in environmental terms. The NEO process means that this responsibility will have a long-term endurance and engage governmental units in 'ecological dialogue' with all relevant actors (see, e.g., SOU 2001:20, passim). This also means that the Swedish efforts towards environmental integration also fulfil one of Lafferty's criteria – (see above, p. 120) – for such integration. Environmental objectives are incorporated into all stages of policymaking in non-environmental policy sectors.

That leaves the criteria of *aggregation* and *consistency*. It was noted above that aggregation means that policies and policy measures are evaluated from some overarching criterion or principle, and that consistency connotes that the components of the policy are in agreement. As I have tried to show in earlier chapters, the Swedish government has increasingly emphasised that its pursuit of sustainable development also includes the ecological dimension. The 1996 policy platform of the Social-Democratic Cabinet assumed that goal conflicts among sectoral objectives could be resolved through strategies of ecological modernisation. By making 'green' an overarching criterion for economic and technological development, economic growth and socially and ecologically sustainable development could be brought into consistency with each other.

Much has been said about the shortcomings of ecological

modernisation as a strategy for policy integration to achieve sustainable development (see, e.g., the overview in Carter 2001:211 ff.). As shown above, the Swedish Government's pursuit of this strategy seems to have been more of a short-term, stopgap measure to grab the political initiative on environmental issues. Some features of the LIP program implied that environmental objectives were indeed subsidiary – in overall political terms – to those in economic and labour market policies (see above, p. 78).

The NEO process and the agencies' sectoral responsibility for ecologically sustainable development go much further in meeting the aggregation and consistency criteria of policy integration. To paraphrase Lafferty, these central features in Sweden's ecological governance do in effect provide a 'basic mandate' for environmental and ecological concerns, politically determined by the Parliament and the Cabinet. They become comprehensive societal objectives, and the sectoral responsibility forces all units of government to analyse and take into account presumed environmental consequences in the overall evaluation of their decisions. As stated earlier, Lafferty argues that this is '*the* essential difference between *environmental* policy integration and policy integration in general' (Lafferty 2001:10).

Still, we are left with the most fundamental question concerning environmental policy integration, i.e., that of its *strength*. The fact that sectoral agencies show signs of effective 'ecologisation' does not automatically mean that there is a political, inter-sectorally applied principle lending a privileged position to ecological concerns. Let us assume that the sectorally responsible agencies' analyses of some sectoral decisions find that there are contradictions between ecological concerns for the sustainability of life-support systems on the one hand, and traditional sectoral objectives on the other. What do the Cabinet and Parliament have to say about how such conflicts are to be resolved? In Lafferty's words, we ask whether there exists an explicit 'basic mandate for environmental *privilege*', i.e., a political commitment to minimise contradictions between environmental and sectoral policies by giving some recognised priority or strength to the former over the latter (Lafferty 2001:10; italics mine).

As we saw in the former section, central government – read the Cabinet – does use regulatory, economic and informative instruments to steer the sectoral agencies towards taking ecological concerns into account in their work. What we are looking for here is whether some of these measures also function as weighting devices. Quite clearly, the Letters of Regulation do exhibit such functions. The Cabinet (a) attaches ecological conditions to the agency budget allocations, (b) specifies certain environmental objectives to such sectoral policies as agriculture, forestry, transport, and housing and planning, and furthermore (c) demands specific feedback reporting on agency performance. This in effect means that central government gives specific weight to ecological concerns and values pertinent to sectoral policies.

The strong political backing for the NEO strategy and its generational perspective on ecologically sustainable development also implies the weight given to ecological concerns in the political and administrative decision-making. There are also some mechanisms for administrative co-ordination among the agencies with specific and/or NEO responsibilities of some importance here. The Environmental Objectives Board in operation since early 2002 is charged with developing and issuing guidelines for how all NEO-responsible agencies should monitor and evaluate progress towards the NEOs. The Board is also mandated to provide a comprehensive and co-ordinated annual NEO report to the Cabinet (www.environ.se).

Still, there will be conflicts between sectoral and environmental objectives. Expressions such as 'Sweden should continue to be a forerunner in the transformation to sustainable development' that includes not just economic and social but also ecological aspects which are 'interdependent and must be weighted in a balanced way' does not provide precise guidance as to how such conflicts are to be handled (Cabinet Communication 2001/02:50, p. 5). What then about the recent authoritative statement on Sweden's 'National Strategy for Sustainable Development', prepared for the Johannesburg meeting? One key passage is worth quoting at length:

> The society of the future must be formed within the limits set by nature, environment and human health. To reach this long-term objective, economic growth, social consensus and environmental protection must be co-ordinated in a mutually enforcing manner. The strategy for sustainable development views the concern for environment as an important driving force for growth, development

and employment. The transformation demands new solutions, new and environmentally friendly technology, environmentally adapted production of goods and services, new methods of transportation and new ways of producing energy. An active social policy, competitive business, and a stable economic growth are important building blocks for transforming Sweden into an ecologically, socially and economically sustainable society ... A renewed and long-term sustainable policy for welfare and social justice does not contradict economic growth, but is rather a condition for our long-term common welfare. (Cabinet Communication 2001/02:17)

Could this be read as 'a commitment to minimise contradictions between environmental and sectoral policies by giving priority to the former over the latter' (see Lafferty 2001: 10)? My answer is a tentative 'Yes'. We have seen earlier that statements from the Swedish Government indicate that the three aspects of sustainable development should be given equal weight in the efforts to transform Sweden into a sustainable society. What we find in the Swedish Johannesburg Report may well be seen as a further step forward. The first sentence of the quote explicitly places long-term social welfare and economic growth *within* the limits of nature. There is also an explicit view of environmental concern as a long-term *driving force* for social and economic development, and as a *condition* for long-term common welfare. Together with the statement that the three aspects of sustainable development should be managed in a *mutually enforcing* manner, one must conclude that, at least in principle, the Swedish Government places the ecological aspects of sustainable development at the centre. Temporally rational ecological governance recognises the limits of the commons, and co-ordinates all aspects of long-term sustainable development to protect the natural base of social welfare and economic growth.

As noted above, the Cabinet holds the view that in practice, the final and authoritative balancing of policy and sectoral objectives should come through the overarching budgetary and regulatory decisions by the Parliament and the Cabinet (Cabinet Bill 2000/01:130, p. 23). What remains to be seen is thus to what extent Parliament and the Cabinet are prepared to use their budgetary and regulatory powers to influence the final and authoritative weighting of environmental and sectoral objectives to keep environmental concerns at the centre of future resolutions of conflicts among societal objectives. The common yardsticks described earlier, and even more so the common accounts now introduced and used in the Cabinet's annual Finance Plan, do indeed provide means for enlightened political decisions.

There are thus clear attempts in Sweden to aggregate presumed ecological consequences into an overall evaluation of future policies, i.e., the common cause, the common yardstick, the common account. At the same time, we find remnants of ecological modernisation's win-win-assertions; policy-driven green technological change will provide important building blocks for 'Sustainable Sweden' and thus promote both economic growth and social welfare. For those acquainted with Sweden's political history since the 1930s, in particular the building of the social welfare state, this should come as no surprise. Even as a forerunner in the march towards an ecologically sustainable society, Sweden heads for the 'middle way'.

# 6
# Democracy and ecological governance – a balancing act

## Sustainability and democracy: a political dilemma

*Legitimising the balance between sustainability and autonomy; the need for democratic politics*

As pointed out in Chapter 1, this book builds on the normative argument that ecologically rational governance must strive for sustainability *within* the limits set by democracy and individual autonomy. The relationship among these values is quite complex. On the one hand, effective and in the longer term successful ecological governance relies on quite radical changes in present values and behaviour in the direction of substantial restrictions on individual autonomy of choice. This could be used as an argument for constraints on democratic participation in order to prevent political conflicts and ease the introduction and implementation of radical measures (see Lafferty and Meadowcroft 1996:257). On the other hand, the very fact that progress towards sustainability presupposes far-reaching value changes implies that citizen participation would be a necessary prerequisite for successful ecological governance. Comprehensive value changes simply cannot achieve political legitimacy without widespread democratic participation in the process of change.

However careful the balance is struck between sustainability and autonomy in the practical implementation of ecological governance, there will be 'winners' and 'losers' in the conflicts over when, how, why and by whom resources should be used. The stronger the value of autonomy is pursued at present, the more individual actors today can utilise natural resources in ways not compatible with the need for long-term, sustainable resource management. Or to turn this argument around; the stronger the pursuit of long-term ecological sustainability, the more threatened may be the value of individual autonomy. While ecological governance for sustainability must profoundly affect all and everyone in order to be successful, it cannot achieve legitimacy without offering each and everyone a possibility to participate in the formation and implementation of such governance. Susan Baker has succinctly summarised this dilemma of ecological governance:

> If new governance is to be increasingly relied upon as a way of governing the crisis of environmental governability, then new ways will have to be found to ensure greater societal participation in environmental policy-making while at the same time guarding against any erosion of the principles of democratic government. (Baker 2001:121)

Baker's last words are important; attempts to make ecological governance both effective and democratically legitimate are made in a context of traditional democratic processes. When a larger number of groups and interests are brought into such governance, 'special' interests are bound to appear. Such interests are often entrenched in policy communities or issue networks based on values contrary to sustainability, and might not necessarily take a favourable view of sustainable development. But locking out some groups from participation would mean a break with the values of democracy and individual autonomy. So, the efforts to bring about ecologically rational governance must ultimately observe the limits on their legitimacy drawn by the values of democracy and individual autonomy. Only when formulated and implemented in an open, participatory process of democratic decision-making could massive policy changes deeply affecting individual autonomy be considered legitimate and thus *politically* sustainable.

### Participation and autonomy for whom: market actors or democratic citizens?

As the earlier chapters reveal, ecological governance for sustainability does have important spatial, temporal, cognitive, and integral implications for both the democratic process and its outcomes in terms of individual autonomy. Such governance creates new levels and new entities of governance, thus providing several new points of access for public participation in the policy process. It opens up new temporal dimensions, implying that the democratic process should take into consideration the interests of future generations not yet appearing on the political scene. By bringing in cultural traditions and local knowledge of man-nature relationships, widened participation challenges traditional methods of policy-making, where science and technology are used to determine 'objectively' the problems to be addressed. Perspectives of public participation and individual autonomy challenge the implementation of sustainability not just on whether or not integrative mechanisms effectively promote that value, but also on whether such mechanisms are consistent with individual freedom of choice and rights to self-determination.

How, then, could democratic participation be promoted and individual autonomy safeguarded in a system of governance geared towards ecological sustainability? In the latter half of the 1990s, it was increasingly argued that this question was wrongly put. Proponents of ecological modernisation held that promotion of green growth would do away with the presumed conflict between sustainability and individual freedom of choice. By promoting green growth, governments could provide a win-win solution in tune with the prevailing logic driving actors in the market (see Jansen, Osland and Hanf 1998:291 ff.). However, this view has been questioned on grounds of both sustainability and autonomy. As for sustainability, ecological modernisation 'follows, in essence, past patterns of economic development, particularly the equation of economic growth with human social progress' (Barry 1999:252 f.). A comparative study of West European environmental governance furthermore found evidence that 'none of the most active promoters of ecological modernisation will achieve its goals in terms of the central categories and criteria of environmental policy' (Jansen, Osland and Hanf 1998:319).

In terms of democracy and individual autonomy, ecological modernisation is criticised because its strong emphasis on market-based instruments addresses individuals and groups in society as producers and consumers rather than as 'democratic citizens under the law' (Barry 1999:227). It encourages people to think in terms of marginal behavioural change guided by the criterion of individual economic gain. This, argue the critics of ecological modernisation, is not compatible with the massive change in cultural values necessary to achieve ecologically sustainable development. Such changes must be based on free and informed deliberations on what the institutionalised societal values should really be about. This implies a concern with measures for participatory democracy where autonomous citizens are 'encouraged to consider the interests of all those potentially affected by the democratic process' (Barry 1999:228 f.).

When individuals are addressed as *citizens*, their sphere of autonomy is widened. They are empowered to participate in, and deliberate over which collectively binding decisions should be made with respect to resource use and management. Democratic governance, in which citizens also have a guaranteed sphere of influence over collective matters, is after all 'a process in which we all come to internalise the interests of each other and indeed of the larger world around us' (Goodin 1996:18). Goodin's words point out the dual nature of the sustainability-autonomy relationship. A participatory democratic process offers the promise of respect for the integrity of the commons (citizens taking responsibility for the fate of the larger world surrounding them) as well as for the value of autonomy (citizens coming to respect the rights of other individuals). In conclusion, I agree with the argument that only through democratic participation can society create 'a shared public basis on which to ground the legitimacy of restrictions and corrections' that are considered necessary to achieve ecologically sustainable development (Achterberg 1993:91).

*Solving the dilemma: measures for participatory and legitimate ecological governance*

Much has been done to create such a basis since environmental policy became a policy field in its own right in the 1960s. The field has been marked by a distinctive drive for new means and channels of participation. Some argue that following the Rio Summit and the Agenda 21 process of the 1990s, 'citizen participation is seen as the defining characteristic of sustainable development' (Baker 2001:119). Compared to the 'traditional' policy-making process, many innovative measures have been

introduced to bring different actors and the public together in free
and open discourse to reach decisions through the strength of the
better argument (Dryzek 1995:302).

Right-to-know legislation has been extended, and brought into
use in processes of physical and infrastructural planning. The
same is true for public hearings; it would nowadays seem almost
unthinkable to launch large development projects without open
hearings that involve affected interests. Environmental NGOs
have enjoyed a firmer legal standing and widened possibilities of
appeal. The concept and procedures of Environmental Impact
Assessment, once introduced in the US National Environmental
Policy Act, have found their way into a host of national legisla-
tions, thereby enlarging the public's possibilities of participation
and influence. Environmental mediation and regulatory negotiation are examples of efforts to bring relevant actors and
affected interests into the decision-making processes of ecological
governance.

It should be noted that by being in essence a multi-level system
of 'nested enterprises', ecological governance is dependent for its
democratic legitimacy on *each level* having spheres of autonomy
that allow for meaningful popular participation (Ostrom 1990:
89 f.). Decentralisation and delegation of authority and responsibility are called for in this respect, as are specific programmes
directly addressing local and ecosystem-based entities of
governance with recognised spheres of competence. The inter-
generational perspective of ecological governance calls for
mechanisms to enhance the interests of future generations. There
are proposals to give rights to future generations in order to guarantee sustainability (see Wissenburg 1993). To pass the test of
legitimacy, however, ecological governance must not only be 'just
in time' but also 'just now', i.e., it must observe the rights and the
autonomy of present generations. In line with the argument made
on pages 148 ff. we could view several of the measures for
increased participation as ways of safeguarding those values.

With respect to the democracy and autonomy aspects of
ecological governance, the following criteria can be formulated:

• Governance is ecologically rational in terms of democracy to
  the extent that the management of environment and natural
  resources is subjected to political debate and decision-making

in democratic processes open to meaningful public participation at all levels of governance.

- Governance is ecologically rational in terms of individual autonomy to the extent that the choices of policy measures used in such governance are made with a view to safeguarding individual rights both now and in the future.

In the following, I first of all analyse the formal regulations surrounding citizen access to public information in general, and on environment-related issues in particular, as well as the rules safeguarding individual rights and freedom of choice. Then I look into the points and channels of access and participation in the process of policy formation, followed by a study of participation in two processes of local ecological governance. The chapter then traces the official views of participation in future ecological governance, and ends with an analysis and judgement of how the discovered Swedish patterns correspond to the criteria just outlined.

## Formal ecological governance in Sweden; access to the commons and enclosures for individuals

*An open political process; common access to information*
The *Public Access to Information Principle* has been a fundamental part of Swedish law since 1776. The present rules on public access to official documents are found in one of Sweden's constitutional laws – the *Freedom of Press Act*. They guarantee the right of Swedish citizens to obtain access and insight into administrative documents and activities. The principle furthermore means that the public and the mass media – newspapers, radio and television – have the right to obtain information about state and municipal activities (the following builds on Government Offices 2000). The principle is expressed in various aspects of access, freedom of expression and communication:

- Access to official documents;
- Freedom of expression for civil servants and others;
- Communication freedom for civil servants and others;
- Access to court hearings;
- Access to meetings of decision-making assemblies.

The public access concerns *official* documents. A document is official if it is *held* by a public authority, or can be regarded as having been *received* or *drawn up* by a public authority. Drafts, written communications or other working material are not considered official if the draft is not used when the issue is finally decided upon, or if they have not been retained for filing. It is often easy to conclude that written paper documents are 'held' by a certain public authority. Electronically processed data, AV recordings, and the like are considered as held both by the public authority storing the recording, or having a computer terminal link-up, or having facilities to obtain printouts.

The character and topics of certain official documents qualify them as *secret*. This means that the public is not entitled to read the documents and the public authorities are forbidden to make them public. Official documents other than the following ones listed in the Freedom of Press Act may not be kept secret in order to protect interests:

- Sweden's national security and foreign relations;
- Sweden's central financial, monetary and foreign exchange policy;
- public authorities' inspection, control or other supervisory activities;
- prevention and prosecution of crime;
- Sweden's public economic interest;
- protection of individuals' personal integrity or economic conditions;
- preservation of animal or plant species.

Those wishing to obtain an official document (provided it is not judged to qualify as secret) have the right to read the document at the place where it is held. They are not required to describe the document precisely to obtain it. The authority must make available the necessary technical equipment for comprehending the document. Claimants are also entitled to obtain a transcript or a copy of the document for a fixed fee. As for computerised documents or data, authorities should provide printouts. Requests to obtain official documents must be dealt with speedily by the authority. Unnecessary delay is not permitted. Authorities cannot demand that persons who wish to obtain an official document identify themselves or state what the document will be used for. If a request relates to a document falling under some provision of the Secrecy Act, the authority has the right to ask the applicant about identity and purpose. If the applicant refuses, he or she relinquishes the possibility of obtaining it. If authorities reject the request for a document, or supply the official document subject to reservations, the applicant is entitled to appeal for a court review of that decision.

There should be no doubt that this constitutionally guaranteed openness is of utmost importance for the democratic character and the protection of individual autonomy in the processes of ecological governance. However, there have been concerns that the privatisation and contracting out of policy implementation as well as the Swedish membership in the European Union might shrink the citizens' possibilities to retrieve information for use in the democratic debate. In its January 2002 Democracy Bill, the Cabinet thus proposed that private firms contracted to carry out public duties, private schools with public financing, and the documents from preparatory bodies under the Municipal Council should fall under the principle of public access to documents. This may in fact be interpreted as a widening of public access from govern*ment* to govern*ance*. Sweden furthermore succeeded in achieving its objective for the leadership term in Spring 2001 to widen public access to EU documents (see Cabinet Bill 2001/02:80, pp. 99 ff., 113).

## Public access to the governance of the commons; the law of the land

To further illuminate the prospects for democracy and individual autonomy in ecological governance, let us now look more specifically into how access, participation and protection of individual rights are formally outlined in legislation pertinent to environmental and natural resource issues.

As mentioned above (see p. 126 f.) the 1998 Environmental Code is construed as an amalgamation of a large number of acts covering – in principle – every aspect of human activity that might have an impact on environmental quality and natural resources. Activities that are expected to have considerable such impacts must apply for permits, granted by the Cabinet, environmental courts, regional administrations, or local governments, depending on the scale of the activity and the scope of expected impacts.

What is of particular interest here is how the Code regulates duties to provide information, as well as rights of participation in such processes. When laying out the law of the land in this respect, we will also be covering physical and infra-structural planning in general.

Descriptions and assessments of environmental impacts of everything from specific projects to general policies have been discussed and used in various ways ever since they were put on the books through the US 1969 National Environmental Policy Act. In ideal fashion, Environmental Impact Assessment (EIA) procedures involve not only descriptions of the proposed activity's potential environmental impacts, but also of such impacts from alternative ways of carrying out that activity. Furthermore, an ideal type EIA includes comparative evaluations and assessments of the environmental acceptability of these alternative courses of action. A basic idea behind the demands for EIAs is to provide possibilities for open debate on the proposed action, involving, e.g., those potentially affected by that action through access to public hearings, and rights of appearance and argument before the decision-making body.

A first, and rather limited version of the EIA procedure was introduced in Sweden in 1981, providing merely for description of potential impacts (EID) of projects needing permits under the Environmental Protection Act. This legislation at the same time made mandatory a procedure of early and active counsel between relevant authorities and affected interests before making decisions on projects potentially harmful to the environment. This thinner EID requirement was gradually made applicable to more and more issues and areas, particularly when several resource-related acts were put under the umbrella of the Natural Resources Act in the late 1980s. A National Audit Office review in the mid-1990s found several flaws in the EID procedures. The general public and environmental NGOs were often getting access too late in the process. EID reports often failed to describe the environmental impact of alternative ways of implementing large resource-related projects. EIDs of large water exploitation projects only described the impacts of profitable alternatives (National Audit Office 1996).

The 1998 Environmental Code contains specific regulation on the procedures and content of environmental impact assessments.

All activities requiring a permit under the Code are subjected to the EIA requirement (Cabinet Bill 1997/98:145, pp. 278 ff.). Both the general public and particularly affected interests have the right to be informed of a pending permit application. They also have the right to comment on both the application and the related EIDs, the content of the latter being specified in the Code (Cabinet Bill 1997/98:145, p. 292). One could describe the new EIA as a two-step process. All actors in the process of applying for a permit must seek early counsel with relevant supervisory authorities, usually the Regional Administrations, and with potentially affected interests. At this stage, the applicant should provide at least a preliminary EID to allow for discussion of environmental impacts. Both affected interests and the general public have the right to present arguments at this stage (Cabinet Bill 1997/98:145, p. 282 f.).

In the second round, the general public and the affected interests have the right to retrieve information on both the application and the full EID, except for such details that can be labelled business secrets. The Code makes it mandatory for responsible authorities to announce publicly that the application is made and that an EID is available. This goes also for site inspections to allow for participation from the public and affected interests. The Code particularly regulates the procedures involving projects with 'considerable' potential effects on the environment. Should the supervisory authority find, after the first round, that this is the case, an enlarged EIA procedure is called for. An enlarged counsel is then mandatory, involving relevant national agencies, local governments, as well as environmental NGOs. Furthermore, all affected interests with a legal standing must be involved, i.e., those with property rights or with ongoing economic activities in the area where the applicant wants to locate the project. In terms of content, the EID must now cover all aspects of relevance, including alternative locations and – where possible – alternative technologies (Cabinet Bill 1997/98:145, pp. 286 ff.).

Seen in combination with the general rules of public access to governmental information, the EID/EIA requirements connected to the permit procedures laid out in the 1998 Environmental Code have increased the opportunities for citizens and potentially affected interests to retrieve information. The procedures guarantee public access to the proceedings of those authorities making decisions on permit applications, in most cases the Environmental Courts. While this could be seen as opportunities for the public to influence decisions in the direction of sustainable development, there is, as we have emphasised throughout this book, also another side to it, i.e., that of safeguarding autonomy. When there are such opportunities to protect and promote the value of sustainability, what happens to the protection of individual rights and the enhancement of individual autonomy in the sense of reasonable freedom of choice?

*Enclosures of the commons. Safeguarding individual rights and freedom of choice*
Much of the governance for sustainability is concerned with protecting and enhancing the viability and productivity of ecosystems. To this end, a common interest can be construed with regard to such values as biological diversity, water quality, etc. What occurs when a government or an authority decides to put certain claims and restriction on part of the territory (see above, p. 62 on the concept of 'national interest' in physical planning) is not just an 'enclosure' of the commons in the name of sustainability. It also constitutes an infringement on individual autonomy. Certain present or prospective economic and social uses of the land are put under restriction. Industrial and exploitative action is prohibited. Citizens used to enjoying the unique Swedish common law practice of Common Right to Access to all land not under cultivation find themselves fenced out or subjected to restrictions on their freedom of movement.

How does Swedish law strike the balance between preserving the integrity of the commons and valuing individual autonomy? Discussing this crucial issue in relation to the new Environmental Code, the Minister of Justice took as his starting point the Swedish constitution which states that to justify intrusions on private property and on individual rights, the common interest identified must be very 'important' or 'urgent'. The principle to be applied in relation to issues of ecological sustainability should, concluded the Minister, be that they are often of such importance or urgency as to motivate intrusions on individual rights. While such intrusions always presuppose a reasonable proportionality between common gain and private loss, the wording of the Code Bill implies that the future balance might be shifted towards a

broader interpretation of common gain (Cabinet Bill 1997/
98:145, pp. 320 ff.).

Thus, the scope or magnitude of intrusions on behalf of
sustainability might increase over time. If intrusions on private
property and individual freedom become broader and more
frequent, the issue of compensation becomes even more crucial
than before. The Environmental Code deals with compensation in
the traditional Swedish way. Compensation is afforded when
decisions to establish areas of nature conservation, biodiversity
and water protection or cultural reserves involve appropriation
of land or make on-going land-use 'essentially more difficult'
in the 'affected part of the property' (Cabinet Bill 1997/98:145,
pp. 546 ff.).

Why this particular delineation of the circle of actors entitled
to compensation? What about the general public suddenly closed
out from areas of common access as a result of new economic
activities permitted under the Environmental Code? To answer
this question, one is forced to analyse the concept of 'legal standing' and its implications for individual autonomy. As we saw
earlier, both the general public and the property owners in an
area affected by a proposed economic activity with potentially
harmful environmental consequences have the right to state their
case in a permit proceeding. But in traditional Swedish legislation
related to natural resources, legal standing in the sense of right to
appear and right of appeal was offered only to those owning adjacent property. As for the Environmental Protection Act, legal
standing in this sense was linked to those caused to suffer defin-
able damage or some other inconvenience from environmentally
harmful activities, not necessarily owning property. The
Environmental Code establishes a more uniform concept of legal
standing, based on this latter interpretation. However, those
made to suffer because there are infringements on the Rights of
Common Access are not afforded legal standing (Cabinet Bill
1997/98:145, p. 485 f.). It goes without saying that this excludes
a large potential circle of actors from legal rights of appearance.

However, the Environmental Code also contains some new
statutes enlarging the possibilities for environmental group
action. This comes in the form of a right to legal standing for
environmental NGOs. Such organisations can, as we saw earlier,
participate in the decision-making processes on permits under the

Code. What is really new is that such NGOs now also have the right to appeal against decisions by permit-granting bodies. Provided such organisations are open to all, have been active for more than three years, and provided further that they have a membership of more than 2,000 persons, they can appeal against permit decisions, and environmental court rulings, as well as decisions to exempt some activity from Environmental Code procedures. They can act on behalf of common environmental interests, or on behalf of some particularly affected interests (Cabinet Bill 1997/98:145, pp. 487 ff.).

To summarise, the law of the land provides citizens and affected interests with several formally guaranteed opportunities for becoming informed and participating in the policy process. There may of course be some unequal distribution of capabilities among different categories of actors and interests to fully utilise these opportunities. What becomes crucial is the extent to which governments at different levels actually live up to the provisions for public participation and the right of individuals to be informed on issues that may affect their rights and future freedom of choice.

**Participation in Sweden's ecological governance: who is, and who should be sharing the commons of policy-making?**

*Commissioned to participate: organised interests and environmental policy-making*

Governmental commissions are very important vehicles for policy formation in Sweden. Working on terms set up by a Ministry, a commission investigates a policy problem and reports back to the Ministry. The composition of commissions may vary depending on the perceived political centrality of the problem. The more crucial the topic in the eyes of the government, the more carefully balanced is the representation. Commissions may be *parliamentary*, meaning that the political parties are represented, or *representative of the interests* perceived to become affected by the reform proposals of the commission, or they may be *expert* commissions to deal with a more technical problem. It is quite usual for commissions to establish close contact with public agencies, industrial branch organisations, NGOs, and individual experts during their period of investigation. They may also arrange hearings on particular topics related to their terms of reference, or use such hearings for testing out some of the proposals contemplated. Commissions are thus very important as a means of bringing in and accommodating the views of different political, economic and social interests in Swedish society. They have been described as vehicles for producing relevant knowledge on social problems, as an arena for crafting compromises and creating consensus, and as a Cabinet instrument for strategic political planning (Johansson 1992:17).

What happens after the Commissions present their reports is equally important for the possibilities of participation in policy-making. The reports are usually sent out to all relevant authorities with a 'request' to comment. 'Invitations' to comment are also sent to branch organisations and NGOs related to the report's topic. In principle, the opportunity to provide written comments is accessible to everyone interested in the topic. Together with the original commission report, these 'remittals', i.e., written comments, are then used as the basis for the Cabinet Bills sent to Parliament (Uhrwing 2001:71 ff.).

Commission reports on issues related to sustainable development are thus of utmost importance for the democratic aspects of ecological governance. The proposals in these reports set the agenda for the further stages of the policy process. In so far as the suggestions of these reports are not vehemently challenged in the remittal process, they usually find their way into a Cabinet Bill. When the Cabinet enjoys a majority in Parliament, the sometimes only slightly modified Commission proposals become the law of the land. In this and the following part, we will look into (a) the scope and reach of participation in commissions related to ecological governance, and (b) the content of recommendations for public participation proposed by the two commissions on NEOs and climate reporting in 2000.

A recent study of three environmental policy-making processes analysed the scope and reach of interest participation, from commissions all the way through to the submission of written comments and appearances before ministers and department officers. Interests are not only represented as members on the commissions. They are also participating through experts working for the commissions. Furthermore, they are invited for counsel and to hearings during the early stages of the commissions' work. But there is also a reverse process. Interest organisations initiate contacts with the commissions both formally and in more informal ways. After the commission report, vast numbers of interest organisations take part in the 'remiss' procedures. This participation comprises not only those organisations invited to give comments, but also those sending in comments on their own initiative. In fact, in two of the three policy-making processes under scrutiny, the number of voluntarily provided comments turned out to be larger than that of those invited. In the case of the commissions reporting on Sustainable Development in Sweden's Mountainous Regions, the number of voluntarily provided written comments was quite large. This was in no small amount the effect of the nation-wide association of snow-scooter owners' campaign to have small local scooter-owner clubs sending in comments to protect their interests of free movement in the mountains (Uhrwing 2001, passim).

Two major commission reports related to sustainable development were presented to the national government in the year 2000. Both the Commission on National Environmental Objectives (NEOs, see above, p. 65 f.) and the Climate Commission were parliamentary. Representatives of the political parties investigated future policy alternatives for sustainable development assisted by experts and representatives of affected interests. Both provide typical examples of how commissions are used for gathering knowledge, creating consensus and help the Cabinet set the political agenda.

The NEO Commission was parliamentary; all parties in the *Riksdag* were represented. The membership further comprised several central agency officers. Of the 19 experts working in the commission, four came from interest groups, while the other 15 represented Cabinet ministries. The Commission took in a large amount of material from a total of 44 governmental agencies and regional administrations. Part of that material was based on a process of counselling between agencies and organised interests. Furthermore, the Commission instituted five thematic Working Groups. These groups arranged seminars involving both experts and organised interests. The Commission furthermore co-ordinated its work through counselling with no less than 14 other Commissions. Five hearings were held with business organisations and NGOs to provide for consensus and 'anchoring' of the proposals (SOU 2000:52, pp. 93 ff., Apps. III, IV, and VIII).

**Table 6.1** *Categories of suppliers of written comments (Remiss) on the NEO and Climate Commission Reports*

| Report | Suppliers of written comments | | | | | | | | | |
|---|---|---|---|---|---|---|---|---|---|---|
| | Central Agencies | Regional level* | | Local govt's | Labour market org's | Business org's | NGO's | | Courts | Research inst's | Total |
| | | Reg Adm's | County Councils | | | | Env. | other | | | |
| NEO Commission SOU 2000:52 | 43 | 21 | 5 | 14 | 3 | 44 | 6 | 23 | 2 | 19 | 180 |
| Climate Commission SOU 2000:23 | 28 | 5 | 1 | 8 | 6 | 52 | 8 | 9 | 4 | 23 | 144 |

*Remark: Reg Adm's = Regional Administrations, i.e., the regional arms of central government. County Councils = popularly elected regional bodies mainly responsible for the health policy sector.
*Sources*: SOU 2000:1, 2000:23, and 2000:52

The Climate Commission was also parliamentary with all *Riksdag* parties represented. The membership further comprised several central agency officers. Expertise was linked to the Commission in the form of an economist advisory group, and there was close co-operation with relevant central agencies. Two hearings were held with representatives of business organisations and NGOs (SOU 2000:23, p. 1 f.).

The following stage of providing for written comments from central agencies, affected interests, and others affected by and/or interested in the topic, included a very wide spectrum of the Swedish society. The large number of central agencies involved is a reflection of the fact that they are most often requested and not just invited to supply comments, as are all or a specified number of regional administrations. Research institutions are frequent remiss providers. Perhaps the most remarkable pattern from these two reports is the heavy representation of business organisations, while voluntary NGOs, particularly those with an environmental agenda, are less prominent. This is of course very much due to the small number of nation-wide environmental NGOs in comparison to business.

As revealed by Uhrwing's recent study (2001) of interest organisations' access to the corridors of power, however, there are also other, and for the prospects of democratic ecological governance somewhat disturbing factors at work here. Uhrwing seeks to find out for whom participation in these forms and stages of policy formation for ecologically sustainable development really provides means for influence. She concludes that while the remittal of written comments is open to all, it is by and large mostly a *symbolic* form of participation. What really counts is to be a member of, or provide experts to, a Commission. However, she also finds that to get access to such positions in the process, organised interests seem to have to possess certain characteristics. They must be large enough to afford full-time secretariats and to have their own, in-house expertise. It furthermore helps if a business/labour organisation or a voluntary NGO is dominant within an area under investigation by a governmental commission.

By far, however, the most important conditions for access to the innermost rooms of power relate to the nature of expertise that organised interests and others can provide. What Uhrwing calls the *technocratic norm* prevails. This norm builds on the assumption of an 'immense need for information and technical expertise. Therefore, this kind of information and expertise was demanded from interest organisations if they wanted to gain access to the most meaningful forms of participation in the processes' (Uhrwing 2001:301). Not surprisingly, business organisations much more often have the resources necessary to participate on these conditions, and are thus able to get greater access into the corridors of power than NGOs presenting their argument in what would be interpreted as much more value-laden terms.

*Participation in ecological governance: active citizens or incentive-reacting consumers?*
Given Uhrwing's conclusions about the importance of specific organisational resources for effective participation and influence, it is of interest to compare the contents of recommendations for participation in three commission reports issued in the year 2000, all with a bearing on the future of Sustainable Sweden. The very first commission to report in the new millennium was that of the parliamentary Democracy Commission. Entitled *Sustainable Democracy!*, its 300-page report discusses the prospects for a widened democratic citizenship. The Commission leaned heavily on the discourse on deliberative democracy, and contended that representative democracy is not enough. Citizens should be allowed to commonly deliberate on different political solutions and their consequences throughout the policy-making process so that they are provided with real possibilities of influence (SOU 2000:1, Ch. 1).

The Democracy Commission thus saw active citizenship as a condition for sustainable democracy. When citizens discern a clear relationship between participation and the content of public decisions, there are good prospects for a sustainable democracy with trusted political institutions and highly legitimate policy decisions. Given the allusion to sustainability in the title of the Commission's report, one is led to assume that this would particularly hold for the democratic challenges posed by the quest for sustainable development. These challenges are after all prime examples of problems closely related to citizen participation and political legitimacy.

Thus it is of crucial interest to find out how democratic participation is treated in the two major commission reports related to sustainable development and issued in the year 2000. As already pointed out, both the Commission on National Environmental Objectives and the Climate Commission were parliamentary. Representatives of the political parties investigated future policy alternatives for sustainable development assisted by experts and representatives of affected interests. Indeed, the title of the 400-page NEO Commission report – *The Future Environment – Our Common Responsibility* – would seem to indicate a participatory perspective to legitimise political action with a cross-generational time horizon. On the other hand, the Climate Commission's 500-page report – *Proposals for a Swedish Climate Strategy* – leads one to think of an imminent battle rather than common democratic deliberations. As it turns out, both commissions seem to play on themes not totally in harmony with the ideas of democratic citizen participation. Contrary to the perspectives of the Democracy Commission, we are here confronted with a top-down perspective, where actions are to be taken not in dialogue with participating citizens, but for the most part in the form of signals to consumers and customers to change their market behaviour.

A content analysis of the three commission reports confirms this conclusion. As shown in Table 6.2, the Democracy Commission refers to individuals as 'citizens' 250 times, i.e., a rate of nearly once every page. Of the 174 times individuals are referred to in some other capacity the market-related epithet 'customer' appears only seven times. In the two reports on ecologically sustainable development, however, the perspective is opposite. The NEO Commission and the Climate Commission refer to 'citizens' only sixteen times in their total 1,900+ pages.

Indeed, the dominant view of two reports on sustainable development and future ecological governance puts that of the Democracy Commission on its head. Whereas that commission refers to citizens in a positive and active context 119 times, it refers to civic 'duties' only five times. The Climate and NEO Commissions view individuals mainly as customers and consumers, passive in the political sphere and predominantly acting on signals in the market. The NEO Commission refers to active consumers, while the Climate Commission tends to treat individuals as passively reacting to market incentives rather than actively participating in the collective decision-making process.

**Table 6.2** Group references, and initiation and direction of activities, in three future-related Swedish Commission reports issued in the year 2000

| Commission report | Group reference | | Initiation and direction of activity | | | | |
|---|---|---|---|---|---|---|---|
| | Citizen | Customer/ consumer/ individual | Dialogue | From citizen | Towards citizen | From customer/ consumer/ individual | Towards customer/ consumer/ individual |
| Democracy Commission SOU 2000:1 | 250 | 174 | 4 | 115 | – | – | – |
| NEO Commission SOU 2000:52 | 10 | 358 | 5 | – | – | 48 | 18 |
| Climate Commission SOU 2000:23 | 6 | 109 | – | 4 | 5 | 10 | 22 |

*Sources:* SOU 2000:1, 2000:23, and 2000:52

Thus, the commissions on sustainable development seem to act as if the normative issues of ecological governance are already settled. To a large extent, the role of the individual is reduced to one of 'changing behaviour' in response to future policy. This policy is often the result of negotiations over very specific issues of policy implementation among authorities, branch organisations, and individual enterprises. Now, one could of course argue that issues of ecological governance concern problems that are so complex both technically and politically as to render it well nigh impossible to accommodate broad public participation. There is need for expert judgement, and there is need for a distribution of roles between state and market. But as argued above, neither technological expertise, nor business calculi can claim legitimacy when it comes to which values should be guiding the future ecological governance and the society-environment relationship to be achieved by such governance. The question, then, is whether the general pattern found through our content analysis holds up when we analyse how citizens actually participate in the *implementation* of policies related to ecological governance. Two cases are of special interest here; the Swedish Local Agenda 21 process, and the implementation of the government's support to LIPs for sustainable development (see above, pp. 32 ff., 76 ff.).

## With or without the people: democratic ecological governance in practice

### Ecological governance with the people? Sweden and Local Agenda 21

Swedish local governments enjoy a constitutionally guaranteed autonomy on matters related to the welfare of its inhabitants and the development of the municipality. Local governments have a monopoly on physical and infrastructural planning within their boundaries, although such planning is subject to restrictions placed by environmental law and regulations safe-guarding individual rights to welfare, security and property. Local governments also have the right to tax the income of their inhabitants, and to enter into agreements with other municipalities to provide different welfare services (see Lundqvist 1998).

The Swedish Local Agenda 21 process began within a year after the 1992 Rio Conference, and covered most municipalities in Sweden (Cabinet Bill 1993/94:111 p. 64; see Eckerberg et al. 1997; see above p. 33). An internationally unique activity was launched to engage grassroots citizens and interest organisations in outlining visions and developing programmes for local sustainable development. Very early on, in 1994, central government formulated a national plan for Agenda 21, and the Environment Ministry presented a guide for Local Agenda 21 in the same year (Cabinet Bill 1993/94:111; SOU 1994:128). The purpose of the National Committee for Agenda 21 set up in 1995 was to stimulate local work on Agenda 21 as well as to take in data from local experiences. To this end, the National Committee arranged several meetings at the regional level as well as with different sectors of society. The Swedish Association of Local Authorities (SALA) continued to stress the bottom-up approach by collecting information and spreading data in order to support LA 21 activities among its members, i.e., the local governments (Eckerberg 1999:19 f.).

Already in 1996, about half of Sweden's 289 municipalities had employed special LA 21 officers. Two years later, 70 per cent of the local governments had employed a full-time or part-time Agenda 21 co-ordinator. It should be noted that this increase was supported by central government, which used money from the labour market funds to finance local hiring of such co-ordinators. By the end of 1998, 56 per cent of Sweden's 289 municipalities had local Agenda 21 plans. As for the political status of these plans, it is notable that most of them had been formally adopted through decisions by the Municipal Councils. Furthermore, most local governments located responsibility for co-ordination of LA 21 directly with the Municipal Board, i.e., the leading popularly elected Council politicians, whereas only about one tenth located it with the Environment and Health Board (Eckerberg et al. 1997:56 ff.; Eckerberg 1999:16 f.).

This political treatment of the issue and the allocation of co-ordinating responsibilities can be seen as an indication that Agenda 21 was perceived as extending beyond traditional environmental policy to involve all aspects of sustainable development. One close observer of the Swedish LA 21 process argues that there is tendency to emphasise the ecological over other aspects, both at the local level and in national programmes. Agenda 21 is largely perceived as a renewal and expansion of environmental policy, not involving economic and social aspects. Indeed, most LA 21 co-ordinators have been drawn from the community of environmental professionals (Eckerberg 2001:17).

Municipal action on LA 21 did not stop at planning. Four out of five municipalities have allocated special funding towards LA 21 activities. The level of funding increased somewhat since 1995. This said, one should note that while some local governments keep up the funding, others have cut down their LA 21 budgets. However, there is a tendency towards a growing gap between 'pioneering' municipalities and those who have cut down on staff and resources for LA 21. About 30 per cent have reduced their inputs in terms of both funding and staff (Eckerberg 2001:17).

A survey carried out in late 1998 found 97 per cent of the municipalities reporting quite conscious steps to engage citizens and interest groups in the LA 21 process. Two thirds of the municipalities arranged special courses and seminars or held open hearings and discussion meetings. Over 70 per cent of the municipalities provided LA 21 information brochures or leaflets to local households, or arranged exhibition and market events. Voluntary study organisations and environmental movements were engaged in over half of the municipalities. Every second local government made conscious efforts to involve village and community based voluntary organisations. About two thirds of the municipalities reported that they had established some permanent forum for exchange of ideas around LA 21 (Brundin and Eckerberg 1999). Studies of 'pioneer' municipalities further reveal this participatory thrust. One municipality engaged LA 21 workers in home visits to most of the municipality's households. Leading politicians within some local governments have taken part in initiating bottom-up projects (Eckerberg et al. 1997: 69 f.).

What, then, has actually been achieved in terms of public knowledge and involvement? A national survey in 1996 revealed that about 40 per cent of the population had knowledge of the Local Agenda 21 concept. About 20 per cent recognised at least one on-going LA 21 project, while only three per cent were actually involved in such a project (Eckerberg 1999:21). This may seem like a disappointing figure, given the massive information activities. A closer study of local governments that have formed consultation groups for LA 21 indicates the difficulties of citizen involvement in decision-making. The experience is that it is easy to create interest in 'neighbourhood' issues, but more difficult when broader issues are on the agenda. This holds even if the message of sustainable development is made as operational and simple as possible. The study concludes that 'even where great efforts were made to create conditions for participatory democracy, the results are often discouraging in terms of maintaining this interest' (Eckerberg 2001:33).

All in all, however, the major impression of the Swedish LA 21 process is one of strong emphasis on participation and information to the public, and of a conscious interplay between national initiatives and local action. This is not the least revealed in the titles of contributions from Swedish researchers to comparative studies on LA 21 implementation. Sweden has been seen as 'setting the pace', as combining municipal and national efforts for 'quick progress', and as being 'at the leading edge' in the LA 21 process. In a 1999 comparison, Sweden scored highest among the studied countries in terms of timing and broad-based implementation (Eckerberg, Coenen and Lafferty 1999:242 ff.). The crucial question, however, is how strong this local participatory process really is. What happens to citizen participation when Swedish local governments are targeted for central government funding to promote local investment programmes for sustainable development?

## Ecological governance without the people? Local management of the LIP process

When the Social-Democratic Cabinet launched its programme to fund Local Investments Programs (LIPs) for Sustainable Development in 1997 (see above, pp. 78 ff.), municipal governments were, as we have seen, amidst the LA 21 process. Almost three out of five Swedish municipalities had adopted Agenda 21 action plans for sustainable development by 1998, and most of these plans were adopted during 1997, i.e., just about the same time as the central government launched the LIP process. The central government's view of the relationship between the LIPs and the LA 21 process was summarised by the 1997 *National Agenda 21* Commission's report. LIP 'is directly linked to the Local Agenda 21 process. In this way, a linkage has also been established between the local level and the central decision-making functions of the Cabinet and the Parliament' on issues of sustainable development (SOU 1997:105, p. 11). In its budget bill for 1998, the Cabinet stated that 'local support is required in order for the ecological dimension within societal development to succeed' and that 'local Agenda 21 work should be brought into the investment programme' (Government Bill 1997/98:1, Spending Area 18, p. 43).

One would thus expect a rather close relationship in content between municipal LA 21 plans – many of them worked out in dialogue with local citizens, NGOs and other associations – and the LIP applications sent in to the Environment Ministry. One could also interpret the Cabinet's wordings as an expectation of an LIP process on the local level as participatory as that of LA 21. However, nation-wide surveys of the LA 21 co-ordinators do not seem to corroborate these assumptions. These key actors seem doubtful about the connections between the two programmes. This holds both for municipalities receiving grants as well for those not succesful in getting grants. Only five per cent of the LA 21 co-ordinators considered the two programmes closely connected, while close to half said they were partly connected. Ten per cent reported no connection whatsoever, and two out of five co-ordinators did not know of any such connection. Having focused on 'soft' sectors and broad citizen participation in the LA 21 process, local governments now looked to 'hard' sectors and to local business elites in the LIP programme (Brundin and Eckerberg 1999). Whereas the LIP programme focused on ecolog-ical efficiency through ecological modernisation, LA 21 was concerned with a much broader range of activities (see Eckerberg 2001).

The two programmes also seem to differ substantially in terms of local participation, particularly when it comes to what groups or circles of actors were involved. Only one third of the local branches of the Swedish Nature Conservancy Organisation – the leading Swedish environmental interest group – were invited by local governments to comment on LIPs in the first round of appli-cations (Kågesson and Lidmark 1998). When preparing for the second, 1999 round of LIP applications, one fourth of the local governments engaged their citizens in the process through the creation of networks and other methods. However, contacts with local business were much more lively. As many as three out of four municipal LA 21 co-ordinators reported that local industry and business had been involved in the process of applying for a LIP grant. This is quite different from the LA 21 process, where just over one third of the municipalities reported a high degree of business involvement. The grassroots perspective so evident in the LA 21 process was thus much less prominent in the LIP process (Brundin and Eckerberg 1999).

In fairness, however, one should point out that there are variations to this pattern. The National Audit Office found both municipalities with broad involvement from the population, and others where the links to the local scene were quite weak (National Audit Office 1999b:53 ff.). One reason given by local governments was that the short time for LIP applications made it difficult to 'establish a broad citizen participation' in the process (Auditors of Parliament 1998/99:52). Given this, there would seem to have been all the more reason for the municipalities to build upon the already available LA 21 plans that enjoyed broad popular recognition and support from local networks. Evidently, however, many local governments actually preferred to put forward other projects – often involving infrastructural developments based on energy efficiency and increased employment – in co-operation with local economic interests. In a quite considerable number of cases, the LA 21 achievements thus seem to have been neglected. The LIP process thus came close to 'governance without the people', and – in effect – also local 'implementation from above' (see Lundqvist 2001a).

We thus encounter two local processes and two patterns of participation. One is geared towards citizen involvement all the way from ideas and visions to practical measures. The other seems more linked to socio-economic interests with resources of importance to the success of the local investment programmes. A most crucial question thus arises: Given these patterns, and given further the inclination towards market-based action to achieve sustainable development found in our content analysis of recent commission reports, what is the official view of participation and involvement in Sweden's future ecological governance?

**Sustainability and democratic participation: does Sweden solve the political dilemma?**

*Towards sustainable public participation? National government and the 'new ecological governance'*
Already the title of the NEO Commission's report – *The Future Environment – Our Common Responsibility* – makes allusions to participation for all and everyone. And the opening phrases of the report's chapter on 'The New Environmental Work' (a literal translation; my remark) seem to corroborate this impression:

> The objective of solving the large environmental problems of today within one generation demands widespread participation. It cannot be unilaterally realised by legal and administrative action. It is necessary for all to take on this responsibility. (SOU 2000:52, p. 115)

This is reiterated in the Cabinet's NEO bill accepted by Parliament. Legal and administrative action may provide a basis for action, but that action must involve all and everyone. At the same time, there is an undercurrent indicating that the objectives of widespread responsibility may not solely be to guarantee individuals some influence as subjects in the structures and processes of ecological governance. The diffusion of responsibility is part of a conscious effort to establish consensus and co-operation around specific views and strategies for sustainable development:

> The new NEO structure provides for comprehensive and effective environmental management with participation from all strata in society. A common framework of objectives *gives the direction* for how to achieve an ecologically sustainable society through management by objectives and results. (Cabinet Bill 2000/01:130, p. 18; italics mine)

When we turn to how and in what capacities these 'strata in society' are to participate and take responsibility, a very special pattern emerges. The Cabinet actually begins its outline of the new environmental governance by discussing environmental behaviour from the viewpoint of the individual as a market actor responding to economic signals. Thus, economic and communicative policy instruments are seen as major ways of distributing responsibilities in accordance with the environmental load caused by the individual. Furthermore, the Cabinet sees pressures from customers and market demands as equally important driving forces for business as regulatory and administrative measures (Cabinet Bill 2000/01:130, p. 18 f.).

Indeed, firms and enterprises stand out as very important actors. By responding to customer pressures and market demands through measures such as EMAS, environmental certification, and eco-labelling of products, and by assuming the producer liability throughout the product's lifecycle, these economic actors are at the centre of 'new environmental governance'. The concept of 'sectoral responsibility' is central to the achievement of the NEOs. Public authorities and business share 'sectoral responsibility' for NEO achievement in the respective sectors. And while the Environmental Code and ensuing legislation and administrative guidelines provide the basis for environmental governance, regulatory power should be used sparingly, and complemented by other strategies. Indeed, the NEO bill foresees a specific mode of governance that both echoes Sweden's historic adherence to welfare state corporatism and resembles modes of environmental governance found in, e.g., the Netherlands. A core element in 'new environmental governance' will consist of voluntary agreements between government and business, where 'affected firms and sectors take a large responsibility for active environmental management' (Cabinet Bill 2000/01:130, pp. 19 ff.).

What then, about voluntary organisations and NGOs as representatives of individuals and groups interested in or affected by the ecological governance just outlined? The Cabinet Bill accepted by Parliament deals explicitly with such organisations and their role in a mere 12 lines out of a total of 10 pages discussing 'new environmental governance'. The Bill acknowledges that voluntary NGOs have for decades carried out activities of great value for the environment. On such issues as nature conservancy and eco-labelling, they have even spearheaded policy development. Continues the Bill:

> It is the Cabinet's view that free, active and radical environmental NGOs, networks and other organisations acting on the basis of voluntary engagement will play important roles also in future environmental governance. Thus, environmental NGOs should also in the future act autonomously and independently of government, at the same time as they enjoy recognition and support from the authorities. (Cabinet Bill 2000/01:130, p. 19)

When going more deeply into the Government's argument on who should be at the centre of future ecological governance, we thus find corroborated the pattern revealed by the content analysis of key Commission Reports. Individuals are primarily viewed as market actors responding to market signals. These signals will increasingly be formed in accordance with agreements among the actors really occupying centre stage in Sweden's 'new ecological governance', i.e., public authorities and business organisations sharing and acting out their 'sectoral responsibility' for NEO achievement.

*Democracy and autonomy in Sweden's ecological governance; what will elites and citizens share in common?*
What, then are the prospects for democracy and individual autonomy in ecological governance? To say the least, we have discovered a mixed pattern. On the one hand, we have found that the law of the land is quite generous. The public's right to get access to official documents related to broad policy-making or to particular decisions affecting individuals, groups, or their environment is wider and more far-reaching than in most other countries. Affected interests enjoy the right to early counsel on resource- or environment-related issues requiring permits under the Environmental Code, as well as to take part in public hearings and site inspections. The concept of legal standing in such processes now also includes those affected interests not owning adjacent property, thus enlarging the enclosure around individual rights and individual autonomy. And – most notable in the Swedish context – environmental NGOs have been afforded legal standing as plaintiffs; they can appeal against decisions on behalf of the common interest. Furthermore, we have found that the policy process is quite open. Organised interests regularly participate as members. All such interests, as well as any individual interested in a policy proposal formulated through a governmental commission, are free to provide written comments to the government.

On the other hand, we have found that in reality, these formal possibilities are not used in full, or envisaged to be used in full, to create deliberative democratic ecological governance characterised by widespread participation. Started with much fanfare and backing from central and local government, and seeing more grassroots activity than in most other countries, the Swedish Local Agenda 21 process has lost some of its momentum to become – at best – a routine activity entrenched in municipal bureaucracy. When central government began waving wads of money before local governments to engage them in the LIP process, many municipalities seemed to skip the participatory LA 21 process for that of BAU – Business As Usual. This meant working out local LIPs emphasising jobs and infrastructure development in co-operation with local elites. And – most notable – the future 'new environmental governance' envisaged by major Commissions and acknowledged by Parliament seems to build on a triumvirate. Carrying out their joint 'sectoral responsibilities', governmental agencies and organised business interests are expected to interact to provide customers with economic incentives and communicative signals to change towards more sustainable behaviour. The Swedish wordings on the future role of environmental NGOs could in fact be interpreted as 'an invitation with the elbow'. They are 'allowed' to continue their activities as voluntary organisations within ecological governance.

This mixed pattern lends itself to different interpretations. If we adopt an 'elite-centred' view of participation, Sweden's 'new environmental governance' might look like *co-operative management regimes*. Such regimes involve 'a number of social partners in a collaborative attempt to resolve specific environmental difficulties'. The use of Commissions, the *remiss* procedure, and the public access to official documents could be taken as corresponding to one characteristic of a regime that rests on processes of open, discursive consensus formation. Furthermore, the sectoral responsibility shared among governmental agencies and organised sectoral interests – officially viewed as a core element in the 'new environmental governance' – implies that once the parties have come to some agreement, they assume some joint responsibility for implementing that agreed-upon strategy. It may even be argued that by incorporating the 'mobilisation, compliance-enhancing and legitimating potentials' of crucial socio-economic organised interests, central government tries to ensure that *co-operative management* sectoral regimes of ecological governance actually succeed in terms of sustainability, thus enhancing the legitimacy of such policies (see Lafferty and Meadowcroft 1996:257 f.).

However, if we adopt the 'citizen-centred' view of democratic participation outlined in the beginning of this chapter, several of the features of Sweden's existing and 'new environmental governance' could be questioned. It is true that the right of access to information covers all and everyone. It is furthermore true that the *remiss* procedure is in principle open to all. And it is true that the efforts made to plant LA 21 processes firmly with the grassroots on the local level have been remarkable successful by international comparison. It is, however, equally true that many of these rights and processes are, or have turned out to be, symbolic in character. The channels for citizen participation do not on the whole prove meaningful in terms of actual influence. Instead, the more resourceful actors participating at different stages in the process stand the best chances of actually influencing decisions. As for the future, citizen-centred participation in the NEO processes and climate strategies is best characterised as one where voluntary environmental NGOs are expected to play a mostly complementary role relative to governmental agencies and organised socio-economic sectoral interests.

It may, of course, be argued that this is politically the most realistic way of involving citizen-centred participation in ecological governance. Public participation then functions as a complement to, and a control on, democratically elected representatives at different levels as they make decisions on policies for sustainable development, and as an additional input to ecological problem-solving.

However, problems of legitimacy may arise when ecological governance comes to involve specific channels for compromise and accommodation between governmental bodies and organised sectoral interests. Based on Uhrwing's findings, we may argue that resourceful and thus influential as they are, socio-economic sectoral interests could be assumed to use their position to try to change the balance of the management by objectives strategy for ecological governance to make it more advantageous to them. Indeed, the Cabinet's NEO Bill does not formalise, but only loosely outlines the procedural features of this strategy. The agreements may therefore come to be concluded without the kind of early counsel and public hearings required for permit procedures under the Environmental Code, and may not be fully accessible through citizens' rights to retrieve information, because of the possible secrecy of business information. Citizens and environmental NGOs cannot therefore be sure that sectoral agreements actually observe 'the parameters within which co-operative management regimes' are expected to operate under Sweden's NEO strategy (see Lafferty and Meadowcroft 1996:260 f.).

What happens, then, when we confront these mixed patterns and interpretations of Sweden's 'new environmental governance' with our criteria for democratic and participatory ecological governance observing individual autonomy? To begin with individual autonomy, the formal aspects of Sweden's ecological governance seem to have widened the respect for individual integrity and freedom of choice. Ownership of property is no longer the sole condition for legal standing and right to compensation when people experience harm from others' environmental and resource use. When looking at the envisaged 'new environmental governance', one could contend that the pronounced preference for market-based and communicative policy measures changes the context of choice, but leaves much room for individuals to autonomously determine the content of their choices. This might serve to enhance the political legitimacy for the state and its role within ecological governance (see Lundqvist 2001b).

When we turn to democracy and citizen participation, we must conclude that by almost any formal standard, the Swedish process is very open. It provides for widespread citizen and interest group participation, built on general access to rich information, all the way from policy formation to the implementation of specific decisions. In reality, however, the envisaged future structure and process of ecological governance show features that are more elite- than citizen-centred. While both organised sectoral interests and the general public utilise and are bound to the Swedish commons, the former will enjoy a much closer relationship with governmental agencies than the latter. Citizens and environmental NGOs will have a much more complementary role in the structure and processes of ecological governance. Given that the core of Sweden's ecological governance – the NEO strategy – is less formalised, the prospects for citizen and NGO insight and influence will depend heavily on what willpower and resources they can muster. If these groups find themselves fenced off from the commons of NEO processes, the 'new environmental governance' could meet with problems in terms of the legitimacy of policies and measures. There is thus every reason to return to this problem of democracy and legitimacy in ecological governance (see below, pp. 197–200).

# 7

# Where the buck stops: governmental power and authority in democratic ecological governance

### Ecological governance and the authority of government

The preceding chapters analysed what Sweden has done, and how far that country has come, in creating structures and processes of governance for the sustainability of the commons and the autonomy of the individual within the limits of democracy. One conclusion is that while the logic of ecological rationality may seem attractive in terms of sustainability and autonomy when laid out as an ideal type, its practical implementation will most certainly involve conflicts and compromises on both accounts. Compared to historic patterns of resource management and behaviour, ecological governance for sustainability implies 'winners' and 'losers' in terms of individual autonomy and freedom of choice different from those we are used to identifying in traditional struggles over social and economic issues of development.

Governments engaging in efforts to bring about sustainable development will thus encounter political opposition and competition among conflicting values and interests. The pursuit of ecological sustainability adds new dimensions to the steering of human behaviour, and brings to the fore crucial issues about the ecology of governance itself. When push comes to shove, the political legitimacy of the 'sustainable society' project depends on how government can and does use its political *authority* towards other crucial actors in society to bring about ecologically rational governance.

Political authority involves power to make decisions that are binding on others and to force these others to act according to the

intentions of those holding power. Those in charge of political
government can exercise coercion to bring about the desired reactions among the others. In modern democracies, the scope and
wielding of such power is intimately linked to legitimacy.
Although the possibility of using force to achieve compliance is
always present, liberal democracies ideally strive to have authoritative decisions accepted with maximum consent and minimum
coercion (see Raphael 1990:74 ff.; Birch 1993:31). Political
authority

> is best described as a combination of political power and legiti-
> macy, where power is the ability to get things done and legitimacy
> is the quality of ascribed entitlement to exercise that power. (Birch
> 1993:32)

This means that although authoritative political action through
government may be necessary to achieve certain objectives, such
action is subject to limitations set by democratic norms of individual freedom and autonomy. This study of the Swedish
experience shows that the quest for ecologically sustainable development – (and, by implication, also its social and economic
aspects) – implies that political government should be vested with
far-reaching power and authority. At the same time, norms of
individual autonomy, i.e., individuals' right to make their own
choices of the 'good life' call for restraints on governmental
authority. In liberal democracies, the norms of autonomy and
freedom of choice place restrictions on the legitimate use of such
authority (see, e.g., Jones 1994:124 ff.).

The govern*ance* perspective brings out quite succinctly the
problems of balancing the authority of democratic govern*ment* so
that such authority is at the same time both enough to provide for
development towards desired objectives *and* limited enough to
allow for the individual autonomy necessary to provide legitimacy. But whereas the normative reasoning just presented seems
to have broad acceptance, empirical treatises on the actual
authority of government in governance show some contradicting
patterns.

One line of research on governance treats central government
as one among other players in a system of self-organising, steer-
ing-resistant networks, increasingly dependent on bargaining
skills rather than legal authority in a process of negotiation over

policy content. The core of governance consists of inter-linked networks and communities with both public and private sector participants, mutually interdependent on each other for resources such as money, expertise, and legitimacy. Key figures are those who hold nodal positions in the wider decision network and make judgements about linkages or what to communicate to whom. This would seem to indicate that some actors are more powerful than others in the processes of mutual adjustment among actors and networks striving to control crucial resources. However, networks are first and foremost self-organising and self-governing entities, 'not controlled by any single superordinate actor, not even the government' (Kickert 1993:275). As cited already in Chapter 1, this view holds that because 'integrated networks resist government steering, develop their own policies and mould their environments', governance comes close to 'governing without government' (Rhodes 1996:652, 658).

Against this view of the government as a team player, another school holds that the state indeed retains the role of umpire in the political game. The government has a legitimate hold on such crucial resources as forcing sanctions, enabling it to 'steer' policy objectives and outcomes through conscious use of structural and processual strategies. Governments *do* 'establish the basic parameters within which markets, and even social groups, function' (Pierre and Peters 2000:25, 39). Indeed, the state continues to function as the 'needle's eye' in the nested, multi-level institutionalisation of the logic of ecological rationality. Upward to the international and global levels, the state has the power to enter into binding agreements and assume duties in the common pursuit of global sustainability. Downward to regions and municipalities, the state can delegate responsibilities or issue mandates for implementing these internationally agreed measures. The state is vested with constitutionally legitimised resource-mobilising capacity and coercive competence and authority in its own right. These powers place government in the key position in the processes of governance (Lundqvist 2001a).

Sustainable development presents complications to both the normative delineation of *legitimate* political authority and the empirical views of government's role in governance. The magnitude of the problems to be solved and the entangled web of societal relations touched by the challenge of sustainable development seem to make necessary an expansion of governmental authority. The tradition of the modern welfare state has provided experiences and fostered expectations that government should actively provide *opportunities* to their citizens to make autonomous choices of the 'good life'. And unless political government is vested with authority to secure ecologically rational resource management to provide such opportunities, then as a consequence the possibilities for individuals to exercise autonomy are circumscribed.

To this we must add the different dimensions of rational ecological governance discussed in earlier chapters. The temporal dimension would seem to speak in favour of strengthened political authority to make legitimately binding long-term commitments for society as a whole. At the same time, the spatial dimension calls for multi-level governance, involving several governmental levels as well as non-governmental actors (see Hirst 2000:22 ff.). This logically calls for a diffusion of *state* authority, upward and/or sideways to the international level as well as downward to regional and local governmental levels. The scale of such a problem as climate change necessitates a global approach; 'ecologism in one country' is certainly not a sustainable option. The variation in eco-system scales means that management authority has to be vested in several levels below the state, some of which may already enjoy legitimate spheres of power and authority on their own. Ecologically rational governance also involves self-governing by actual resource users. This may be good for autonomy, but implies a dilution of political authority to bring about sustainable development.

The knowledge dimension challenges political authority from a somewhat different angle. Whereas politicians are elected and administrators are appointed to exercise authority, scientists have special knowledge that make them authorities in their own right within their specialties (see Birch 1993:30). What is 'sustainable' development is beleaguered with uncertainties that call for scientific research, evaluation, and recommendations. When the issues up for decision are particularly marked by such characteristics, it could mean that political authority becomes somewhat of a hostage to the authority of knowledge. Also the organisational and administrative dimension of ecological governance is crucial. Integration of ecological concerns into sectoral policies and bureaucracies may lead to confusion as to where the buck really stops, thus detracting from governmental authority to effectively pursue sustainable development. Last but not least, we have seen that the pursuit of sustainability has important implications for the democratic dimension of ecological governance and the legitimisation of governmental authority.

In the rest of this final chapter, I will discuss how the emerging system of ecological governance in Sweden affects the political authority of democratic national government. As the previous chapter indicated, governmental authority plays a crucial role in protecting individual autonomy and providing the means for democratic participation. My analysis of effects on political authority will be made with this in mind. This will pave the way for an assessment in the final chapter as to whether the Swedish government is actually straddling the fence over to sustainable development, and whether this expands or limits citizens' opportunities to make autonomous choices of the good life. To refer once again to my opening question, I want to find out whether the Swedish example does tell us something about the possibilities to *'govern ourselves so as to value democracy and individual autonomy and still retain the integrity of the commons'.*

## Fencing out or fenced in? Governmental authority and the governance of space

The spatial dimension of ecological governance puts governmental authority to the test. As for sustainability, spatially rational ecological governance must adapt to relevant ecological scales. Governmental authority may have to be transferred upward from the national level, downward to regional and local levels, as well as reallocated across those levels, all in order to manage the health and sustainability of ecosystems. As for autonomy, norms of democracy point towards configurations of authority in spatially rational ecological governance that recognise the right of individuals – stakeholders, resource users, or groups valuing certain ecological features – to devise their own allocations of authority for governing a commonly shared resource.

The Swedish response to the ecological challenges to governmental authority has so far been somewhat wavering. There are some conscious moves towards ecosystem-relevant allocation of authority with respect to coastal zone management, and a catchment approach to water management will be implemented within the next few years. The major pattern so far, however, is to contain governmental authority within traditional, man-made geographical boundaries (see Chapter 2).

To fully appreciate these tensions among sustainability, autonomy and governmental authority, it seems appropriate to look more closely at the problem of multi-level governance. The reader may by now have thrown her or his hands in the air many times, asking in frustrated terms why there is no treatment of the relations between Sweden and the EU in the different chapters, despite obvious linkages to the European dimension. Membership of the EU changes and irrevocably meshes governance in both the Union and its member states. The principles of regional integration and subsidiarity do indeed have significant implications for governmental authority in ecological governance, not just for the national but also for lower, intra-national levels.

The present Swedish process of implementing the EU Framework Water Directive provides a most vivid illustration of the tensions for governmental authority created by spatial ecological governance. In anticipation of the coming Directive, the Cabinet in 1996 appointed a Special Commission to propose a new system for water administration. The October 1997 report recommended that Sweden be divided into ten *Catchment Districts*, each with a special Catchment Authority comprising two or three regional administrations and all local governments within the district. This unit should have authority to decide on collectively binding management plans and issue permits under the Environmental Code. Within the District's major catchments, local governments should consolidate water issues into one decision-making unit per catchment (SOU 1997:99, pp. 49 ff., 69 ff.).

These recommendations resemble Ostrom's model of 'nested enterprises' (Ostrom 1990:90) in that they were knit to the existing allocation of authority among regional administrations and local governments. However, the Commission also recognised the water users' legitimate right to organise for a common management of the shared resource. Public authority could be delegated from the Catchment Authority to 'local environmental management co-operatives', but only if they fulfil certain criteria for joint associations laid down in the Swedish Constitution (SOU 1997:155, p. 81 ff.).

The EU Water Directive became effective in Sweden on 1 July, 2001. In October of that year, the Swedish Government appointed a special commissioner to work out proposals to establish Swedish water catchment districts as required under the EU Directive. His terms of reference clearly indicate the tensions created by the Directive's demand for special levels and units and proper allocation of authority to bring about ecologically rational water management. The catchment-based Water Districts demanded under the EU Directive should build primarily on the existing 21 Regional Administrations, with some 10 to 12 of these being designated to have authority over entire Catchment Districts, thus even for the geographical areas outside the administrative borders. Special Catchment Delegations set up within those Regional Administrations should be vested with authority to promulgate water action plans, following co-ordination and counsel with local governments in the Water District. To further 'nest' the enterprise of new catchment-based water management within existing structures of authority, the Commissioner should also evaluate the need for Cabinet or central agency confirmation of Water District management plans. As for water stakeholders and their right to organise for self-management, the Commissioner was expected to suggest concrete forms for 'water management co-operation'. In particular, the legal aspects of delegating authority to such co-operative networks, be they voluntary or established through administrative proceedings, should be illuminated (Directives M2001:01).

We thus have a situation where the authority of national government is fenced in by this authoritatively binding, supranational EU decision aimed at securing the sustainability of water resources through an organisation based on nature-given boundaries. In reaction to this, the Swedish Government seems to be busy building this new structure without totally compromising traditional lines of authority. In terms of effective pursuit of sustainability, one could of course say that this is an appropriate strategy. The competence, overview and co-ordination necessary for relatively swift production of management plans and concrete measures are already vested in the Regional Administrations and the local governments.

It would seem that autonomy is less well off than is sustainability in the directives for water governance presently discussed.

What is surprising is that this occurs amidst good examples of ecologically rational management of Swedish water resources. Landowners with water rights are entitled by law to establish their own Fishing Management Areas in collectively owned lakes and streams. From all we know, these FMA associations are quite successful examples of local co-operative management of vital ecosystems (SFS 1981:533; see Olsson and Folke 2001; Lundholm 1999). The competence and local knowledge built up in the Water Management Associations presently doing most of the monitoring of water quality in lakes and streams would also seem to provide a good basis for local ecosystem management units. They could thus be charged with considerable authority to govern common water catchments (see Gustafsson 1995).

In a preparatory report presented in June 2002, the commissioner went to some length in arguing for only four very strong Catchment Districts, while discussing arguments for stakeholder self-governance more superficially (Water Administration Commission 2002). This view of what constitutes an 'appropriate' authority distribution indicates that *effectiveness* in the pursuit of sustainability is a powerful underlying argument for securing strong governmental authority in ecological governance. It implies that the *democratic* argument of transferring authority to those actually using or sharing ecosystems is still met with political hesitation, as if increasing autonomy might jeopardise the achievement of sustainable development by allowing people too much space for decision-making.

### Going slow by running too fast? Political authority and the governance of time

We have defined temporally rational ecological governance as governance adapted to ecological cycles. This exposes governmental authority to some formidable cross-pressure. The political authority of democratic governments is linked to election periods. Those in power may feel forced to institute as much of their political ideas as possible into laws, regulations and administrative processes, all in the hope of binding subsequent political majorities to development paths of longer duration. However, this built-in propensity towards short political time horizons becomes quite problematic to temporally rational ecological governance as it depends on authority that can be sustained over a longer period of time than usual political cycles.

At issue here is how the authority of government can be used to handle this conflict between short-term *political* conditions and longer-term *ecological* desirables. We have seen how Sweden's national government has tried several ways to achieve temporally rational ecological governance. What are the prospects for the longer term with respect to governmental ability to wield political authority over and within governance? Do certain strategies tend to confirm long-term governmental authority, while others tend to squander it in the political eagerness to pursue such governance?

First and foremost, some of the strategies used to 'save' time by constraining the choices of present in favour of those in the future rest firmly on governmental authority. Physical planning has been used over the past decades to regulate, and often determine with a high degree of finality, the use of Sweden's ecosystems and resources. Ratified by Parliament and resting on the Environmental Code, nation-wide planning decisions have imposed authoritative long-term restrictions on land use. The national governmental purse is also used to wield long-term binding authoritative decisions. Funds for securing biodiversity – including buying valuable areas – more than tripled around the millennium shift, representing the fastest increase among budget items for environment after 1998 (Cabinet Bill 2002:100, p. 35). At the local level, the municipalities' monopoly on physical planning within their geographical territory gives them formidable authority. It should be noted, however, that the last decade has found local governmental planning authority more and more dependent on negotiating with private interests for the realisation of local development objectives.

This would seem to indicate that as we move from rather clear-cut govern*ment*-dominated situations to govern*ance* situations involving efforts to bring other actors 'on schedule' through persuasion, negotiation and bargaining, governmental authority might become less affirmative and less identifiable. At first sight, the Swedish NEO strategy seems firmly based on governmental authority. A Cabinet Bill passed by Parliament confirms the political intent of government to move society towards sustainable development 'within one generation'. However, the implementa-

tion of temporal ecological governance through NEOs presupposes that non-governmental actors perform roles that might
otherwise have been within the realm of public bureaucracies. In
such a process of reaching *negotiated ecological consensus* with
key actors and target groups in society at large, it may well be that
authoritatively formulated political objectives and targets become
adapted to the options acceptable and the capacities available to
the actual NEO implementers.

Two alternatives of temporal ecological governance provide
cases in point here. The 'closing of eco-cycles' presumes political
authority to be essential to initiate and promote such measures to
'save time' through infrastructural measures and incentives.
However, the success is in no small measure a matter for market-
related processes of demand and supply of recycled/recyclable
materials and products. If government wants to speed up
processes through authoritative decisions, it might find itself
going into domains of autonomy and individual choice viewed as
essential to democratic government, and experience losses in the
legitimacy upon which that authority ultimately depends.

An even more challenging case for governmental authority is
the one of eco-efficiency, i.e. of 'beating time'. This concerns
global processes of economic and technological change, large-
scale processes of market behaviour and market developments.
To put it euphemistically, it seems very problematic that national
democratic governments elected on short terms would be able to
provide authoritative incentive structures for governance to steer
these global, long-term processes.

Temporally rational ecological governance thus presents two
particularly formidable challenges to governmental authority.
One is time itself. The cross-generational horizon necessitated
when taking sustainable development seriously means that the
much shorter politically relevant time periods make problems for
*continuous* affirmation of governmental authority. Governments
trying to institutionalise as much of their strategy as they can
within the mandate period, in the hope of setting the course
firmly for sustainable development, expose themselves to political
risks. Too much output from government in too short a time may
lead to implementation deficits (see O'Toole, Jr. 2002). This
would lead to questioning of the legitimacy of the strategy and
thus a loss of political authority for government.

Another is the circle of actors in ecological governance; the wider that circle of actors, and the more dependent the government becomes on their long-term co-operation, the more problematic becomes a *consistently* upheld strategy based primarily on governmental authority. The NEOs, and the eco-cycle and eco-efficiency strategies embedded in Sweden's drive towards ecological governance, all rest heavily on the will among firms and business organisations, stakeholder groups and the general public to take on designated roles in ecological governance. A strong flexing of governmental authority would – as the literature on conditions for successful implementation clearly illustrates – have negative repercussions on that will. Therefore, governments may find themselves forced to accommodate the views of those groups, either from the outset with a view to at least get off to a relatively quick start, or gradually as the intricacies and problems of strategy implementation unfold. Either way, there is reason for recycling Hamlet's words: '[E]nterprises of great pith and moment, with this regard their currents turn awry, and lose the name of action'.

The Swedish case is of interest on both accounts. The epitome of Sweden's flirt with ecological modernisation – the LIP programme – is a prime example of how government used its political authority to speed up the country's turn onto the path to a sustainable society. But what comes across from the account of the case is first and foremost that you can go slow by running too fast. The desires for swift implementation of the programme led to strong exercise of central governmental authority. This may have seemed quite logical for strategic political reasons, but the results in terms of sustainable development have not been overly successful.

The other example is the ongoing process of implementing National Environmental Objectives. Intended to run for the next 20 to 25 years, and involving all strands in society, this programme confronts government with the problem of keeping the processes and structures of temporal ecological governance active as well as consistently working towards the agreed objectives. To make all these possibly conflicting interests and actors go along, however, government may have to adapt both the intensity and the pace of the long march towards sustainability. And in retrospect, at the perceived end of that march, it may turn out that governmental authority could have been more consistently affirmed. To quote a conclusion by the Dutch government after three successive rounds of National Environmental Plans with heavy use of negotiated ecological agreements with target groups: Those agreements 'did – in fact – result in increased efficiency, but *in retrospect, the impression is that the stakes could have been set higher*' (NEPP 4 2001:9; italics mine). Negotiations aimed at agreements tolerable to target groups may be good from an autonomy point of view. However, they run the risk of watering down objectives and requirements, and thus dimming the prospects of achieving sustainable development within the time frames originally established.

## On tap or on top? Political vs. scientific authority in ecological governance

Democratic political authority involves the ability to legitimately use (the threat of) coercion by those who are elected to be in authority, or those appointed to exercise authority through some form of delegation of political authority from elected representatives. When we move from politics to science, we are dealing with another type of authority. Scientists have special knowledge that *makes* them *personal* authorities within their fields (see Birch 1993:30). The scientifically grounded views from frontline researchers on what constitutes the most effective 'solutions' to 'problems' of ecologically rational governance are authoritative in this sense.

Issues of sustainable development are particularly marked by uncertainties that call for scientific research, evaluation, and recommendations. At the same time, 'political authority in the modern state is wielded by identifiable and fallible human beings' (Birch 1993:30). Elected politicians in power most often do not possess special knowledge or qualities that lend them personal authority in the sense just outlined. To wield political authority in a system of ecological governance involving experts, technicians as well as target groups thus forces political representatives to come out from behind their veils of ignorance to make sure their decisions are accurate enough to make them legitimate in the eyes of the citizens. One should not forget, however, that they have an asset not available to others, i.e. the legitimate right to exercise authority backed by democratic legitimacy. As Birch puts it, having such right 'is four fifths of the battle' (Birch 1993:30).

Using this advantage to force political decisions could mean losses in legitimacy, particularly if the knowledge base of those decisions becomes so thin as to make the outcomes non-transparent to affected interests and the public. Good governance presupposes adequate policy theories. There is thus a need to strike the balance between the two bases of authority. On normative grounds, the balance should be in favour of governmental authority. Scientific and expert knowledge *is* necessary on issues of ecological governance, but it 'should not be used to authoritatively *determine*, as opposed to *inform*, either the "problem" or the "solution". Once these major issues have been democratically decided, then technical considerations may be appropriate. Experts ought 'to be "on tap, not on top", as it were'. (Barry 1999:200)

What is, then, the evidence from the Swedish case? Has that country been able to craft a system of governance that is ecologically rational in the sense that scientific knowledge and expertise is brought in to support political judgement on how best to use and manage natural resources to achieve sustainable development?

The pattern found seems to support Birch's view of the upper hand of political authority. By using the traditional Swedish process of establishing investigatory commissions with specified terms of reference, the government brings qualified scientific advice and counsel into the policy process, but reserves the last word for political judgement. For a small country like Sweden, this could mean that political authority sometimes has to rely on a very thin base of relevant knowledge. To resolve this, the Swedish government has acted much in accordance with the old Roman device 'Divide et impera'. Gone is the dominance of research directed through programmes written by environmental bureaucrats, and funded by boards closely knit to the Swedish Environmental Protection Agency. Those wielding the ultimate governmental authority nowadays have on tap a wider and more pluralistic community of research and expertise for the decisions on how to organise governance for sustainable development.

This should not be taken to mean that even if it is on top, governmental authority is always inclined to tap all available science and expertise to strike an ecologically rational balance with the authority of knowledge. We have seen from chapter 4 that considerations of political gain (the LIP process) and/or of economic gain (the Hallandsås Tunnel) have led government to shove aside and even ignore well-founded scientific or expert advice that – if heeded – might have been more beneficial to local environments and longer-term sustainable development. It should be noted, though, that the early Swedish process on climate change reveals a very intimate, and quite fruitful interaction between the two types of knowledge. On the other hand, the later stages in the process of ironing out the Swedish position on climate change indicate a move from on top to on tap. Using Birch's metaphor, one could say that political authority in the guise of top-level Ministry officers began to cover 'four fifths of the battle'.

What these findings reflect is that the balance between the authority of knowledge and the authority of political government is always precarious, because of the different sources and charac-teristics of these two types of authority. What this implies for ecologically rational governance is that the balance may have to be somewhat indeterminate, and also changing with the issues at hand. It is clear, however, that both are necessary, given the long-term perspectives and the wide latitude of uncertainty linked to issues of sustainable development. What is equally clear is that longer-term legitimacy of governmental authority in rational ecological governance is dependent on its wise use in two aspects. First, government must secure a dynamic climate for developing scientific knowledge on all aspects of sustainable development. Second, government must ascertain that this knowledge base is wisely tapped into ecological politics. If not, the legitimacy neces-sary for upholding a continued authoritative position in ecological governance, i.e., for democracy to stay on top without the threat or actual use of coercion may dwindle, according as there is evidence that the integrity of the commons is compromised.

## Whose table? Political authority and the integration of ecological concern

Integration of ecological concerns into the structures and processes of governmental agencies is promoted in order to make the governmental role in ecological governance as effective as possible in the pursuit of sustainable development. At the same time, this integration puts new and quite strenuous burdens on the agencies, dedicated as they are towards promoting other sectoral objectives on the basis of quite special, and over a longer term achieved knowledge and expertise. We also know that policy implementation is replete with accounts of great expectations becoming ruins of hope in the mazes of bureaucracy.

The fate of governmental authority in ecological governance is closely linked to that of integration. Enabled to legitimately use (the threat of) coercion through some form of delegation of political authority from elected representatives, agencies and bureaucrats may gain or lose legitimacy – and thus the foundation of authority – depending on how the quality, consistency and transparency of their decisions and actions are conceived by those affected and by the general public. After all, people may reject governmental authority because of 'objections to specific policies pursued by the government' (Birch 1993:36). There is all the more reason to assume that such situations could occur with regard to policies for sustainable development, since these policies will most probably include measures and outcomes that are re-distributive in relation to the present relationship between governmental policies and different societal interests.

This problem of authority makes itself felt in at least two ways. One is internal. Will the environmental concerns be integrated in such a way as to actually have an impact on the decisions of different sectoral agencies? That is, will a specific agency's decisions reflect an apprehension of these concerns that render them legitimate in the eyes of the affected interests and the general public? The other is external. It concerns how conflicting perspectives on policy 'privilege' are reconciled to allow for both individual agencies and the governmental apparatus at large to appear to speak with one voice on matters of ecologically sustainable development. At issue is the prevention of situations where governmental authority dwindles because agencies discredit the legitimacy of government's drive for sustainable development through actions revealing a 'not my table'-attitude towards environmental concerns.

Furthermore, governmental authority may become diffused as an effect of target group participation in policy implementation.

Many measures presuppose that non-governmental actors – business, producers in industry and agriculture – perform roles that might otherwise have been within the realm of public bureaucracies. As evidenced in so many other cases, it is perfectly possible that ecological governance may also give rise to issue networks, policy communities that are able to adapt policy measures to the options acceptable and the capacities available to them as actual implementers of public policy (see Daugbjerg 1998). This may cause losses of legitimacy for those measures, and thus ultimately losses in governmental authority in ecological governance.

How has governmental authority fared in the Swedish efforts to integrate ecological concern into sectoral policies and agencies? The account in Chapter 5 indicates that sectoral policies are nowadays always integrating the 'common cause' of sustainable development. This sectoral integration means that 'economic and other considerations are interwoven with ecological concern in planning and decision-making'. Agencies with specific sectoral responsibilities thus have to 'integrate ecological concerns and resource management in their actions and promote work towards ecological sustainability within their whole sector' (Cabinet Bill 2001/02:172, p. 106). The continuous Greening of Agencies Programme involves 'common yardsticks' of green performance, and 'common purses' in the form of green procurement and green tender programmes.

The annual reports of the agencies reveal a preparedness to observe and implement the new ecological responsibilities bestowed upon them by government. However, the duty to mix ecological with economic and other considerations might lead to difficulties. Ultimately, conflicts of interest may occur both within the agency and among sectoral actors. Does government succeed in avoiding situations where agencies with green sectoral responsibilities tend to 'pass the buck' from their tables, i.e., is government effective in authoritatively asserting 'where the buck stops'?

My tentative answer to this question is yes. The Swedish national government has at its disposal an institutionalised capacity to make sure not only that agencies take their ecological responsibilities seriously, but also that there is a balancing of ecological and other concerns compatible with centrally determined priorities. The historically developed mix of legal, economic and other incentives and checks is also actually used to make the infusion of ecological concern effective and durable. The Letters of Regulation attached to budget allocations to the agencies have a key role here, in particular since the administrative culture is traditionally very much geared towards abiding by these detailed instructions from government.

Still, integration may cause problems for governmental authority in ecological governance on two accounts. One concerns the relationship between central and local government. Since Sweden's municipal governments enjoy far-reaching self-determination in taxation and – particularly crucial here – physical planning, questions may arise about which governmental table the buck should stop at. If demands for locally determined ecological management are not adequately dealt with, or if local ecological activities seem to count for little (as experienced in the clash of principles of the LIP and LA 21 programmes), losses of legitimacy may occur, thus affecting governmental authority across levels of governance. The other problem concerns the legitimacy of central government in the governance for sustainable development. The prestige put into the long-term programme for 'Sustainable Sweden' makes it extremely important that the processes and measures infused by government into ecological governance prove successful. If they do not, the blame will particularly fall on national government, which may lead to losses in the legitimacy of that programme.

## No trespassing? Political authority and individual autonomy in ecological governance

The question of how we should govern ourselves so as to value democracy and individual autonomy and still retain the integrity of the commons directs our attention to three things. First, 'to govern ourselves' refers to 'governing' and 'governance'. The concept of governance traditionally connotes the 'act or process of governing', but has nowadays come to comprise all the mechanisms and instruments that can be used to direct social development in directions reflecting the authoritative will of the community (see Lafferty 2002). Second, such an authoritative will here concerns the quest for changing society towards ecologically sustainable development. Governance should be ecologically rational in its use of mechanisms and instruments to retain the integrity of the commons. Third, the 'how' directs our attention to how governmental authority could be exercised in such ecological governance. To gain legitimacy, government must act within limits set by the values of democracy and individual autonomy.

But is it possible to lay down precise limits for the 'enclosure' around individual autonomy necessary to secure a democratically legitimate exercise of governmental authority? This is particularly relevant for ecological governance in the pursuit of sustainable development, literally concerned as it is with the survival of the commons, without which any such enclosures would be impossible as well as void of meaning.

Arguably, the limits to governmental authority cannot be laid out in some purely 'physical' fashion. What governmental authority can be used to achieve is – as we have repeatedly pointed out – dependent on what those subjected to that authority *judge* as legitimate, even in the face of formal democratic rights and duties. Governments in liberal democracies use their authority to promote certain objectives, most often by way of providing opportunities for citizens to choose and enjoy the good life. But while this may become the case for some, one must not forget that inherent in that exercise is the potential restriction on others' freedom of action and/or expression. These are central aspects of *democratically* legitimate governance. If government goes far in promoting *ecologically* rational governance, it may restrict one part of the good life at the expense of another (see Raphael 1990:74 ff.).

In line with this, we early on argued that in democratic ecological governance, government should steer with 'minimum coercion and maximum consent'. But this balance is extremely precarious. Valuing democracy and individual autonomy very highly might compromise the integrity of the commons, and the opposite may lead to losses of democratic legitimacy. As I have argued elsewhere, the ecological state should appear as 'a green fist in a velvet glove' (Lundqvist 2001b).

What, then, are the conclusions from the Swedish experience to date? The traditionally generous formal 'enclosures' around individual autonomy and individual rights have actually been widened. The rights of access and information make Swedish citizens privileged in comparison to those of many other countries.

Legal standing in environmentally related decision-making is provided to wider circles and in more cases. On this score, it would thus seem as if the national government has used its authority to promote individual rights and freedoms of action and expression within the policies for sustainable development.

When we turn to the exercise of those freedoms, i.e., actual public participation in the emerging structure of ecological governance, the picture becomes more shaded. True enough, the broad public participation in the Local Agenda 21 process has rightfully earned Sweden a favourable record in comparison with many other countries. It is also true that by way of participating in NGOs or other interest organisations, Swedish citizens have access to the process of policy-making, e.g., in the commissions and during the *remiss* process. They may thus be able to influence how governmental authority should be used to achieve sustainable development. And it is furthermore true that in the 'New Environmental Work' envisaged by national government, public participation is foreseen as a vehicle for successful implementation of strategies for sustainability.

There are, however, also tendencies for public participation to become an icon, or a symbol, in the actual pursuit of ecological governance. When central government pushed its LIP programme, municipal governments do not seem to have consciously used the potential for participation developed in the LA 21 process. In the central policy documents outlining in detail the strategies for ecological governance over the next two decades, 'New Environmental Work' takes on a different meaning. Government will use – and share – its authority to promote sustainable development in co-operation with such organised interests as business and producers in industry and agriculture. We find that members of the public are more frequently addressed as customers and consumers in the market place than in their capacity as citizens in a polity.

We thus see two patterns here. There is a generous formal enclosure protecting citizen freedom of action and expression. But there is also a tendency not to fully use this potential for democratic input from the citizens into the actual future protection of the integrity of the commons. To reuse the metaphor on the role of scientists in ecological governance, citizens are not 'on tap', as it were. This peculiar Swedish mix of governmental authority and individual autonomy has deep roots in the development of both democracy and the welfare state. There is a long-standing consensual political culture in which highly *organised interests* play a central role in public policy-making as 'caretakers' of different aspects of the good life. This has made it possible to proceed with maximum consent and minimum coercion *without* lively individual citizen participation.

But should not citizens as autonomous individuals be 'on top' in *democratic* ecological governance? In the representative democratic sense they of course are. But the deliberative recipe of 'simply increasing the participation of citizens in democratic decision-making is no guarantee that they will act responsibly, motivated by concern for the common ecological good'. What that good is, and what does or does not lead to ecologically sustainable development, is too surrounded by extreme uncertainty to easily lend itself to definition through popular majority vote. What is important in terms of participation is first and foremost 'the possibility of *transforming* unecological preferences in the light of debate' (Barry 1999:232). It is above all for such reasons that the balance between authority and autonomy in Swedish ecological governance may have to be reconsidered as the cross-generational striving for sustainable development proceeds in the years to come.

# 8
# Straddling the fence: on the possibility of sustainability and democracy in advanced industrial nations

At the heart of this study of Sweden and its efforts to create structures and processes for ecologically rational governance has been the political dilemma posed by sustainable development. Taking as my point of departure the normative question of 'How are we to govern ourselves so as to value democracy and individual autonomy and still retain the integrity of the commons?' and by measuring the empirical evidence of Sweden's ecological reforms against several criteria for rationally ecological governance, I have sought to answer the following question: *To what extent do policy measures taken in Sweden to achieve ecologically sustainable development shape and/or rearrange the structures and processes of governance in such a way that the collective outcome is ecologically rational* and *democratically acceptable?*

The choice of Sweden as the single case for an empirical study of the compatibility of democratic and ecological governance was made on mainly two grounds. One was consciously *heuristic*; Sweden is viewed in recent scholarly debate as a forerunner on matters of environmental and ecological policy, and its launching of the programme for 'Sustainable Sweden' seemed to corroborate that view. If any country has come anywhere near meeting the criteria for ecologically rational government, Sweden might be that country. Given the evidence laid out in the preceding chapters, what remains to be assessed here is whether this is actually the case. The other was concern for *cumulativity*; much has been written on how ecological governance or an ecological state should be designed and function, as well as on the pros and cons of the probability for such governance to emerge. However, there is not a whole lot of empirical research on whether and how such governance is actually working. The question, then, is how the evidence from the empirical 'front' case of Sweden squares with recent scholarly statements on governance for sustainable development, and how this might influence the current discourse.

Clearly, much of the Swedish strategy for a 'sustainable society' is still in the making. Still, enough has been done to (a) warrant some conclusions as to the prospects for *ecologically rational* governance; (b) address some salient issues for *democratic* ecological governance, and (c) outline some crucial aspects of *governance* as a conceptual framework for studying how societies try to solve their relationships to the natural environment. This will be done in a two-pronged way. First, I summarise and evaluate the Swedish case by juxtaposing the empirical evidence presented in the previous chapters with the general criteria for ecologically rational governance presented in the first part of Chapter 1.

Second, I confront the Swedish case with arguments put forth in recent comparative studies of environmental politics and policies for sustainable development. One line of argument concerns the possibility for democracies in advanced industrial states to actually get over the fence to the greener side, i.e., to organise for *sustainability*. The editors of *Governance and Environment in Western Europe* argue that democratically elected politicians are locked into the logic of competition in global markets. The need to secure continued economic growth and social welfare for the citizen forces them to secure hegemony for the strategy of ecological modernisation. This fencing in of the discourse makes environmental policy fully compatible with the logic of global market competition, thus most probably blocking the move towards rational ecological governance (Jansen, Osland and Hanf 1998:292 ff., 313 ff.). Another view is found in *Implementing Sustainable Development – Strategies and Initiatives in High Consumption Societies*. Building on the different national reports, the editors of that volume conclude that the expanded normative conceptual scope of sustainable development *has* been taken seriously and that governments – at least among the 'enthusiastic' states – are committed to 'carrying forward and deepening the quest for "sustainability"', thus going beyond the strategy of ecological modernisation (Lafferty and Meadowcroft 2001b:454 ff.).

Another line of argument deals with the *democratic* aspect of ecological governance. In *Environmental Governance in Europe. An Ever Closer Ecological Union?* the authors argue that the models for achieving ecological governance within the European Union actually come a long way in bringing about such a union. At the same time, the procedures by which this is done – governmental negotiations to find contingent majorities, Commission initiatives, little input or participation from the European Parliament, etc. – point to a democratic deficit (Weale et al. 2000). Drawing on that discussion, I analyse whether such 'EU-like' elements of the Swedish strategy as the NEO implementation process can sustainably uphold the criteria for autonomy and democracy that we have here defined as part and parcel of ecologically rational governance.

### Straddling the fence; Sweden on the move towards ecologically rational governance

As the logic of ecological rationality has been defined throughout this book, the pursuit of sustainability is normatively constrained by the value of democracy and individual freedom and autonomy. To enable conclusions about the extent to which Sweden is approaching ecologically rational governance, four *normative*, and ideal-type set of criteria for ecologically rational governance have guided the analysis:

- Ecologically rational governance is adapted to ecologically relevant boundaries.
- Ecologically rational governance is adapted to natural eco-cycles and to the safeguarding of inter-generational equality without sacrificing norms of socio-economic justice embraced by the present welfare state.
- Ecologically rational governance has institutional capacities to interpret and effectively transform scientific sustainability-directed arguments into integrated and collectively binding policies and decisions legitimised by representative democratic government.
- Ecologically rational governance effectively brings socio-economic activities within the scale of the ecological resource base with minimum coercion and maximum consent and without fettering initiatives conducive to efficient resource use.

As for *spatial* rationality, we have first of all found that there are changes occurring toward units based on nature-given rather than man-made borders. The remarkable thing here is that it is an external factor – the EU Water Directive – that seems to be the prime mover towards spatial reforms of the Swedish administration, on the basis of the catchment concept. However, there are also signs that such rationality is not easily implemented. Even in areas where such reforms are particularly called for, such as climate change, old administrative fences are still standing and directing the path. To take just one example, the 2002–04 national subsidy programme for local climate measures is primarily following municipal boundaries. Concerns for experience, expertise and effectiveness still speak very strongly in favour of minimal administrative changes and against dramatic societal reorganisation.

With respect to *temporal* ecological rationality, it is remarkable that the democratic political system in Sweden has managed to commit itself to a time frame for ecological governance that stretches as far as one generation into the future. Furthermore, there are precise timetables for most of the first decade in terms of what should be achieved when and by whom. Admittedly, many of the details are still to be worked out together with target groups and affected interests. This leaves room for compromises that could detract somewhat from the projected strategies and achievements. At the same time, the long process leading to these time tables may have created a sense of commitment among involved actors and interests that can not be broken without incurring considerable social costs in terms of trust and reciprocity. Future developments are furthermore dependent on a steady flow of reliable, complementary and yet critical knowledge on progress as well as on new or unsolved problems. The eternally uneasy relation between authority based on scientific knowledge and authority based on political legitimacy will thus continue to be a crucial issue for ecologically rational governance.

Governmental bureaucracies at all levels will in all likelihood continue to occupy a central position in ecological governance. It is thus vital that they can continuously watch and take care of the ecological dimension of sustainable development. The Swedish case provides valuable insight on how *integration* of ecological concern can reach all corners of the public sector. The 'sectoral responsibility' mechanisms established over the last few years – above discussed as common 'cause', 'yardstick', 'account' and 'purse' – all impose on different bureaucratic units a duty to constantly observe and assess the ecological consequences of their actions, and act to protect ecological values under the Environmental Code and the NEO programme. It is important to note that this imposition is based on central government's willingness to continuously use the means at its disposal to authoritatively enforce its strategies for sustainable development.

The question that emerges here is why this infusion of ecological concern into sectoral administrations seems to have been so relatively easy to achieve in Sweden. Earlier studies of environmental politics in developed countries contend that long-term strategies for sustainable development cannot be launched without highly developed systemic capacities for co-ordination and direction (see Jänicke 1997). As an advanced industrial nation, Sweden possesses both the economic as well as the scientific and organisational capacity necessary for pursuing innovative strategies for ecological governance. One should particularly emphasise the comparative advantage of a unitary political system in formulating and pursuing coherent policies; the number of possible veto points within such a system is low compared to federal systems.

However, structural systemic characteristics and capacities do not suffice as an explanation. They may bring innovation and effectiveness to strategies for sustainable development but at the same time score low on legitimacy. To achieve both effectiveness and legitimacy, explicit, orderly and continuous involvement of target groups in implementation is an important factor. Such involvement seems to warrant specific preconditions in terms of political culture (see Jänicke 1997). Both the introduction and the success of such involvement are dependent on collective memories on both sides of the public-private divide. In political systems where relations between government and target groups have historically developed through processes of consensus, the political culture is much more favourable to solutions building on high degrees of target group involvement.

Sweden's political culture has traditionally built firmly on consensus and cooperation. The development of the post-war welfare state, metaphorically referred to as the 'People's Home',

was in large measure achieved through neo-corporatist co-operation between the state and large organised interests (Rothstein
1992; see also Tilton 1990:125 ff.). The picture of the 'Green
People's Home' can be seen as instrumental in getting acceptance
for the further 'consensualisation' of environmental politics that
is in effect embedded in the involvement of well-organised target
groups in implementation of the Swedish strategy for solving all
major environmental problems 'within one generation'. This
involvement all the way from investigatory Commissions to the
operationalisation of sectoral, regional and local environmental
quality objectives no doubt helps in gaining acceptance and legitimacy for measures taken within ecological governance.

This brings us up close to the *democratic* aspects of ecological
governance. We have found that while providing a comparatively
generous enclosure of individual autonomy in terms of rights of
access and information, the emerging Swedish system of ecological governance is more keen on *organisational* than on *citizen*
participation. True enough, there are provisions for public hearings during the decision-making process, and there was at first
quite lively public participation in Local Agenda 21 activities.
However, other studies strongly suggest that in the formally very
open process of policy-making, well-organised special interests
tend to gain favoured positions thanks to their superior resources
compared to individual citizens and loosely formed action groups
(Uhrwing 2001). Furthermore, we have interpreted the envisioned
'new environmental work' of implementing ecologically sustainable development, e.g., through the NEOs, as treating members of
the public more as members of interest organisations or market-
based actors reacting to stimuli from industry and business than
as citizens engaging in collective ecological management.

What we have here is a rather clear-cut example of path
dependence. As was just said, the 'Swedish model' that developed
when Sweden was building the social welfare state involved close
co-operation between the democratic and administrative organs
of the state on the one hand, and organised social and economic
interests on the other. The post-war Swedish politics aiming at
sustainable social welfare and economic growth is best characterised as a search for collectivist and corporatist rather than
individualistic and pluralistic processes and solutions. When the
Social-Democratic government evoked the vision of a 'Green

People's Home' to gain acceptance for its LIP programme of ecological modernisation, it deliberately used this quite successful historic process to legitimise this way of organising the society-nature relationship. The historically developed organisation of social governance thus stakes out, but also fences in, the path for the broader future-oriented processes in ecological governance. It is part of a cluster of factors that bias a country 'in a more supportive direction for sustainable development' (see Lafferty and Meadowcroft 2000b:424).

On balance, then, how far has Sweden come towards ecologically rational governance? As for the spatial dimension, it is fair to say that there *are* moves to change man-made jurisdictional boundaries and adapt to scales compatible with the boundaries of natural ecosystems. In temporal terms, Sweden already scores high in adapting socio-economic processes to natural eco-cycles. The process of implementing the National Environmental Objectives is quite unique. It represents the so far most pronounced commitment of present and future generations to intergenerational equality, at the same time as it safeguards the norms of socio-economic justice of the present welfare state. Sweden has built up, and continues to develop institutional capacities for interpreting and transforming scientific sustainability-directed arguments into integrated measures for sustainable development. Those measures are legitimised and made collectively binding through decisions in democratically elected bodies.

One should not, however, hasten to conclude that Sweden is nearly over to the other greener side of the fence. There are still some hurdles in the way. We have seen that validated scientific and expert arguments are not always given attention in policy decisions and resource management. And the core problem of ecological governance is still there; do the steps taken so far provide for both autonomy and sustainability? The NEO strategy can be interpreted as an effort to bring about ecologically sustainable development with minimum coercion and maximum consent, and without fettering initiatives conducive to economically effective resource utilisation. It is important to note the path dependency of that strategy. The 'corporatist' governance through co-operation between national government and organised interests that helped build the social welfare state is now envisaged as the vehicle also for building the sustainable society.

The real test is whether this political strategy really could effectively bring socio-economic activities within the scales of the ecological resource base. As already said, this is too early to tell. But as a 'forerunner' and an 'enthusiast' with respect to issues of sustainable development, Sweden is now straddling the fence to get over to the greener side. The experience of Sweden can thus provide important stimuli to the scholarly debate on the problems and possibilities for ecological governance to achieve sustainability while upholding individual autonomy, public participation and democracy. To assess the usefulness of the Swedish case for future comparative studies, let us therefore confront it with some recent inputs into the comparative study of policies for environmental quality and ecologically sustainable development.

### Forever fenced in? The prospects of governance for sustainability in advanced industrial countries

The editors of *Governance and Environment in Western Europe* present a grim view of the possibilities for democratically elected politicians in capitalist nations to opt for ecologically rational governance. In order to win elections, they have to establish a record of delivering the economic and social welfare citizens aspire to. Therefore, the political leadership has to make the national economy stable and competitive, so that tax income increases enough to pay for continued economic and social welfare for the citizenry. To take seriously the arguments made by biologists and ecologists for radical structural changes could seriously threaten the national economy and thus the deliverance capacity of the political leadership. In short, political leaders in democratic and industrialised nations are fenced in by the logic of competition in global markets.

Consequently, political leaders have to find ways of handling the ecological problematic in ways compatible with the market logic. The solution, argue the volume editors, is to secure discursive and political hegemony for the strategy of ecological modernisation. Policy-makers seek to convince key socio-economic interests that environmental protection can be turned into a 'positive-sum game' by providing incentives that help create new eco-technological markets. In this way, industry finds anticipatory development of green technology profitable, and the politicians can preach 'green growth'. Indeed, the editors conclude that the 'strategy of ecological modernisation is not only compatible with, but may even be seen as part of the overriding project of the ruling policy elites to expand the logic of the institutional order of the market.' (Jansen, Osland and Hanf 1998:313 ff.; quote from p. 318).

The editors of *Implementing Sustainable Development – Strategies and Initiatives in High Consumption Societies* disagree with 'the triumph of this sort of eco-modernist perspective'. Instead, the globally expanded commitment to sustainable development functions as a normative external force that makes governments, particularly in the 'enthusiastic' states, incorporate sustainable development 'as a high-profile, officially sanctioned standard, against which environment and development initiatives can be weighed.' This is furthermore 'associated with innovation in the environmental policy domain, and governments remain formally committed to carrying forward and deepening the quest for "sustainability"' (Lafferty and Meadowcroft 2001b:454 f.).

This should not, however, be taken to mean that sustainable development is achieving the kind of unilateral discursive and policy hegemony ascribed to ecological modernisation by Jansen et al. First of all, the sustainable development discourse leaves more open the *scope* of institutional reform, such as internalisation and participation. The steps taken even by forerunner states are best seen as 'pragmatic efforts at implementation ... to match the ambitious' language of the UNCED programme. Second, the engagement in sustainable development has had a more pluralist character. But the direction of the movement is clear: 'True sustainable development has been broadly accepted as a legitimate goal – and this has a determinate normative and policy content' to move the governance of the society-environment relationship beyond the strategy of ecological modernisation (Lafferty and Meadowcroft 2000b:452 f.).

To sum up: The 'eco-modernist' interpretation encloses nations within the parameters drawn up by the competitive market logic. It is politically impossible for the individual country to proceed beyond ecological modernisation. The 'sustainabilist' interpretation views nations as politically and morally committed to a globally acknowledged agenda to achieve economically, socially and ecologically sustainable development. This prods the individual country to proceed beyond present policies to bring about ecologically rational governance.

Sweden presents a critical case for testing the eco-modernist view. It is a highly industrialised state, heavily dependent on its competitiveness in international markets for economic stability and resource mobilisation for the social welfare state. At the same time, it has a record of being a forerunner and enthusiast in the global and regional search for sustainable development. In order to systematise this assessment, some core characteristics of ecological modernisation and sustainable development identified in recent discourse are outlined in Table 8.1.

**Table 8.1** *Ecological modernisation and sustainable developments: a comparison of core elements*

| Problem/issue/ dimension/ relationship | Major approach/views of | |
|---|---|---|
| | *Ecological modernisation* | *Sustainable development* |
| Geographical dimension | Primarily national, 'enclosure' within traditional boundaries | Global and national, 'commons' define appropriate areas |
| Character of environmental problem | Sectoral, 'medial' problems possible to control and contain | Long-term, global, cross sectoral high-consequence- risk potential |
| Economy/environment relationship | Growth can be 'greened' through technological development | Shifts in pros/cons patterns necessary, changes in quality of growth through decoupling |
| Policy instruments | Mainly economic, but also regulatory incentives for green technology; use of voluntary agreements | Regulatory action a necessary base for all other measures |
| Social dimension | Win-win solutions possible, thus implying harmony among interests | Conflicts unavoidable, distributive justice must be part of ecological measures |
| Institutional/ Administrative dimension | Existing institutions can handle the problems through effective internalisation | Significant modifications are called for, and structural changes may be needed |

*Source:* Builds on Jansen et al. 1998; Langhelle 2000; Lafferty and Meadowcroft 2000b

There are several aspects of the Swedish case that might first tempt us to conclude that what has actually been achieved is nothing more than a 'Swedish model' of ecological modernisation. The very first speech of the newly elected leader of the governing Social Democratic Party in 1996 struck that note. Win-win solutions were seen as possible, growth could be greened, and the perspective of *national* gain from such a strategy was evident. The Local Investment Programmes introduced in 1997 certainly built on the possibilities to achieve green growth and greening of technology. The programmes for eco-cycling introduced in the early 1990s and later expanded, are in many cases built on utilising the commercial potentials of recycling and reusing goods and materials. These measures, as well as the quest for increased eco-efficiency, and the early introduction and subsequent expansion of green taxation could all be interpreted as fully within the logic of competitive markets.

However, the evidence indicating that Sweden has proceeded beyond ecological modernisation is strong. The use of sustainable development as both a valid concept and a long-term objective for environmental policy can be found as early as around 1990 in the major governmental bills. This was followed by a stream of governmental bills and parliamentary decisions establishing sustainable development as the overarching objective across traditional societal sectors from about 1996 on. The Cabinet's reports to Parliament on the state of the environment shifted from discussing sectoral and/or medial pollution problems to outlining measures for sustainable development within and across such boundaries. There was a comprehensive integration of all resource-related legislation into one major code, building explicitly on the objectives and principles contained in sustainable development, thus providing strong legal ground for all other environmental measures. Sweden's swift introduction and development of Agenda 21 activities after the Rio summit also points in the same direction.

Furthermore, the spatial, temporal and social justice aspects of sustainable development are in clear evidence in the Swedish case. Several of the opening arguments of the Cabinet Bill on National Environmental Objectives, passed by Parliament in 2001 imply that Sweden has indeed incorporated sustainable development as a high-profile, officially sanctioned standard against which environment and development initiatives can be weighed. After having quoted the Brundtland Commission's definition of sustainable development, the Cabinet states that

Work for the environment must be seen in a dynamic and global perspective. Experience shows the difficulty in foreseeing future environmental problems. (Thus) the precautionary principle, as expressed in the Environmental Code, should have precedence ... an ecologically sustainable development in one part of the world cannot be had at the expense of environmental and social welfare in some other part. (Cabinet Bill 2000/01:130, p. 11 f.)

Now, could not all this be dismissed as nothing but some rattling at the fences, 'a rhetorical cover for a policy stance that in practice looks much more like "ecological modernisation"' (Lafferty and Meadowcroft 2000*b*:451)? The most crucial part of assessing the Swedish case in this respect is the NEO process of management by objectives. Although founded on the principles and rules of the Environmental Code, and despite its long-term, cross-generational perspective on social justice and sustainable development, it depicts many of the trappings of ecological modernisation. The 15 National Environmental Objectives are very broad in character. Their operationalisation into sectoral, regional and local targets with specified deadlines for achievement is subjected to negotiations and agreements among authorities and important producer and consumer interests in various socio-economic sectors.

Evidently, there is a possibility that issues of market competitiveness might enter this process, and lead to a watering down of the NEOs to make them compatible with that logic. However, there are several nuts and bolts installed into the process to keep it on track towards solving the major environmental problems within one generation. The interim targets are formulated by Parliament, thus formally binding and committing agencies and actors further down the line that are involved in the process of developing goals and targets to carry forward and deepen the quest for 'sustainability'. Having invested so much in the NEO process, it is most probable that agencies and authorities also come to feel morally bound to use sustainability as the common yardstick for their work.

My conclusion is that the direction of the Swedish movement is clear: 'True sustainable development has been broadly accepted as a legitimate goal – and this has a determinate normative and policy content'. (see Lafferty and Meadowcroft 2000b:452 f.) The Swedish example shows beyond doubt that it *is* possible for advanced industrial nations to go beyond ecological modernisation and commit future policy-making and implementation to the full range of sustainability issues. At the same time, it shows that the ways and methods for getting further can be both varied and as yet indeterminate in terms of outcome. A most interesting aspect of Sweden's movement towards sustainability is that so much of future 'environmental work' (the Cabinet's term) is to be entrenched in the governmental bureaucracy and their negotiations with affected organised interests to further elaborate these objectives. Within the NEO process of management by objectives, present bureaucrats actually uphold the function as 'ombudsmen' for future generations. If it turns out that the sub-goals and targets come to reflect judgements of administrative feasibility and implementability as much as considerations of levels and conditions necessary for sustainable development, this would affect the autonomy of future generations. We then come up against the ultimate question guiding this study: What are the prospects for autonomy and democracy within multi-level and long-term binding ecologically rational governance aimed at saving the integrity of the commons?

*Getting over in style? The prospects for democracy in ecological governance*
We started out from the normative argument that ecologically rational governance for sustainability must be sought within the limits drawn by democracy and the value of individual autonomy. We assumed that ecologically sustainable development is not possible to achieve without conflicts over how to use or not use scarce resources. There will be winners and losers in that process. The necessary redistribution of resources, positions and power cannot gain political legitimacy if it is not decided upon and implemented through democratic procedures open to public scrutiny and participation.

Sweden's progress towards sustainability has been achieved with a somewhat mixed record in terms of democracy and participation. True enough, there are comparatively generous rights of citizen access to information, policy-making and implementation of issues related to the management and quality of natural resources. Furthermore, Sweden has been at the leading edge in engaging citizens in Local Agenda 21 activities. It is equally true, however, that much of the future 'new environmental work' seems to be copied from the corporatist arrangements evolving when building the social welfare state. A dominant strategy is for government to seek consensus and agreements with established and securely entrenched organised interests, while the role of individuals is to a considerable extent seen as that of customer and consumer reacting to carefully orchestrated policy incentives and market signals. It is furthermore true that the projected water management organisation to be introduced in order to implement the EU Framework Water Directive involves a centralisation of power and authority at levels above the present local and regional ones in Sweden.

Could it be that *effective* governance for sustainable development implies some basic problems or conflicts with *democracy*? As pointed out in the analysis of the spatial dimension (see Chapter 2), an ecologically desirable adaptation to natural scales means that ecological governance is inherently multi-level in character. We end up with a system of nested enterprises, all the way from 'super-local' eco-system management units to global regimes for such gigantic problems as climate change. This of course also means that the issue of what is the 'appropriate' distribution of authority, participation and influence becomes crucial if we want both effective and democratic ecological governance.

At issue, then, is what standard should be applied to determine what is appropriate. When the standard of *functional effectiveness* is applied, the logic may easily become one of centralisation. The argument is two-pronged. Most problems facing rational ecological governance – such as diffuse pollution affecting ecosystems over long distances, and climate change – are such that their effects and consequences cannot be contained and handled at the level of origin. Their solution demands treatment at national and often international levels. This is further accentuated by the increasing demands for internationally and globally valid common regulations and conditions for economic activities. Ecologically motivated measures to save, protect and manage natural resources and environmental quality should thus as far as possible be common across not only regional but also international political and administrative boundaries.

Applying the principle of functional effectiveness to distribute authority, participation and influence will have repercussions for democracy. There are different constituencies at different scales, meaning that democratic participation is faced with differing opportunities and obstacles at each level. The further up authority is moved for the sake of functional effectiveness, the more difficult it may be for ecological governance to actually be rational in the sense of valuing individual autonomy and democracy. The principle of *subsidiarity* could be applied here. As I interpret this principle, it is applicable within *any* multi-level system of governance. In its most general form, it means that authority to take action should be allocated to the level where the objectives of a given policy can be sufficiently achieved. The application of subsidiarity would then be a decentralising force. If lower levels can sufficiently handle an issue related to ecological governance, then that is where authority should be allocated. Needless to say, this will have positive implications for the possibility of citizen and interest participation in governance (see Weale et al. 2000:494).

It is interesting here to compare the patterns of ecological governance we have found in Sweden to those of the European Union. The authors of a recent study of EU environmental policy conclude that the complex EU system of ecological governance has gained capacity to make significant choices for the European environment. Environmental concern has moved from obscurity to centre stage in EU very much because the strive to widen and consolidate the single market has made member states see it as functionally effective to support common approaches and measures to ecological problems, as much as or more than opting for subsidiarity as the guiding principle. However, the procedures by which this centralisation has come about – government level negotiations to find contingent majorities, Commission initiatives, little input or participation from the European Parliament, etc. – are such that environmental issues have not been subjected to political competition and are characterised by low democratic accountability. They may thus not fully 'approximate the interest of the citizens of Europe' (Weale et al. 2000:437, 440).

It seems as if both subsidiarity and functional effectiveness have been applied as guiding principles in the emerging system of ecological governance in Sweden. There has been some scaling down of authority to local government. There was an initial and strong move to incorporate citizens in the Local Agenda 21 activities. There will be moves to arrange new entities at the local and 'super-local' level with respect to the management of ecosystems such as small water catchments. And there is, as we have seen, a comparatively generous and liberal formal regulation of citizen access to the public policy process.

Yet, important as these signs of subsidiarity may be for the democratic and participatory character of ecological governance, there are very strong indications of functional effectiveness as a major principle for distributing authority, participation and opportunities to influence such governance. The LIP process involved traditional local and business elites, but was exceptionally centralised in that the Cabinet itself made the implementing decisions on how to allocate funds. The NEO process builds very much on developing nation-wide targets and deadlines in co-operation with organised sectoral – read producer – interests.

From the perspective of functional effectiveness, these patterns of incorporating crucial socio-economic interests in processes to reach nation-wide agreements on measures could be seen as efforts to secure progress towards sustainability. However, problems of democratic accountability and legitimacy arise if ecological governance comes to involve specific channels for compromise and accommodation between government and organised sectoral interests. As was seen from the recent study of organised interests' access to the policy process in Sweden, the stages to which citizens have access provide mostly for symbolic participation, whereas the most resourceful organised interests can wage real influence.

It would seem as if both the EU and the Swedish processes tend to follow a similar pattern. There is a push upward in terms of the levels and scales where final decisions are taken, as well as where and by whom participation and influence is exercised. This could spell difficulties for how to get over to the greener side in a democratically acceptable style, i.e., through an open political process with lively public participation and rich possibilities to hold those involved accountable. In a wider perspective, the similarities of the two processes point to a feature of modern advanced societies that further studies of ecological governance must address, i.e., the fact that they are so highly and thoroughly *organised*.

## Governing the commons; negotiated ecological governance in modern highly organised societies

This high degree of organisation colours the ultimate lessons from Sweden's struggle towards ecologically rational governance. On the side of sustainability, Sweden's experience points to the political readiness to incorporate the conceptual framework of sustainable development into the political process, as well as much of the arsenal of measures seen as necessary for its practical implementation. At the same time, we have found that the Swedish governmental efforts to implement sustainable development seem to follow the maxim of minimum coercion and maximum consent; the dominant form for ecological governance is co-operation with organised interests and persuasion of the general public.

While having advantages in terms of sustainability, this governance pattern is also problematic. First, as a co-operative, agreement-seeking and long-term directed strategy, the Swedish NEO (read management by objectives) process may ease the implementation of sustainability measures. However, it may at the same time be based on policies setting the stakes lower than those claimed necessary by those possessing expert knowledge, all because of the value policymakers put on political feasibility and acceptance among target-groups. Second, the co-operative, agreement-seeking and long-term directed NEO strategy is formally based on easy access and rich opportunities for participation, which would speak in favour of democracy in ecological governance. However, the real pattern found in crucial policy-making processes is one of special and resourceful highly organised interests, talking the right 'technocratic' language, and getting further into the corridors of power than citizen and action groups promoting broad societal and value changes.

This latter characteristic seems to be particularly at odds with much of the argument put forth on the relationship between sustainability and democracy in the discourse of green political theory. Ecologically rational governance for sustainability is said to necessitate a new communicative rationality in a discursive democracy characterised by lively citizen involvement (see summarising discussion in Barry 1999:226 ff.). At the risk of sounding somewhat biased, I would argue that many green political theorists have approached this issue almost wholly from an individualistic and pluralistic angle. Their view comes close to classic liberalism. The democratic political system consists of elected representatives and electing citizens with the latter standing in a direct, individual relationship to government. Insofar as there are discussions and examples of organisations in civil society as intermediary aggregators of group interest, they mostly concern associations in a civil society working to protect individuals from both the state and the market, not to positively influence future governance (see Barry 1999:237).

This means that many of the normative designs of governance for sustainable development often tend to neglect, or perhaps better put, wish away the existence in advanced societies of strong socio-economic and other interest organisations. Across all possible expressions of human life we find special interest organisations, actively fighting to influence public policy with whatever resources they have and appearing wherever they can get access to processes of governance seen as relevant to their interests. This further means that *empirical* studies of ecological governance that do not take into account that modern society is thoroughly *organised* are also bound to miss important points. There is also evidence from comparative research implying that industrially advanced countries with high capacities for environmental policymaking and implementation seem to favour 'sophisticated forms of governance based on high public-private interaction instead of command-control regulation or self-regulation' (Enevoldsen 2001:104). To sum up this line of argument, the democratic state in modern advanced societies is increasingly engaged in establishing some form of 'negotiated social governance' with large hierarchically managed organisations (Hirst 2000:20).

This thoroughly organised character of modern advanced societies must thus be given close attention when we analyse how ecological governance is organised to deal with both sustainability and autonomy. Greening the commons to achieve sustainable development in such thoroughly organised modern societies as Sweden does indeed resemble a steeplechase. The commons is criss-crossed by enclosures claimed or defended by strongly organised special interests, often with historically gained status as keepers at the gates to specific natural resources. To prevent these claims from becoming fences that place the greening of society beyond political feasibility, negotiations with those interests have to be carried out, and resulting agreements must be made politically legitimate.

Of central concern, then, is how inherently multi-level ecological governance is organised to allow for interplay between governmental authority and organised interest activities (necessary for the successful implementation of adopted policies) and still preserve the *political* legitimacy and accountability of 'negotiated' ecological governance. Two things are of crucial importance here. First, it must be remembered that not all organisations are as internally democratic as to provide citizens with appropriate opportunities for participation and influence. Second, the democratic government should preserve the ultimate authority and remain the ultimate source of legitimacy for such elaborate division of labour in the greening of the commons.

The most salient lesson from the review of the Swedish case is that it points to both opportunities and conditions for securing the legitimacy of negotiated ecological governance. Founded on a base of broadly co-ordinated regulation, where the Environmental Code covers the full spectrum of the society-environment relationship, the Swedish approach to ecological governance has involved organised interests from all walks of life. This holds all the way from policy formulation and selection of strategies to the implementation of detailed measures all the way down to the ecosystem level. As shown in the preceding chapters, this negotiated form of ecological governance has promoted policy and action beyond ecological modernisation and towards a path of sustainable development.

We have argued that the selection and success of the negotiative approach to ecological governance is very much a matter of path dependence. Organised interests engaged in activities with potentially heavy impact on natural resources and the environment, such as industry, agriculture and transport are historically used to participating in negotiations with government on policy formulation and implementation ever since the building of the social welfare state. This inherited legitimacy of co-operative negotiated governance has both directed the construction, and legitimised the continued process of ecological governance in Sweden. Here, it seems appropriate to return to the 1997 words of Prime Minister Göran Persson when setting the 'Sustainable

Sweden' programme in motion. The Swedish welfare state – the People's Home – was built through 'broad consensus on the conditions for production, increased standards of living, and security for everyone.' In a similar way, he said, '[w]e will realise the vision of a *green* welfare state'.

The attentive reader might object that the negotiated approach could lead to the stakes being set lower than might be necessary for sustainability. After all, the strongest and most resourceful interests involved in negotiating the actual implementation of the NEO strategy of management by objectives are those who stand to lose substantially from a more radical change of values that some deem crucial to 'real' progress towards sustainable development. These interests are also the ones found to get closest to influencing government and the way its authority should be used to direct future developments.

To this it must be said again that it is too early to judge how far negotiated ecological governance will help Sweden in retaining the integrity of the commons. What could be said, however, is that just as no country could get over to the greener grass on the other side alone, no national government could command its people to sustainability. Legitimacy for a unilateral commandeering system of ecologically rational government would be hard to accept in democracies valuing individual autonomy. To this should be added what research on implementation convincingly shows, i.e., that interest participation increases the effectiveness and efficiency of governance.

What *is* the real problem for the latter approach is that the unevenly distributed resources and historically achieved power positions of different affected interests may detract from the legitimacy of negotiated ecological governance. Again, the historic record is an important conditioning factor. The success and legitimacy of negotiated governance are crucially dependent on the degree of trust and reciprocity on both sides of the public-private divide. When such values are part and parcel of the collective memories among actors in negotiated governance, there is a potential for getting over the fence to attain ecologically *rational* governance, i.e., one that *both* values democracy and individual autonomy *and* still retains the integrity of the commons.

# References

## Books and articles

Achterberg, W. (1993) 'Can Liberal Democracy Survive the Environmental Crisis? Sustainability, Liberal Neutrality and Overlapping Consensus', pp. 81–104 in Dobson, A. and Lucardie, P. (eds.), *The Politics of Nature. Explorations in Green Political Theory.* London and New York: Routledge.

Adam, B. (1994) 'Running out of Time: Global Crisis and Human Engagement', pp. 92–112 in Redclift, M. and Benton, T. (eds.), *Social Theory and the Global Environment.* London: Routledge.

Arwidsson, B. (1999) 'Miljömålen, miljöbalken och samhällsplaneringen' (National Environmental Objectives, the Environmental Code, and Physical Planning) *Miljösekvensen* No. 2:8–9.

Auditors of Parliament (Riksdagens Revisorer) (1998/99) *Statligt stöd till lokala investeringsprogram för en ekologiskt hållbar utveckling* (State Grants to Local Investment Programs for Ecologically Sustainable Development). Stockholm: Swedish Parliamentary Record.

Baker, S. (2001) 'Evaluating the Swedish Local Investment Programme: A Comparative, European Perspective', pp. 106–36 in Hanberger, A. et al. *Lokala investeringsprogram – en förstudie inför utvärderingen* (Local Investment Programs – A Preview for the Evaluation). Umeå: Umeå Centre for Evaluation Research, #10.

Barry, J. (1999) *Rethinking Green Politics.* London: Sage.

Berkes, B. and Folke, C. (2000) 'Linking Social and Ecological Systems for Resilience and Sustainability', pp. 1–25 in in Berkes, F. and Folke, C. (eds.), *Linking Social and Ecological Systems. Management Practices and Social Mechanism for Building Resilience.* Oxford: Oxford University Press.

Berry, J., et al. (1998) 'Closing the Gap Between Ecosystem Management and Ecosystem Research', *Policy Sciences* 31:55–80.

Birch, A. (1993) *The Concepts and Theories of Modern Democracy.* London and New York: Routledge.

Board for Sustainable Development of the National Research Council (1999) *Our Common Journey. A Transition to Sustainability.* Washington D.C.: National Academy Press.

Bookchin, M. (1982) *The Ecology of Freedom: The Emergence and Dissolution of Hierarchy.* Palo Alto: Cheshire Books.

Brundin, P. and Eckerberg, K. (1999) *Svenska kommuners arbete med Agenda 21: En enkätundersökning* (Swedish Municipalities and their Work on Agenda 21: A Survey). Stockholm: Svenska kommunförbundet.

Brunsson, K. (1995) *Dubbla budskap – Hur riksdagen och regeringen presenterar sitt budgetarbete* (Double Messages – How the Parliament and the Government Present their Work on the Budget). Stockholm: University of Stockholm, Department of Business Administration.

Brussard, P. F., Reed, J. M. and Tracy, C. F. (1998) 'Ecosystem Management: What is it Really?', *Landscape and Urban Planning* 40:9–20.

Cabinet Bill 1987/88:85 *Miljöpolitiken inför 90-talet* (An Environmental Policy for the 90's). Stockholm: Swedish Parliamentary Record.

Cabinet Bill 1990/91:90 *En god livsmiljö.* (A Good Living Environment). Stockholm: Swedish Parliamentary Record.

Cabinet Bill 1991/92:100 *Förslag till statsbudget för budgetåret 1992/93, Del 15* (State Budget Proposal Fiscal Year 1992/93 part 15). Stockholm: Swedish Parliamentary Record

Cabinet Bill 1991/92:92 *Om utskiftning av löntagarfonderna* (On the Dissolution of the Wage Earner's Funds). Stockholm: Swedish Parliamentary Record.

Cabinet Bill 1992/93:100 *Förslag till statsbudget för budgetåret 1992/93, Del 15* (State Budget Proposal Fiscal Year 1992/93 part 15). Stockholm: Swedish Parliamentary Record.

Cabinet Bill 1992/93:170 *Forskning för kunskap och framsteg* (Research for Knowledge and Progress). Stockholm: Swedish Parliamentary Record.

Cabinet Bill 1992/93:171 *Om forskning i frontlinjen* (Frontline research). Stockholm: Swedish Parliamentary Record.

Cabinet Bill 1992/93:180 *Riktlinjer för en kretsloppsanpassad samhällsutveckling* (Principles for an Ecocycle Adapted Societal Development) Stockholm: Swedish Parliamentary Record.

Cabinet Bill 1992/93:226 *En ny skogspolitik* (A New Forestry Policy). Stockholm: Swedish Parliamentary Record.

Cabinet Bill 1993/94:111 *Med sikte mot hållbar utveckling: genomförandet av besluten vid UNCED* (The Aim is Sustainable Development: Implementing the UNCED Decisions). Stockholm: Swedish Parliamentary Record.

Cabinet Bill 1994/95:230 *Kommunal översiktsplanering enligt plan-och bygglagen m m* (Municipal Overview Planning under the Planning and Building Act). Stockholm: Swedish Parliamentary Record.

Cabinet Bill 1996/97:1 *Förslag till statsbudget för 1997* (Proposed State Budget for 1997). Stockholm: Swedish Parliamentary Record.

Cabinet Bill 1996/97:5 *Forskning och samhälle* (Research and Society), Stockholm: Swedish Parliamentary Record.

Cabinet Bill 1996/97:22 *Statliga stiftelser* (State Foundations). Stockholm: Swedish Parliamentary Record.

Cabinet Bill 1996/97:84 *En uthållig energiförsörjning* (Sustainable Energy Provision). Stockholm: Swedish Parliamentary Record.

Cabinet Bill 1996/97:150 *1997 års ekonomiska vårproposition* (1997 Spring Economic Bill). Stockholm: Swedish Parliamentary Record.

Cabinet Bill 1996/97:172 *Hantering av uttjänta varor i ett ekologiskt hållbart samhälle – ett ansvar för alla* (The Handling of Waste in an Ecologically Sustainable Society – Everyone's Responsibility). Stockholm: Swedish Parliamentary Record.

Cabinet Bill 1997/98:1 *Förslag till statsbudget för 1998, Utgiftsområde 18* (Proposed State Budget for 1998, Spending Area 18). Stockholm: Swedish Parliamentary Record.

Cabinet Bill 1997/98:2 *Hållbart fiske och jordbruk* (Sustainable Fisheries and Agriculture). Stockholm: Swedish Parliamentary Record.

Cabinet Bill 1997/98:3 *Kulturpolitik* (Cultural Policy). Stockholm: Swedish Parliamentary Record.

Cabinet Bill 1997/98:13 *Ekologisk hållbarhet* (Ecological Sustainability). Stockholm: Swedish Parliamentary Record.

Cabinet Bill 1997/98:45 *Miljöbalk, Del 1* (Environmental Code, Part 1). Stockholm: Swedish Parliamentary Record.

Cabinet Bill 1997/98:56 *Transportpolitik för en hållbar utveckling* (Transportation Policy for Sustainable Development) Stockholm: Swedish Parliamentary Record.

Cabinet Bill 1997/98:90 *Lagändringar till följd av miljöbalken* (Legislative Changes Pursuant to the Environmental Code). Stockholm: Swedish Parliamentary Record.

Cabinet Bill 1997/98:119 *Bostadspolitik för uthållig utveckling* (Housing Policy for Sustainable Development). Stockholm: Swedish Parliamentary Record.

Cabinet Bill 1997/98:145 *Svenska miljömål. Miljöpolitik för ett hållbart Sverige* (Swedish National Environmental Objectives. Environmental Policy for A Sustainable Sweden). Stockholm: Swedish Parliamentary Record.

Cabinet Bill 1997/98:150 *1998 års ekonomiska vårproposition*

224                                                      *References*

*Utgiftsområde 18* (1998 Spring Economic Bill Spending Area 18). Stockholm: Swedish Parliamentary Record.

Cabinet Bill 1999/2000:81 *Forskning för framtiden – en ny organisation för forskningsfinansiering* (Research for the Future – a New Organisation for Research Funding). Stockholm: Swedish Parliamentary Record.

Cabinet Bill 2000/01:1 *Budgetproposition för 2001 Utgiftsområde 20* (Budget Proposal for 2001, Spending Area 20). Stockholm: Swedish Parliamentary Record.

Cabinet Bill 2000/01:3 *Forskning och förnyelse* (Research and Innovation). Stockholm: Swedish Parliamentary Record.

Cabinet Bill 2000/01:130 *Svenska miljömål – delmål och åtgärdsstrategier* (Swedish National Environmental Objectives – Targets and Strategies for Action). Stockholm: Swedish Parliamentary Record.

Cabinet Bill 2001/02:100 *2002 års ekonomiska vårproposition* (The 2002 Spring Economic Bill). Stockholm: Swedish Parliamentary Record.

Cabinet Bill 2001/02:172 *Nationell strategi för hållbar utveckling* (National Strategy for Sustainable Develoment). Stockholm: Swedish Parliamentary Record.

Cabinet Bill 2001/02:80 *Demokrati för det nya seklet* (Democracy for the New Century). Stockholm: Swedish Parliamentary Record.

Cabinet Communication 1996/97:50 *På väg mot ett ekologiskt hållbart samhälle* (On the Road Towards an Ecologically Sustainable Society). Stockholm: Swedish Parliamentary Record.

Cabinet Communication 1997/98:67 *Konsumenterna och miljön en handlingsplan för hållbar utveckling* (Consumers and the Environment. An Action Plan for Sustainable Development). Stockholm: Swedish Parliamentary Record.

Cabinet Communication 1998/99:5 *Hållbara Sverige uppföljning och fortsatta åtgärder för en ekologisk hållbar utveckling* (Sustainable Sweden. Evaluation and Further Measures for an Ecologically Sustainable Development). Stockholm: Swedish Parliamentary Record.

Cabinet Communication 1999/2000:13 *Hållbara Sverige – uppföljning av åtgärder för en ekologiskt hållbar utveckling* (Sustainable Sweden – Evaluation of Measures for an Ecologically Sustainable Development). Stockholm: Swedish Parliamentary Record.

Cabinet Communication 1999/2000:114 *En miljöorienterad produktpolitik* (An Environmentally Oriented Products Policy). Stockholm: Swedish Parliamentary Record.

Cabinet Communication 2000/01:38 *Sustainable Sweden – a Progress Report on Measures To Promote Ecologically Sustainable Development*. Stockholm: Swedish Parliamentary Record.

Cabinet Communication 2001/02:50 *Hållbara Sverige – uppföljning av åtgärder för en ekologiskt hållbar utveckling* (Sustainable Sweden – Evaluation of Measures for an Ecologically Sustainable Development). Stockholm: Swedish Parliamentary Record.

Cabinet Communication 2001/02:172 *Nationell strategi för hållbar utveckling* (National Strategy for Sustainable Development). Stockholm: Swedish Parliamentary Record.

Cabinet Policy Platform (1996) Stockholm: Swedish Parliamentary Record, September 17.

Caldwell, L. K. (1990) *Between Two Worlds. Science, the Environmental Movement, and Policy Choice.* Cambridge: Cambridge University Press.

Carter, A. (1993) 'Towards a Green Political Theory', pp. 39–62 in Dobson, A. and Lucardie, P. (eds.), *The Politics of Nature.* London: Routledge.

Carter, N. (2001) *The Politics of the Environment. Ideas, Activism, Policy.* Cambridge: Cambridge University Press.

CEIS (1991) Chief Environmental Inspector Survey. Göteborg University: Department of Political Science.

CESP (Kommittén för ekologiskt hållbar upphandling) (2001) *Ett levande verktyg för en ekologiskt hållbar upphandling* (A Functional Tool for Ecologically Sustainable Procurement). Stockholm: The Environment Ministry.

Cohen, M. J. (1998) 'Science and the Environment: Assessing Cultural Capacity for Ecological Modernization', *Public Understanding of Science* 7:149–167.

Collier, U. (1994) (1994) *Energy and Environment in the European Union.* Aldershot: Ashgate.

Cortner, H. J. et al. (1998) 'Institutions Matter: The Need to Address the Institutional Challenges to Ecosystem Management', *Landscape and Urban Planning* 40:159–66.

Crepaz, M. M. L. (1995) 'Explaining Variations of Air Pollution Levels: Political Institutions and Their Impact on Environmental Policy-making', *Environmental Politics* 4:391–414.

Daugbjerg, C. (1998) *Policy Networks under Pressure. Pollution Control, Policy Reform and the Power of Farmers.* Aldershot: Ashgate.

DESD (Delegationen för ekologiskt hållbar utveckling – Delegation for an Ecologically Sustainable Development) (1997) *Ett hållbart Sverige* (A Sustainable Sweden). Also retrievable as Cabinet Bill 1996/97:150 *1997 års ekonomiska vårproposition Bilaga 5 Ett hållbart Sverige* (The Spring 1997 Budget Bill, Part 5, A Sustainable Sweden). Stockholm: Swedish Parliamentary Record.

Directive 2001:25 'Tilläggsdirektiv till Miljöbalkskommittén' (Additional Mandate to the Environmental Code Committee). Stockholm: Ministry of Environment, March 2001.

Directive 2000:28 *Översyn av producentansvaret samt förslag till garantier för producentansvarets fullföljande och funktion* (Analysis of Producer Liability and Suggestions to Guarantee its Maintenance and Functioning). Stockholm: Ministry of Environment.

Directive 2001:01 *Utredningen svensk vattenadministration* (Commissioner to Investigate a New Swedish Water Administration). Stockholm: Ministry of Environment.

Dobers, P. (1997) *Organising Strategies of Environmental Control*. Stockholm: Nerenius and Santérus.

Dobson, A. (1990) *Green Political Thought*. London: Routledge.

Dryzek, J. S. (1987) *Rational Ecology. Environment and Political Economy*. London: Basil Blackwell.

Dryzek, J. S. (1990) *Discursive Democracy: Politics, Policy, and Political Science*. Cambridge: Cambridge University Press.

Dryzek, J. S. (1995) 'Democracy and Environmental Policy Instruments', pp. 294–308 in Eckersley, R. (ed.), *Markets, the State and the Environment. Towards Integration*. Melbourne: Macmillan.

Eckerberg, K. (2001) 'Sweden: Problems and Prospects at the Leading Edge of Local Agenda 21 Implementation', pp. 15–39 in Lafferty, William M. (ed.) (2001). *Sustainable Communities in Europe*. London: Earthscan.

Eckerberg, K., Coenen, F. and Lafferty, W. M. (1999) 'The Status of LA21 in Europe: A Comparative Overview', pp. 241–61 in Lafferty, W. M. (ed.), *Implementing LA21 in Europe. New Initiatives for Sustainable Communities*. Oslo: ProSus.

Eckerberg, K., Forsberg, B. and Wickenberg, P. (1997) 'Sweden: Setting the Pace with Pioneer Municipalities and Schools', pp. 51–83 in Lafferty, W. and Eckerberg, K. (eds.), *From Earth Summit to Local Forum: Studies of Local Agenda 21 in Europe*. Oslo: ProSus.

Eckerberg, K. and Lafferty, W. M. (1997) 'Comparative Perspectives on Evaluation and Explanation', pp. 267–93 in Lafferty, W. M. and K. Eckerberg (eds.), *From Earth Summit to Local Forum. Studies of Local Agenda 21 in Europe*. Oslo: ProSus.

Eckersley, R. (1995) 'Markets, the State and the Environment: An Overview', pp. 7–45 in Eckersley, R. (ed.), *Markets, the State and the Environment. Towards Integration*. Melbourne: Macmillan.

Eckhoff, T. (1983) *Statens styringsmuligheter. Særlig i resurs- og miljøspørsmål* (State and Governance in Resource and Environmental Matters). Oslo: Tanum-Norli.

Ecocycle Commission (Kretsloppsdelegationen) (1997) *Strategi för kret-*

*sloppsanpassade material och varor* (A Strategy for Ecocycle Adaptation of Goods and Materials). Stockholm: Environment Ministry, Swedish Ecocycle Commission Report 1997:14.

Ecocycle Commission (Kretsloppsdelegationen) (1998) *Företag i kretslopp – en lägesredovisning av företagens kretsloppsanpassning* (Industries and Ecocycles – A Progress Report on Industrial Ecocycle Adaptation). Stockholm: Environment Ministry, Swedish Ecocycle Commission Report 1998:23.

Edelman, M. (1998) *Constructing the Political Spectacle*. Chicago: University of Chicago Press.

Edenman, L. (1990) *Planeringsunderlag, former för vattenplanering m. m. En bakgrundsbeskrivning med kommentarer* (Material and Forms of Water Planning. A Commented Background). Solna: Naturvårdsverket Rapport 3832.

Edman, S. (1998) *Världens Chans! Ny möjlighet för Sverige: en bok om ekologi, teknik och solidaritet* (The Chance of a Lifetime! New Possibility for Sweden: A Book on Ecology, Technology and Solidarity). Stockholm: Atlas.

EEA (1999) *Making Sustainability Accountable: Eco-efficiency, Resource Productivity and Innovation*. Copenhagen: European Environment Agency, Topic report No. 11.

Ekengren, M. (1998) *Time and European Governance. The Empirical Value of Three Reflective Approaches*. Stockholm: University of Stockholm, Department of Political Science.

Elzinga, A. and Nolin, J. (1998) *Climate as Research and Politics. The Case of Sweden*. Göteborg: Göteborg University, Department of Theory of Science and Research, Report #197.

Emmelin, L. (1998) 'Evaluating Nordic Environmental Impact Assessment – Part 2: Professional Culture as an Aid in Understanding', *Scandinavian Housing and Planning Research* 15:187–209.

EndterWada, J., Blahna, D., Krannich, R. and Brunson, M. (1998) 'A framework for understanding social science contributions to ecosystem management', *Ecological Applications*, 8:891–904.

Enell, M. et al. (1988) *Samordnad recipientkontroll 1987–1988*. (Coordinated Recipient Control 1987–1988). Stockholm: IVL, B-publ. 902.

Enevoldsen, M. (2001) 'Rationality, Institutions and Environmental Governance', pp. 73–111 in Beckerman, S. C. and Kloppenberg Madsen, E. (eds.), *Environmental Regulation and Rationality. Multidisciplinary Perspectives*. Aarhus: Aarhus Universitetsforlag.

Engen, T. (1996) *På kommunernas villkor. Lokal organisering och interkommunalt samarbete om Västerhavets marina miljö*. (At the Mercy of Local Governments. Local Organisation and Inter-municipal Co-operation on the Marine Environment of the Swedish West Coast). Göteborg: Department of Political Science.

Environment Ministry (1998) Press Releases spring 1998.

Environmental Advisory Board (Miljövårdsberedningen) (1998) *Lägesrapport till regeringen angående skärgårdsuppdraget.* Stockholm: EAB.

Esselin, A. and Arvidsson, F. (1998) *Miljöforskning i förändring* (Changes in Environmental Research). Umeå: Memo, available from the authors.

Falkemark, G. (1998) 'Hallandsåsen och höghastighetens pris' (The Halland Ridge and the Price of High Speed), encl. 3 in SOU 1998:134 (see below).

FORMAS (2001) Board Meeting June 19. Proceedings (mimeo). Stockholm: FORMAS.

Freemuth, J. (1996) 'The Emergency of Ecosystem Management: Reinterpreting the Gospel?', *Society and Natural Resources* 9:411–17.

Funtowicz, S.O. and Ravetz, J. R. (1993) 'Science for the post-normal age', *Futures* 27:739–55.

Geus, M. de (1996) 'The Ecological Restructuring of the State', pp. 188–211 in Doherty, B. and Geus, M. de (eds.) *Democracy and Green Political Thought.* London: Routledge.

Gipperth, L. (1999) *Miljökvalitetsnormer* (Environmental Quality Standards). Uppsala: Uppsala University.

Glasbergen, P. (1992) 'Seven Steps towards an Instrumentation Theory for Environmental Policy', *Policy and Politics* (20):191–200.

Goodin, R. (1996) 'Enfranchising the Earth and its Alternatives', *Political Studies* 44:835–49.

Gouldson, A. and Murphy, J. (1997) 'Ecological Modernization: Restructuring Industrial Economies', pp. 74–86 in Jacobs, M. (ed.), *Greening the Millennium? The New Politics of the Environment.* Oxford: Blackwell Publishers.

Government Offices (2000) *Public Access to Information and Secrecy with Swedish Authorities.* Stockholm: Regeringskansliet.

Gustafsson, J.-E. (1995) *Avrinningsområdesbaserade organisationer som aktiva planeringsaktörer* (Catchment-based Organisations as Active Planners). Stockholm: KTH.

Haas, P. M. (1993) 'Epistemic Communities and the Dynamics of International Environmental Cooperation', pp. 168–201 in Rittberger, V. (ed.) *Regime Theory and International Relations.* Oxford: Oxford University Press.

Haas, P. M. (1997) 'Scientific Communities and Multiple Paths to Environmental Management', pp. 193–228, in Brooks, L. A. and VanDeveer, S. D. (eds.) *Saving the Seas: Values, Scientists, and*

*International Governance*. Maryland: Sea Grant College.

Hagevi, M. (1999) *Kommunalpolitikens professionalisering? Kommunalt förtroendevalda 1999* (Professionalisation in Local Politics? Local Councillors 1999). Stockholm: Svenska Kommunförbundet.

Hajer, M. A. (1995) *The Politics of Environmental Discourse. Ecological Modernization and the Policy Process*. Oxford: Clarendon.

Hanf, K. and Jansen, A.-I. (1998) 'Environmental Policy – the Outcome of Strategic Action and Institutional Characteristics', pp. 1–16 in Hanf, K. and Jansen, A.-I. (eds.), *Governance and Environmental Quality. Environmental Administration, Policy and Politics in Western Europe*. London: Longman.

Hayward, B. M. (1996) 'The Greening of Participatory Democracy: A Reconsideration of Theory', *Environmental Politics* 4:215–36.

Hirst, P. (2000) 'Democracy and Governance', pp. 13–35 in Pierre, J. (ed.), *Debating Governance: Authority, Steering, and Democracy*. Oxford and New York: Oxford University Press.

Holling, C. S., Berkes, F. and Folke, C. (2000) 'Science, Sustainability and Resource Management', pp. 342–362 in Berkes, F. and Folke, C., (eds.), *Linking Social and Ecological Systems. Management Practices and Social Mechanism for Building Resilience*. Oxford: Oxford University Press.

Hydén, H. and Baier, M. (1998) 'När kunskapen blir onödig – om normative asymmetri i fallet Hallandsåsen' (When Knowledge becomes Unnecessary. On Normative Asymmetry in the Halland Ridge Case), encl. 4 in SOU 1998:134 (see below).

Jagers, S.C. (2002) *Justice, Liberty and Bread – For All? On the Compatibility between Sustainable Development and Liberal Democracy*. Göteborg University: Göteborg Studies in Politics 79.

Jahn, D. (1998) 'Environmental Performance and Policy Regimes: Explaining Variations in 18 OECD-countries', *Policy Sciences* 31:107–31.

Jänicke, M. (1985) *Preventive Environmental Policy as Ecological Modernization and Structural Policy*, Discussion Paper IIUG dp 85–2, Internationales Institut für Umwelt und Gesellschaft, Wissenschaftszentrum Berlin für Sozialforschung (WZB).

Jänicke, M. (1997) 'The Political System's Capacity for Environmental Policy', pp. 1–24 in Jänicke, M. and. Weidner, H. (eds.), *National Environmental Policies. A Comparative Study of Capacity-Building*. Berlin: Springer.

Jänicke, M. and Jörgens, H. (1998) 'National Environmental Policy Planning in OECD countries: preliminary lessons from cross-National comparisons', *Environmental Politics* 7 (2):27–54.

Jänicke, M., Kunig, P. and Stitzel, M. (1999) *Umweltpolitik. Politik, Recht und Management in Staat und Unternehmen.* Bonn: Dietz.

Jansen, A.-I., Osland, O. and Hanf, K. (1998) 'Environmental Challenges and Institutional Changes. An Interpretation of the Development of Environmental Policy in Western Europe', pp. 277–325 in Hanf, K. and Jansen, A.-I. (eds.), *Governance and Environmental Quality. Environmental Administration, Policy and Politics in Western Europe.* London: Longman.

Jasanoff, S. (1990) *The Fifth Branch. Science Advisors as Policymakers.* Cambridge, Mass.: Harvard University Press.

Johansson, J. (1992) *Det statliga kommittéväsendet. Kunskap, kontroll, konsensus* (The Swedish Commission System. Knowledge, Control, Consensus). Stockholm: Stockholm University, Department of Political Science.

Jones, J. R., Martin, R. and Bartlett, E. T. (1995) 'Ecosystem management: the U.S. forest service's response to social conflict', *Society and Natural Resources* 8: 161–8.

Jones, P. (1994) *Rights.* London: Macmillan.

Kågesson, P. and Lidmark, A.-M. (1998) *Konsten att använda 5,4 miljarder. En kritisk granskning av stödet till de lokala investeringsprogrammen för hållbar utveckling.* (The Art of Spending 5.4 billions. A Critical Evaluation of the State Support to Local Investment Programs for Sustainable Development). Stockholm: Svenska Naturskyddsföreningen Rapport 9423/98.

Kalmar County (1997/1999) *Stadgar, årsrapporter rörande länets luftvårdsförbund.* (Statutes and Annual Reports of the County Air Quality Association). Kalmar: Länsstyrelsen.

Kickert, W. (1993) 'Autopoiesis and the science of (public) administration: essence, sense and nonsense', *Organisation Studies* 14:261–78.

Kjellerup, U. (1997) 'MKB-proceduren – offentlighet och aktörer' (The EIA Proces – Openness and Actors), pp. 374–86 in Andersson, H. E. B. (ed.), *Trafik och miljö: Forskare skriver om kunskapsläge och forskningsbehov* (Traffic and the Environment – Researchers on Knowledge Base and Research Needs). Lund: Studentlitteratur.

Knoepfel, P. (1995) 'New Institutional Arrangements for the Next Generation of Environmental Policy Instruments: Intra- and Interpolicy-Cooperation', pp. 197–233 in Dente, B. (ed.), *Environmental Policy in Search of New Instruments.* Dordrecht: Kluwer Academic Publishers.

Konjunkturinstitutet (National Institute for Economic Research) (1998) *Miljöräkenskapsprojektet vid Konjunkturinstitutet 1992–1997* (The NIER Work on National Environmental Accounts 1993–1997) Stockholm: KI report 1998:10.

Kronoberg County (1997/1999) *Stadgar, årsrapporter rörande länets luftvårdsförbund.* (Statutes and Annual Reports of the County Air Quality Association). Växjö: Länsstyrelsen.

Lackey, R. T. (1998) 'Seven pillars of ecosystem management', *Landscape and Urban Planning* 40 (1–3):21–30.

Lafferty, W. M. (1996) 'Democracy in an Ecological State: Problem and Prospects', Paper prepared for the Conference on the 'Ecological State', Seville, Spain, Nov. 28–Dec. 1, 1996. Oslo: ProSus notat.

Lafferty, W. M. (2001) 'Adapting Government Practice to the Goals of Sustainable Development: The Issue of Sectoral Policy Integration', Paper prepared for presentation at the OECD seminar on 'Improving Governance for Sustainable Development', Paris, 22–23 November, 2001.

Lafferty, W. M. (2002) 'Governance for Sustainable Development: The Challenge of Adapting Form to Function: Introduction', Paper to the ProSus Workshop of 'Governance of Sustainable Development', Lillehammer, Norway, 25–28 April.

Lafferty, W. M. and Meadowcroft, J. (1996) 'Democracy and the Environment: Prospects for Greater Congruence', pp. 256–72 in Lafferty, W. M and Meadowcroft, J. (eds.), *Democracy and Environment: Problems and Prospects.* Cheltenham: Edward Elgar.

Lafferty, W. M. and Meadowcroft, J. (2000a) 'Introduction', pp. 1–22 in Lafferty, W. M. and Meadowcroft, J. (eds.), *Implementing Sustainable Development. Strategies and Initiatives in High Consumption Societies.* Oxford: Oxford University Press.

Lafferty, W. M. and Meadowcroft, J. (2000b) 'Concluding Perspectives', pp. 422–59 in Lafferty, W. M. and Meadowcroft, J. (eds.), *Implementing Sustainable Development. Strategies and Initiatives in High Consumption Societies.* Oxford: Oxford University Press.

Langhelle, O. (2000) 'Why Ecological Modernization and Sustainable Development Should Not Be Conflated', *Journal of Environmental Policy and Planning* 2:303–22.

Lee, K. N. (1993) *Compass and Gyroscope. Integrating Science and Politics for the Environment.* Washington D.C.: Island Press.

Liberatore, A. (1997), 'The Integration of Sustainable Development Objectives Into EU Policymaking: Barriers and Prospects', pp. 108–26, in Baker, S. et al., *The Politics of Sustainable Development,* London: Routledge.

Lidskog, R. (1996) 'Miljöfrågans uppgång – och fall? Kritiska synpunkter på kretsloppsanpassad utveckling, grön produktion och global miljöpolitik', *Nordisk Samhällsgeografisk Tidskrift* Nr 22:3–25.

Ligteringen, J. J. 1999. *The Feasibility of Dutch Environmental Policy Instruments.* Enschede: Twente University Press.

Lindh, A. (1997) *Morgondagens miljöpolitik – en väg till nya möjligheter* (Tomorrow's Environmental Policy – A Road to New Possibilities). Speech by the Environment Minister delivered January 29. Earlier available at www.sb.gov.se_info.rosenbad under '*Statsråden*', '*Miljöminister Anna Lindh*', '*Tal m.m.*'.

Loftsson, E. et al. (1993) *Svensk miljöpolitik* (Swedish Environmental Politics). Lund: Studentlitteratur.

Lundholm, A.-M. (1999) 'Fiskevårdsområden: En hållbar förvaltnings-form för resursen fisk?' (Fishing Management Areas – A Sustainable Form for Managing Fish Resources?). Göteborg: Statsvetenskapliga institutionen. Term paper.

Lundqvist, L. J. (1971) *Miljövårdsförvaltning och politisk struktur* (Environmental Administration and Political Structure). Lund: Prisma/Verdandidebatt.

Lundqvist, L. J. (1972) 'Sweden's National Physical Planning for Natural Resources Management', *Environmental Affairs* 2:487–504.

Lundqvist, L. J. (1979) 'Environmental Impact Assessment in Sweden – Status, Problems, and Proposals for Change', *Policy and Politics* 7:245–68.

Lundqvist, L. J. (1994) 'Environmental Cooperation among Swedish Local Governments. Professional Networks and the Evolution of Institutions for Collective Action', *International Journal of Public Administration* 17:1733–66.

Lundqvist, L. J. (1995) 'Municipal Sewage Treatment in Sweden 1960–1990. From Bans on Bathing to Schools of Salmon', pp. 43–59 in Jänicke, M. and Weidner, H. (Hrsg.), *Successful Environmental Policy – A Critical Evaluation of 24 Cases*. Berlin: edition sigma.

Lundqvist, L. J. (1996) 'Sweden', pp. 259–338 in Munk Christiansen, P. (ed.), *Governing the Environment: Politics, Policy, and Organizaton in the Nordic Countries*. Copenhagen: Nordic Council of Ministers, NORD 1996:5.

Lundqvist, L. J. (1998) 'Local-to-Local Partnerships among Swedish Municipalities: Why and How Neighbors Join to Alleviate Resource Constraints', pp. 83–101 in Pierre, J. (ed.), *Partnerships in Urban Governance: European and American Experiences*. London: Macmillan 1998.

Lundqvist, L. J. (2000) 'Capacity-Building or Social Construction? Explaining Swedish Environmental Policy Change', *GeoForum* 31:21–32.

Lundqvist, L. J. (2001a) 'Implementation from Above? The Ecology of Sweden's New Environmental Governance', *Governance* 14:319–37.

Lundqvist, L. J. (2001b) 'A Green Fist in A Velvet Glove: The Ecological State and Sustainable Development', *Environmental Values* 10:455–72.

Meadowcroft, J. (1997a) 'Planning for Sustainable Development: Insights From the Literature of Political Science', *European Journal of Political Research* 31:427–54.

Meadowcroft, J. (1997b) 'Planning, Democracy, and the Challenge of Sustainable Development', *International Political Science Review* 18:167–89.

Michanek, G. (ed.) (1991) *Lagbok i miljörätt 1991* (Environmental Legislation 1991). Stockholm: Allmänna förlaget.

Milbrath, L. (1984) *Environmentalist: Vanguards for A New Society*. Albany: SUNY Press.

Ministry of the Environment (1993) 'A Greener Sweden: The Environmental Strategy of the Swedish Government'. Stockholm: Ministry of Environment and Natural Resources.

MISTRA (1997) *Miljöstrategisk forskning. Inriktning och resurser 1998–2002* (Strategic Environmental Research – Direction and Resources 1998–2002). Stockholm: MISTRA.

Murphy, J. (2000) 'Ecological modernization', *Geo-Forum* 31:1–8.

National Audit Office (1996) *Miljökonsekvensbeskrivningar i praktiken* (EIA in Practice). Stockholm: Riksrevisionsverket RRV 1996:29.

National Audit Office (1999a) *Miljarden som försvann – en granskning av kretsloppsprogrammet* (The Billion that Disappeared – An Assessment of the Ecocycle Program). Stockholm: Riksrevisionsverket RRV 1999:28.

National Audit Office (1999b) *De lokala investeringsprogrammen i praktiken – en uppföljning av kommunernas arbete* (The LIPs in Practice – a Follow-up on Municipal Activities). Stockholm: Riksrevisionsverket RRV 1999:37.

National Audit Office (2000) *Miljömålen och återrapporteringen – en felande länk i resultatstyrningen* (Feedback on Progress towards the NEOs – A Missing Link in the Management by Results). Stockholm: Riksrevisionsverket report 2000:29.

NEPP 4 (2001) 4th *National Environmental Policy Plan. Where There's a Will There's a World. Summary*. The Hague: VROM.

NHBP (National Housing and Planning Board) (2001) *Årsrapport 2000* (Annual Report 2000). Karlskrona: Boverket.

Norman, K. (1997) *Nationell inventering av samordnad vattenplanering* (National Inventory of Coordinated Water Planning). Stockholm: Swedish Environmental Protection Agency.

O'Riordan, T. and Voisey, H. (1997) 'The Political Economy of Sustainable Development', *Environmental Politics* 6:1–23.

O'Toole, Jr. L. J. (2002) 'Implementation Theory and the Challenge of Sustainable Development:The Transformative Role of Learning on both Theory and Practice', Paper to the ProSus Workshop of 'Governance of Sustainable Development', Lillehammer, Norway, 25–28 April.

OECD (1999a) *Report by the Environmental Policy Committee on Implementation of the 1996 Recommendation on Improving the Environmental Performance of Governments* Paris: OECD C(99) 33/ FINAL

OECD (1999b) *Trade Issues in the Greening of Public Purchasing.* Paris: OECD COM/TD/ENV(97)111/FINAL

Olsson, P. and Folke, C. (2001) 'Local Ecological Knowledge and Institutional Dynamics for Ecosystem Management: A Study of Lake Racken Watershed, Sweden', *Ecosystems* 4:85–104.

Ophuls, W. (1977) *Ecology and the Politics of Scarcity Revisited.* San Francisco: Freeman.

Ophuls, W. and Boyan Jr., A. S. (1992) *Ecology and the Politics of Scarcity Revisited.* New York: W.H. Freeman.

Östergötland County (1997/1999) *Stadgar, årsrapporter rörande länets luftfårdsförbund* (Statutes and Annual Reports of the County Air Quality Association). Linköping: Länsstyrelsen.

Ostrom, E. (1990) *Governing the Commons. The Evolution of Institutions for Collective Action.* Cambridge, Cambridge University Press.

Paehlke, R. and Torgerson, D. (1990) 'Environmental Politics and the Administrative State', pp. 285–302 in Paehlke, R. and Torgerson, D. (eds.), *Managing Leviathan. Environmental Politics and the Administrative State.* London: Belhaven Press.

Parliament Housing Committee (1998/99) *Statens stöd till lokala investeringsprogram för hållbar utveckling* (State Support to Local Investment Programs for Sustainable Development) Stockholm: Swedish Parliamentary Record.

Pavlikakis, G. E. and Tsihrintzis, V. A. (2000) 'Ecosystem Management: A Review of a New Concept and Methodology', *Water Resource Management* 14:257–83.

Persson, G. (1997) 'Så gör vi Sverige till ett föregångsland för ekologisk hållbarhet!' (This Is how We Make Sweden a Forerúnner in Ecologically Sustainable Development!) Prime Minister's speech at SSU:s och Byggnads Environmental Seminar, 11 April. Earlier available under '*Statsministern*', '*Tal m.m.*', at www.sb.gov.se_info.rosenbad

Pierre, J. (2000) 'Conclusions: Governance beyond State Strength', pp. 241–46 in Pierre, J. (ed.), *Debating Governance: Authority, Steering and Democracy.* Oxford: Oxford University Press.

Pierre, J. and Peters, B. G. (2000) *Governance, Politics and the State*. London: Macmillan.

Porritt, J. (1984) *Seeing Green: The Politics of Ecology Explained*. Cambridge: Blackwell.

Pritchard, Jr., L. et al. (1998) *The Problem of Fit between Ecosystems and Institutions*. Bonn: International Human Dimensions Programme on Global Environmental Change (IHDP) Working Paper No. 2.

Raphael, D. D. (1990) *Problems of Political Philosophy*. London: Macmillan.

Rhodes, R.A.W. (1996) 'The New Governance: Governing without Government', *Political Studies* 44:652–67.

Rothstein, B. (1992) *Den korporativa staten. Intresseorganisationer och statsförvaltning i svensk politik* (The Corporatist State. Interest Organisations and Public Administration in Swedish Politics). Stockholm: Norstedts.

Sale, K. (1984a) 'Mother of All: An introduction to Bioregionalism', in Kumar, S. (ed.), *The Schumacher Lectures*, Vol. 2. London: Blond and Briggs.

Sale, K. (1984b) 'Bioregionalism: A New Way to Treat the Land', *The Ecologist*, 14 (4).

SAP (Swedish Social Democratic Party) (1997) *Steget in i 2000-talet – en socialdemokratisk politik i förändringens tid*. (Into the 21st Century – Social-Democratic Politics in A Time of Change). Party Board's Platform Proposal to the 1997 Party Congress. Stockholm: SAP, June 24. Earlier available at www.a-torget.org/sappolitik/kapitel2.htm#2.3 Hållbara Sverige

SCB (Statistics Sweden) (2001) *Sustainable Development Indicators for Sweden – A First Set*. Örebro: Statistics Sweden.

SEPA (Swedish Environment Protection Agency) (1996) *Research and Development for a Better Environment 1996. A Report from Thirteen Financiers of Environmental Research*. Stockholm: SEPA.

SEPA (Swedish Environmental Protection Agency) (1997) *Ren luft och gröna skogar – förslag till nationella miljömål* (Clean Air and Green Forests – A proposal for National Environmental Objectives). Stockholm: SEPA.

SEPA (1999) *System med indikatorer för nationell uppföljning av miljökvalitetsmålen* (System for National Monitoring of the National Environmental Objectives). Stockholm: SEPA.

SEPA (2000a) *Scenarier för framtida (år 2013) vattenförvaltning med ett ramdirektiv* (Scenarios for Future (2013) Water Administration under the Framework Water Directive). Stockholm: SEPA, Vattenprojektet 2000–12–20.

SEPA (2000b) *Miljöforskningsnämnden Programförklaring för 2001* (The Environment Research Board. Statement of Intent 2001). Stockholm: SEPA (available at www.environ.se).

Sexton, W. T. and Szaro, R. C. (1998) 'Implementing Ecosystem Management: Using Multiple Boundaries for Organizing Information', *Landscape and Urban Planning* 40:167–72.

SFS (Swedish Code of Statutes) 1981:533 *Lag om fiskevårdsområden* (Law on Fishing Management Areas).

SFS 1994:1235 *Förordning om producentansvar för förpackningar* (Ordinance on Producer Responsibility for Packages).

SFS 1995:1322 *Verksförordning* (Government Agency Ordinance).

SFS 1998:23 *Statliga bidrag till lokala investeringsprogram som ökar den ekologiska hållbarheten i samhället* (State Grants to Local Investment Programs for Sustainable Development). Stockholm: Ministry of Environment.

SFS 1998:808 *Miljöbalk* (Environmental Code).

Slocombe, D. S. (1998) 'Lessons from Experience with Ecosystem-Based Management', *Landscape and Urban Planning* 40:31–40.

Smeets, E. and Weterings, R. (1999) *Environmental indicators: Typology and Overview*. Copenhagen: EEA, Technical Report no 25.

Smith, R. J. (1996) 'Sustainability and the Rationalisation of the Environment', *Environmental Politics* 5(1):25–47.

SOU 1983:56 (Statens Offentliga Utredningar, Investigative Committee Reports) *Naturresursers nyttjande och hävd* (The Use and Management of Natural Resources). Stockholm: Ministry of Agriculture.

SOU 1987:32 *För en bättre miljö*. (For a Better Environment). Stockholm: Ministry of Environment and Natural Resources.

SOU 1992:68 *Långsiktig miljöforskning* (Long-term Environmental Research). Stockholm: Ministry of Environment.

SOU 1993:19 *Kommunerna och miljöarbetet*. (The Municipalities and their Work for a Good Living Environment). Stockholm: Ministry of Environment and Natural Resources.

SOU 1993:27 *Miljöbalk* (Environmental Code). Final Report of the Environmental Protection Commission, Part I. Stockholm: Ministry of Environment and Natural Resources.

SOU 1994:125 *Samordnad insamling av miljödata* (Coordinated Collection of Environmental Data). Stockholm: Ministry of Environment and Natural Resources.

SOU 1994:128 *Lokal AGENDA 21 – en vägledning* (Local Agenda 21 – Some Guidelines). Stockholm: Environmental Advisory Council.

SOU 1994:138 *Rapport från Klimatdelegationen* (Report from the Commission on Climate Change). Stockholm: Ministry of Environment and Natural Resources.

SOU 1995:96 *Jordens klimat förändras. En analys av hotbild och globala åtgärdsstrategier* (Global climate change. An Analysis of Threats and Counterstrategies). Stockholm: Ministry of Environment.

SOU 1996:112 *Integrering av miljöhänsyn i den statliga förvaltningen* (Integration of Environmental Concerns in Central Agencies). Stockholm: Ministry of Environment.

SOU 1996:153 *Hållbar utveckling i Sverigens skärgårdsområden* (Sustainable Development in Sweden's Archipelagos). Stockholm: Ministry of Environment.

SOU 1997:34 *Övervakning av miljön* (Monitoring the Environment). Stockholm: Ministry of Environment.

SOU 1997:99 *En ny vattenadministration – Vatten är livet* (A New Water Administration – Water is Life). Stockholm: Ministry of Environment.

SOU 1997:105 *Agenda 21 i Sverige. Fem år efter Rio – resultat och framtid* (Agenda 21 in Sweden. Five years after Rio – Results and Future). Stockholm: Ministry of Environment.

SOU 1997:145 *Förvalta med miljöansvar* (Environmentally Responsible Government). Stockholm: Ministry of Environment.

SOU 1997:155 *Miljösamverkan i vattenvården* (Environmental Co-operation in Water Management). Stockholm: Ministry of Environment.

SOU 1998:60 *Kring Hallandsåsen* (About the Halland Ridge). Stockholm: Ministry of Environment.

SOU 1998:137 *Miljö i grund och botten – erfarenheter från Hallandsåsen* (Environment Grounded – Experiencies from the Hallandsås). Stockholm: Ministry of the Environment.

SOU 1998:170 *Gröna nyckeltal för en ekologiskt hållbar utveckling samhälle.* (Green Indicators for Ecologically Sustainable Development). Stockholm: Ministry of Environment.

SOU 1999:127 *Gröna nyckeltal – följ den ekologiska omställningen* (Green Indicators – Follow the Ecological Transition). Stockholm: Ministry of Environment.

SOU 2000:1 *En uthållig demokrati! Politik för folkstyrelse på 2000-talet* (A Sustainable Democracy! Policy for Government by the People in the 21st Century). Stockholm: Ministry of Justice.

SOU 2000:23 *Förslag till Svensk Klimatstrategi* (Proposals for a Swedish Climate Strategy). Stockholm: Ministry of Environment.

SOU 2000:52 *Framtidens miljö – allas vårt ansvar!* (The Future Environment – Our Common Responsibility). Stockholm: Ministry of Environment.

SOU 2000:67 Levande skärgård. Utvärdering av de regionala miljö- och hushållningsprogrammen (Living Archipelagos. An Evaluation of the Regional Environmental and Resource Management

Programs). Stockholm: Ministry of Environment.

SOU 2000:7 *Långtidsutredningen 1999/2000* (Long-term Economic Forecast 1999/2000). Stockholm: Ministry of Finance.

SOU 2000:7, App. 2 *Miljö och ekonomi – scenarier fram till år 2015* (Environment and Economy – Scenarios up to 2015). Stockholm: Ministry of Finance.

SOU 2000:7, App. 7 *Vad är hållbar utveckling?* (What is Sustainable Development?) Stockholm: Ministry of Finance.

SOU 2001:2 *Effektiv användning av naturresurser* (Efficient use of Natural Resources). Stockholm: Ministry of Finance.

SOU 2001:20 *Tänk nytt, tänk hållbart! – dialog och samverkan för hållbar utveckling* (Think Anew – Think Sustainable! – Dialogue and Co-operation for Sustainable Development). Stockholm: Ministry of Environment.

SOU 2001:31 *Mera värde för pengarna* (More Value for Money). Stockholm: Ministry of Finance.

Standing Committee on Housing (Bostadssutskottet) (1998/99) *Statens stöd till lokala investeringsprogram för hållbar utveckling – uppföljning av den hittillsvarande fördelningen av ramanslaget E1 under statsbudgetens utgiftsområde 18* (State Grants to Local Investment Programs for Sustainable Develoment – A Review of Allocated Grants). Stockholm: Swedish Parliamentary Record, URD1.

Statistics Sweden (2000) *Naturmiljön i siffror 2000* (The Environment in Figures 2000) Stockholm: Statistics Sweden.

Stavins, R. and Whitehead, B. (1997) 'Market-Based Environmental Policies', pp. 105–17 in Chertow, M. R. and Esty, D. C. (eds.), *Thinking Ecologically. The Next Generation of Environmental Policy*. New Haven, Conn. and London: Yale University Press.

Stoker, G. (2000) 'Urban Political Science and the Challenge of Urban Governance', pp. 91–109 in Pierre, J. (ed.), *Debating Governance: Authority, Steering and Democracy*. Oxford: Oxford University Press.

Stretton, H. (1976) *Capitalism, Socialism and the Environment*. Cambridge: Cambridge University Press.

Sunstein, C. R. (1990) *After the Rights Revolution. Reconceiving the Regulatory State*. Cambridge, Mass. and London: Harvard University Press.

Sveriges Nationalatlas (1991) *Miljön* (The Environment). Stockholm: SNA Förlag.

Swedish Parliamentary Record, Debates March 22, 1996 (Prime Minister Göran Persson).

Szaro, R. C., Sexton, W. T. and Malone, C. R. (1998) 'The Emergence of Ecosystem Management as a Tool for Meeting People's Needs and Sustaining Ecosystems', *Landscape and Urban Planning* 40:1–8.

Thomas, C. and Tennant, T. (1998) *Creating a Standard for a Corporate CO₂ Indicator*. Geneva: UNEP Economics, Trade and Enviornment Unit. Working Document, May.

Tilton, T. (1990) *The Political Theory of Swedish Social Democracy. Through the Welfare State to Socialism*. Oxford: Clarendon Press.

Uhrwing, M. (2001) *Tillträde till maktens rum. Om intresseorganisationer och miljöpolitiskt beslutsfattande* (Access to the Rooms of Power. Interest Organisations and Decision-making in Environmental Politics). Hedemora: Gidlunds.

Underdal, Arild (1980) 'Integrated Marine Policy: What? Why? How?', *Marine Policy*, 4:159–69.

Water Administration Commission (2002) *En ny svensk vattenadministration. Lägesrapport från Utredningen svensk vattenadministration* (A New Swedish Water Administration. Position Paper June 2002). Stockholm: Ministry of Environment.

WCED (1987) *Our Common Future*. Oxford and New York: Oxford University Press.

Weale A. et al. (2000) *Environmental Governance in Europe: An Ever Closer Ecological Union?* Oxford: Oxford University Press.

Wissenburg, M. (1993) 'The Idea of Nature and the Nature of Distributive Justice', pp. 3–20 in Dobson, A. and Lucardie, P. (eds.), *The Politics of Nature. Explorations in Green Political Theory*. London and New York: Routledge.

Wynne, B. (1994) 'Scientific Knowledge and the Global Environment', pp. 169–89 in Redclift, M. and Benton, T. (eds.), *Social Theory and the Global Environment*. London: Routledge.

## Internet addresses

http://helcom.fi/
http://miljo.regeringen.se/index.htm
http://miljo.regeringen.se/M-dep_fragor/hallbarutveckling/LIP
www.environ.se
www.hallbarasverige
www.ivl.se
www.mistra-research.se/
www.ospar.org/
www.repa.se

# Index

244

Index

management by objectives
(MBO), 58, 64–9, 85–6, 174,
212–13, 217, 220
marine pollution, 48–9
materials companies, 70
Meadowcroft, J., 22, 202, 209
Ministry for Industry, 123
Ministry of Agriculture, 123
Ministry of Environmental
Affairs, 123
Unit for Ecological
Transformation
and Development
(MENUET), 107–9
Ministry of Foreign Affairs, 106
MISTRA, 95–102, 106–7, 113
*Monitor* reports, 103
monitoring and evaluation,
environmental,
102–4, 115–16, 133–5, 121
multi-level governance, 4–7, 18–20,
152, 183–6, 214–15, 219
Municipal Act (1991), 31

National Audit Office, 63, 109,
130, 141, 156, 173
National Board for Housing and
Planning, 141
national environmental objectives
(NEOs), 63–8, 82, 85, 103,
115, 130, 133–5,
140–5, 174–5, 189–91,
205–7, 212–13, 216–17, 220
Bills on, 70–1, 75, 104, 211
Commission on, 103, 133–5,
162, 166–7, 174
National Institute for Economic
Research, 136
national interests, 62–4, 82, 128
national parks and national
rivers, 60
National Physical Planning
system, 60–1

national strategies for sustainable
development, 23–4
*Natural Environment in Figures,
The*, 103
Natural Resources Act (NRA),
61–2
Nature Conservancy, 47, 172
nature reserves, 60, 62
nested enterprises, 8–9, 18–20,
25–6, 29, 50–1, 152, 186,
214
Netherlands, the, 192
'new environmental governance',
175–80
'new environmental work', 199,
206, 213–14
'new public management', 58, 64
non-governmental organisations
(NGOs), 159–61, 164–5,
175–9, 199
non-renewable resources, 61
North East Atlantic Marine
Environment, Convention for
the Protection of
(OSPAR), 48–50

official documents, access to,
154–5, 176–7
Ophuls, W., 90
Organisation for Economic
Cooperation
and Development (OECD),
132, 137
organisational change, 15, 29, 32
Osland, O., 17, 150, 202, 208–9
Östergötland, 41
Ostrom, Elinor, 25, 186
overview plans, 62–3
ozone layer, 87

participation in decision-making,
10, 17–18, 21, 27, 56, 63,
135, 148–53, 160,